REGIONS

of the

GREAT
HERESY

WORKS IN ENGLISH BY BRUNO SCHULZ

The Street of Crocodiles
Sanatorium Under the Sign of the Hourglass
Letters and Drawings of Bruno Schulz with Selected Prose
The Booke of Idolatry
The Drawings of Bruno Schulz

WORKS IN ENGLISH BY JERZY FICOWSKI

Sister of the Birds and Other Gypsy Tales
Introduction to *The Street of Crocodiles*
A Reading of Ashes
Gypsies in Poland: History and Customs
Introduction to *Letters and Drawings of Bruno Schulz with Selected Prose*
Introduction and editing, *The Drawings of Bruno Schulz*

REGIONS
of the
GREAT
HERESY

BRUNO SCHULZ
A Biographical Portrait

Jerzy Ficowski
Translated and Edited by
THEODOSIA ROBERTSON

W. W. Norton & Company
New York   London

For information about permission to reproduce selections from this book, write to Permissions, W. W. Norton & Company, Inc., 500 Fifth Avenue, New York, NY 10110

Manufacturing by The Haddon Craftsmen, Inc.
Book Design by Mary A. Wirth

Library of Congress Cataloging-in-Publication Data
Ficowski, Jerzy.
  [Regiony wielkiej herezji. English]
  Regions of the great heresy : Bruno Schulz, a biographical portrait /
Jerzy Ficowski ; translated and edited by Theodosia Robertson.
     p. cm.
Includes index.
  ISBN 0-393-05147-1
  1. Schulz, Bruno, 1892–1942. 2. Authors, Polish—20th century—Biography.
I. Robertson, Theodosia S. II. Title.
PG7158.S2942 F513 2002
891.8'5372—dc21

                                                                2002013885

W. W. Norton & Company, Inc., 500 Fifth Avenue, New York, N.Y. 10110
                              www.wwnorton.com

W. W. Norton & Company Ltd., Castle House, 75/76 Wells Street, London W1T 3QT

1 2 3 4 5 6 7 8 9 0

Contents

❦

"It is worth noting how all things that touched this unusual man somehow retreated into the root of their existence, reconstructed their phenomenon down to the very metaphysical core, somehow returned to the original idea—only to prove faithless to it, veering off into those dubious, risky and ambiguous regions which we shall name here, in short, the Regions of the Great Heresy."

—BRUNO SCHULZ, "TAILORS' DUMMIES," *CINNAMON SHOPS*, 1934

Jest godne uwagi, jak w zetknięciu z niezwkłym tym człowiekiem rzeczy wszystkie cofały się niejako do korzenia swego bytu, odbudowyały swe zjawisko aż do metafizycznego jądra, wracały niejako do pierwotnej idei, ażeby w tym punkcie sprzeniewierzyć się jej i przechlić w te wątpliwe, ryzykowne i dwuznaczne regiony, które nazwiemy tu krótko regionami wielkiej herezji.

TRANSLATOR'S INTRODUCTION

A Living Book

Jerzy Ficowski's biographical portrait of Bruno Schulz, which emerged in its earliest form in Polish in 1967 and is here presented for the first time to American readers, proved to be a watershed for interest in this Polish-Jewish writer of short fiction to whom little attention had been paid in early postwar decades. Bruno Schulz now belongs to the elite of Polish letters, although his published fictional output consists of only two volumes of short stories, *Sklepy cynamonowe*, 1934 (*Cinnamon Shops;* in English, *The Street of Crocodiles*), and *Sanatorium pod klepsydrą* (*Sanatorium Under the Sign of the Hourglass*), 1937. But what short stories they are. Difficult to categorize, Schulz's writing has affinities with European and Polish expressionism, surrealism, and the grotesque. His stories are an extraordinary fictional world with distinctive language and imagery, recurring motifs, sense of time, and view of artistic creation.

Bruno Schulz was born in 1892 in Drohobycz in what was then known as Galicia, a crownland of the Austro-Hungarian Empire since the late eighteenth century. The region returned to Poland after World War I and is now in the western part of Ukraine. Schooled in Polish, Schulz spoke and wrote that language, as well as German. Although his father, a respected merchant with a place in the town synagogue, must have been familiar with Yiddish, Schulz never learned it or used it as a literary medium. Schulz remained provincial by temperament all his life; he traveled little inside Poland and reluctantly outside. He found his creative inspiration mainly in his hometown. The modest fame Schulz had achieved in the 1930s was cut short by World War II and the Holocaust. Today Bruno Schulz is considered one of the most original exponents of twentieth-century Polish prose. In the larger European context he is a striking example of the rich confluence of cultures characteristic of interwar Central Europe.

In *Regions of the Great Heresy*, Jerzy Ficowski reconstructs Bruno Schulz's life, interweaving it with a keen artistic appreciation of the stories Schulz wrote. Through biographical information and discussion of Schulz's fiction, Ficowski evokes Bruno Schulz's family and milieu, his first attempts at writing, his discovery by interwar literati, his struggle to create while teaching, his starvation in a wartime ghetto, and finally his murder. It was in his native Drohobycz that he was killed by a Gestapo officer in 1942, not far from where he was born and had spent his entire life. Himself a distinguished poet, short story writer, and scholar of Gypsy life, Jerzy Ficowski is the foremost chronicler and archaeologist of Bruno Schulz; since 1947 he has patiently searched worldwide for all Schulziana. His efforts and publications kept Schulz studies alive in Poland in the 1950s and 1960s despite enormous political obstacles. His indefatigable documentation—especially this volume of biographical essays—has borne rich fruit in the renewed scholarly and popular interest in Schulz that emerged in the 1970s in Poland and around the world and continues unabated to the present.

Regions of the Great Heresy reveals Bruno Schulz as a frail and introverted artist, erudite far beyond the local gymnasium from which he graduated, knowledgeable in European culture and art and attracted to aspects of both its Jewish and Christian traditions. Schulz's essays and reviews reflect his friendships with the writers of his own day and his distinctive critical evaluation of their writing: the arch and sophisticated Witold Gombrowicz, the flamboyant Stanisław Ignacy Witkiewicz, known as Witkacy, the influential woman writer Zofia Nałkowska, and many other writers known primarily to those familiar with Polish literature, such as the poet Julian Tuwim and the novelists Tadeusz Breza and Maria Kuncewiczowa. Schulz's letters both reveal his literary and artistic temperament and disclose his deep concern for those dear to him. The letters deal with the artistic and mundane; Schulz's timidity in everyday affairs contrasts with his intense absorption in creative life and firm conviction about his own artistic path.

During his lifetime, Schulz's work was appreciated by several famous Polish writers; he was rewarded with a 1935 prize from the Polish journal *Wiadomości Literackie* (Literary News), and in 1938 he received the prestigious Golden Laurel award from the Polish Academy of Literature. His elaborate and sensuous use of the Polish language was characterized as baroque, poetic, and symbolist. A few contemporary critics reacted negatively toward his writing—a barometer of interwar social prejudices and cliques ill disposed toward Schulz's provincial Jewish background and his peculiar, fantastic tales. After the war, interest in Schulz grew only slowly; the poetic prose, style, and subject matter of a Polish-Jewish writer had nothing to do with socialist realism. Yet, despite official discouragement, several landmark studies of Schulz's writing appeared in the decades between the 1950s and the 1970s. Critic Artur Sandauer, who had known Schulz, wrote an essay entitled "Rzeczywistość zdegradowana" (Degraded Reality, 1956) which appeared as a preface to the reprintings of Schulz's stories in the 1960s and 1970s. But it was Jerzy Ficowski's painstakingly researched and eminently readable *Regions of the Great Heresy* that became the primary source of information about Schulz's life and the survival of his writing. During the decade of the 1970s, a handful of articles about Schulz emerged, as well as two Polish monograph studies.[1] These essays and volumes, however, remained known primarily to scholars. Subsequently revised and reissued in 1975 and 1992, *Regions of the Great Heresy* has continued to be the sole biographical study of Bruno Schulz, the book through which Polish readers know the writer and which is now inseparable from Schulz himself.

A new stage in Schulz studies was signaled in 1974 when a young critic named Wojciech Wyskiel organized the first Bruno Schulz conference at the University of Silesia. The conference papers, published in 1976 as *Studia o prozie Brunona Schulza* (Studies in the Prose of Bruno Schulz), reflect trends in literary criticism of the time—psychoanalysis, structuralism, linguistics, and semiotics. The poetic quality of Schulz's writing style, often categorized as surreal or grotesque, was analyzed with rigor and detail. Schulz's work also began to be viewed from a new critical vantage point, that of the Jewish elements in his writing.[2] Although Artur Sandauer had noted salient Jewish allusions in Schulz's stories in 1956, the pervasive connections between Hebrew poetics and Schulz's writing began to be extensively explored during the years of the political ferment in the late 1970s from which emerged the Solidarity movement in 1980–81. Study of the Jewish aspect of Schulz's writing paralleled the phenomenon in Polish intellectual life of renewed interest in the history of Jewish presence in Polish lands, an interest that remains part of the context in which Bruno Schulz and his stories are considered today.

The more than sixty years of criticism of *Cinnamon Shops* and *Sanatorium Under the Sign of the Hourglass* have had their own, often dramatic, historical dimensions connected with the political vagaries of twentieth-century Poland. Research on Schulz's Polish-Jewish milieu between the two world wars in Poland could only be openly treated in the last decade of Communist rule in Poland. The topic of the Jews in Poland, their civilization and contribution to Polish history, and finally their horrific fate in World War II and its inescapable connection with Poland's wartime suffering has long been a political flashpoint in postwar Poland. For many intellectuals of the university generation of the late 1960s, the anti-Semitic "March events" of 1968 (the Polish Communist Party's purge of Jewish members) during their student days was a catalyst in their political development. Evidence of other kinds of interest in Poland's historical Jewish communities surfaced in the 1970s when Catholic student groups in Warsaw undertook the cleaning of the Jewish cemetery there. By the late 1970s and early 1980s, literary journals carried articles on such topics as Polish-Jewish literature or the "Galician theme" in Polish literature.

Public discussion of the Jews in Poland intersected dramatically with literary studies in 1987 when Jan Błoński, an eminent literary critic and professor at Jagiellonian University in Cracow, published an essay in the Catholic weekly *Tygodnik powszechny* (General Weekly) entitled after Czesław Miłosz's poem "The Poor Poles Look at the Ghetto." Błoński challenged Poles to reexamine without self-justification their attitudes toward Jews and their own behavior during wartime and the Holocaust. The ensuing debate and polemics among literary critics, historians, journalists, and politicians was carried out on the pages of various intellectual journals in Poland despite martial law, as well as in the Polish émigré press. In the 1980s, historians, sociologists, journalists, and literary critics explored Polish-Jewish topics at conferences both in Poland and abroad.

In the heady political atmosphere less than one year before the Round Table discussions of February 1989,[3] a seemingly minor event occurred in 1988 in Cracow when a small film series on Jewish themes developed into a Festival of Jewish Culture that was attended by prominent guests such as Nobel laureate Czesław Miłosz. The success of the festival resulted in an annual June tradition concluding with a finale open-air klezmer concert in Szeroka Street in the Kazimierz district, center of Cracow's historic Jewish quarter since the Middle Ages. Young Jewish musicians and singers from abroad, many of them the far-flung descendants of the annihilated community of East European Jewry, perform beneath a starry night sky; Polish and international visitors attend and participate.

When the year 1992 marked the centennial of Bruno Schulz's birth and the fiftieth anniversary of his death, conferences devoted to the writer were held in Poland in Cracow, Gdańsk, Częstochowa, Cieszyn, and in his hometown, Drohobycz in Ukraine. Cracow's Jagiellonian University organized a three-day international symposium that was cosponsored by the now Third Annual Festival of Jewish Culture and the first annual European Cultural Month promoted by the European Communities (CSCE). The opening speaker of the Jagiellonian University symposium was Jerzy Ficowski. In his foreword to the symposium papers, published in Polish as *Czytanie Schulza* (Reading Schulz, 1994), a leading literary critic and Schulz scholar, Jerzy Jarzębski, characterized Jerzy Ficowski's contribution as twofold: the preservation of the relics of Schulz's life and the scattered remnants of his work, and the maintenance of a coherent sense of Schulz's identity, originality, and greatness.

Although Bruno Schulz had been an unapproved writer in the socialist decades of the 1950s and 1960s, his posthumous fame grew as Communist People's Poland disintegrated in the 1970s and 1980s. High school curricula included Schulz's stories, while his complete fiction entered the canon of Polish classics in 1989 by appearing in the definitive National Library series edition, edited and annotated by Jerzy Jarzębski. In 2000, Polish readers placed Schulz's fiction on a list of Best Books of the Twentieth Century to be printed in a popular commemorative series, *Kanon na koniec wieku* (Canon for the End of the Century). Meanwhile, critics explore and debate the extent of Jewish mysticism and kabbalah in Schulz's fiction, the Jewish, Polish, and German society in the Galicia of his time, the relationship between Schulz's art and prose, and the role of women in his creative work. Schulz's popular appeal remains undiminished; his works are found among the regularly stocked titles in Polish bookstores, while Schulz-related studies appear on shelves alongside Polish Judaica and studies of historic minority populations of Poland. Today Bruno Schulz figures prominently in the cultural heritage of Poland's diverse past, and especially the presence of Jewish civilization in Polish-ruled lands.

In the decades since postwar Schulz studies were initiated by the original Polish edition of *Regions of the Great Heresy*, Jerzy Ficowski's volume has grown with changes and additions. *Regions of the Great Heresy* is a living book which grants Schulz a continued existence in two-track time. Not only Schulz's fiction but also his life as evocatively reconstructed by Jerzy Ficowski inspires other writers, as attested by Danilo Kiš's *The Hourglass* (1972), Cynthia Ozick's *The*

Messiah of Stockholm (1987), David Grossman's *See Under: Love* (1989), and Philip Roth's *The Prague Orgy* (1991). The growing field of Bruno Schulz criticism relies not only upon *Regions of the Great Heresy* as the major source of biographical information about Bruno Schulz but upon the art, letters, publications, oral testimony, and materials of all kinds connected with Bruno Schulz which Jerzy Ficowski has continued to publish: *Księga listów* (Book of Letters, 1975), *Okolice sklepów cynamonowych* (Environs of Cinnamon Shops, 1986), *Xięga bałwochwalcza* (*The Booke of Idolatry*, 1988), and *Bruno Schulz: Ilustracje do własnych utworów* (Bruno Schulz: Illustrations to His Own Works, 1992). Jerzy Ficowski has contributed prefaces and forewords to Schulz's writing published in England and America, as well as other Schulz titles in English such as *Letters and Drawings of Bruno Schulz* (1988) and *The Drawings of Bruno Schulz* (1990). Until now, however, the first and fundamental piece in the puzzle of Bruno Schulz was missing: *Regions of the Great Heresy*.

Jerzy Ficowski's heroic labors on Schulz's behalf testify to the close and intimate bond between the researcher and his subject. In his own poetry devoted to the Holocaust,[4] Jerzy Ficowski evokes an entire panorama of Jewish life in Poland. Two of Ficowski's poems, "My Unsaved" (1968) and "Drohobycz, 1920" (1981), are dedicated to the memory of Bruno Schulz. Jerzy Ficowski shapes *Regions of the Great Heresy* as a poet and makes the poet's associative saltos, relying upon poetic intuition long steeped in Schulz's works. The special bond between the scholar poet and his master is poignantly palpable, particularly when Jerzy Ficowski travels to Schulz's Drohobycz to see with his own eyes the locale that Schulz creatively transformed. As Jerzy Ficowski notes in the first chapter of *Regions of the Great Heresy*, he formulates his own Schulz. That Bruno Schulz is now our Schulz as well.

The present edition of *Regions of the Great Heresy* is a uniquely expanded volume. The translation is based upon the 1992 Polish edition, to which two new chapters on Schulz's lost novel *Messiah* and his murals in Drohobycz, a detailed chronology, and a selection of letters have been added. Photographs beyond those in the Polish edition of *Regions* allow the American reader to visualize Schulz's locale, his family and friends, and his art. Newly translated letters (including one letter to Zenon Waśniewski, never before translated into English) provide a glimpse of Schulz's intense epistolary life and its relation to his writing. The extensive chronology of Schulz's life is the product of decades of research. Finally, the most recent history of Jerzy Ficowski's work on Bruno Schulz unfolds here: the mysterious fate of Schulz's *Messiah* and the circumstances surrounding the dramatic discovery of one of Schulz's final art projects are described at last. The case of the theft in Drohobycz and the extent of the devastation wrought by its perpetrators, both culturally and personally, can be fully grasped by the reader. The future peripeteia of *Messiah* will emerge within the evolving political relations among today's Poland, Russia, and Ukraine. Whether the outcry of the international scholarly and cultural community will prevail regarding Schulz's art remains to be seen.

A word is in order about the translations of Bruno Schulz's own writing that appear in this book. All the translations from Schulz's fiction, essays, and letters are my own. Until now, English-speaking readers have known Bruno Schulz's stories as *The Street of Crocodiles* and *Sanatorium Under the Sign of the Hourglass* (both originally part of the Penguin series edited by Philip Roth, "Writers from the Other Europe," then printed in 1990 in one volume as *The Complete Fiction of Bruno Schulz*, and again in separate volumes in 1995 and 1997). When the first English translation of *Cinnamon Shops* appeared in 1963 (subsequently retitled *The Street of Crocodiles*), the translator's mission was to bring Schulz's fiction to the English-speaking audience. At that time, Europe east of the Elbe River was, in Philip Roth's phrase, "the other Europe," mysterious and exotic, a region forced by politics to remain in shadow. Celina Wieniewska's readable translations succeeded admirably in their task, but today Schulz's writing is incomparably better known. The region from which he came has rejoined Europe. Scholars worldwide analyze every line in Schulz's prose; schools of interpretation rise and fall upon a single word or phrase. It is time for a more precise translation, one that does not simplify Schulz's imagery or universalize his references. In Polish, Bruno Schulz's writing is more difficult to read than the English translations suggest. His stylistic arsenal is richly international, replete with oxymorons, Latin terms, and Jewish and biblical allusions. English-speaking readers, accustomed to postmodern and experimental fiction, can read Schulz without having his language trimmed and domesticated. Above all, Jerzy Jarzębski's definitive edition of Schulz's prose (1989), available only decades after the Wieniewska translations, provides the textual basis that is essential in translating a writer whose manuscripts, save for one, have not survived.

We may see the first English appearance of Jerzy Ficowski's powerful book as a celebration. Bruno Schulz lives in its extraordinary pages, which are a vade mecum to his world. The reader who wishes to encounter Schulz will find him in his own time and place in this classic study. There remains no better way to meet Bruno Schulz the man, the artist, and the writer than to enter the misty Galician provinces and the small town of Drohobycz through Jerzy Ficowski's *Regions of the Great Heresy.*

—*Theodosia Robertson*
University of Michigan–Flint

Acknowledgments

With the deepest appreciation, I want to express my sincere gratitude to the three individuals who are responsible for this expanded edition of *Regions of the Great Heresy*. The book is exemplary of the commitment Robert Weil, Norton's executive editor, has made to enhance reader's access to great modern writers. His insistence on making this volume a fully realized introduction to Bruno Schulz has resulted in a rich new work.

Neither Bruno Schulz's prose nor my own stands translation easily, but Theodosia Robertson has been far more than a fine translator in bringing about this volume. Dr. Robertson saw the need for an English-language version and has brought a rare combination of talents and interest to the book. She is herself a highly involved scholar of Schulz, and comes to the literature with training as a historian and special interests in Polish and Jewish subjects.

Alan Adelson, executive director of Jewish Heritage, initiated this edition. Some thirty-eight years after I published the first version of the book in Poland, my friends and colleagues Anna Frajlich-Zając and Henryk Grynberg brought Mr. Adelson to me. He declared his intention of seeing *Regions of the Great Heresy* published in English, and to make an updated and expanded edition available to serve the still-awakening interest in Bruno Schulz around the world. Within a month of my consent, the Norton edition was arranged.

REGIONS

of the

GREAT
HERESY

1

I Found the Authentic

(In Place of a Prologue)

My own enchantment with the writing of Bruno Schulz lies at the heart of this book. When I experienced in 1942 the incomparable emotion which accompanies a first reading of Schulz's works, it turned out to be the last year of his life.

I would like to share with the reader the circumstances connected with the origin of this work, to explain how it was that although I did not know Schulz personally and am not engaged in literary theory or literary criticism, I persisted in my resolve to write *Regions of the Great Heresy*. My desire was not a new one. It had emerged immediately after my initial delight with *Cinnamon Shops*.[1] My first sudden thought was to thank this writer—previously unknown to me, and about whom I knew nothing—and to express to him my appreciation for his existence.

I came across Schulz's address and with all the enthusiasm of an eighteen-year-old, I naively wrote that although it might mean nothing to him, he should know that there was someone for whom *Cinnamon Shops* was the source of intense delight and revelation, that I was embarrassed that up until now I had not known about the "greatest writer of our time," and that he should not disdain this devotion lavished upon him by an unknown young man. I asked some question, thanked him for everything, and expressed my timid hope that he would answer.

I did not know that the address was no longer his or that Schulz, forced into a small room in the ghetto, was near the end of his life. I had no idea how inopportunely timed my letter was. Only in the spring of 1943—several months after Schulz had tragically perished—did news of the terrible loss of his death reach me. No longer able to tell Schulz personally about my experience with *Cinnamon Shops*, I decided to write about him myself. My decision was a kind of irrational act of reader's gratitude. My enchantment required an explanation and demanded some active expression of admiration for Schulz's work. My reading suggested the personality of the kind of genius who sometimes creates great religious systems, or a magician and master of black arts, whose predecessors were burned at medieval stakes.

In a small provincial town, Bruno Schulz, a modest drawing teacher, undertook the lonely creation of a new world. He created a personal and disquieting bible: two collections of stories in which the object of worship is the secret essence of things which transcend their own limitations—the magic of creation. Schulz terms the mythic, lost model of this bible the "Authentic."[2] It is the book of childhood, composed of magic scraps of paper known to us all when we were children and the source of the enchantment of our earliest readings, our first and most profound emotions: an old illustrated paper, a decal, a stamp album. In his story "The Book," which opens his second volume of tales, *Sanatorium Under the Sign of the Hourglass*, Schulz writes:

> I call it simply The Book, without descriptions or epithets, and in this abstinence and limitation there is a helpless sigh, a quiet capit-

ulation before the unattainability of the transcendent, where no word, no allusion is able to sparkle, to scent the air, to drift with this shiver of fear, this sense of things beyond name whose first taste on the tip of the tongue exceeds the capacity of our admiration.

The creative reconstruction of that "Book" is Schulz's major literary postulate. He expresses it in all his fiction and he declares it in his theoretical statements and in his private letters. In the following story, "Age of Genius," the narrator Joseph accidentally discovers that scrap of paper from childhood—the last pages of an old illustrated weekly. He confides to his friend, the town thief, Shloma, "I have to confess to you— . . . I found the Authentic. . . ."

I too found the Authentic—in 1942. It was Schulz's first collection of stories, published in 1934, *Cinnamon Shops*.[3] A book different from all others, it was a discovery for me of the formulation of the elusive sensual contents of my childhood, an artistic and psychological revelation, a complete recreation of the perfection of the irrational "Book." There are writers who are known as the authors of a single book. I turned out to be a reader of a single book, one for which no rival has ever emerged. The attainment of the Schulzian artistic postulate led me to a state of feverish ecstasy. I did not then know of Schulz's letter of 1936 in which he wrote:

> The books which we read in childhood don't exist anywhere; they fluttered away—bare skeletons remain. Whoever would still have in himself the marrow of childhood—ought to write them anew as they were then.[4]

Bruno Schulz did so in his two published books: *Cinnamon Shops*, printed in 1934, and *Sanatorium Under the Sign of the Hourglass*, printed in 1937. The stories in these two volumes are rich, ambiguous, and multileveled, like every brilliant work of art.

And so in 1943 I wrote a small and disorganized essay in which adoration of Schulz went hand in hand with naiveté of expression. The whole work—some thirty-odd pages in manuscript—I bound in canvas cloth, titled even then *Regions of the Great Heresy*. I have kept that little volume as a memento. What has endured from it is primarily my enchantment with Schulz and the title, taken from his "Tailors' Dummies." It was my first step in the direction of the book which would evolve despite all vicissitudes through three editions over the following six decades. Soon after the war, beginning in 1947, I began to search for traces of Schulz's life. I acquired three valuable letters of Schulz's which fortunately I was able to keep. Above all, I collected the testimony of people whom Schulz had known personally in various periods of his life; these were his colleagues and contemporaries, as well as his grateful students from the Drohobycz gymnasium. Thanks to what they remembered and were willing to share with me, I could begin to reconstruct from scraps and fragments more or less precisely the course of Bruno Schulz's life—his spiritual portrait—accumulating details of his life and work not known to the general public or even to literary specialists. The extent of ignorance about Bruno Schulz was extraordinary. Suffice it to say that as late as 1961 his birth date was variously misstated in different publications and what little information was given about his life and death was full of gaps and inconsistencies. The war, the changes in the Polish borders, the deaths of the majority of Schulz's friends, the destruction of his vast correspondence, and the loss of all his manuscripts and signed works—so completely destroyed had been the era of his life and those who witnessed it. All this meant that one had to go about as if blind, often using almost detectivelike or archaeological techniques. My search was not confined to Poland, but extended to Ukraine and the United States. The results have included not only the recollections of Schulz's acquaintances, but also his letters, his drawings, graphics, photographs, and papers. Some of these findings are of minor importance, but ultimately every detail connected with a great writer warrants attention and respect.

So it was that by the late 1940s I had collected stories about Schulz and some papers related to his biography. My first essay was scheduled for publication in 1946 in *Życie Literackie* (Literary Life), a Poznań journal edited by Wojciech Bąk. It never appeared. Soon after I received the news that it was to be printed, the journal ceased publication. In 1949 I attempted to publish an expanded version of my essay about Schulz's life and work, this time in the Cracow *Dziennik Literackie* (Literary Daily). On October 17 of that year I received a letter from Wilhelm Mach in which he wrote:

The problem [of the essay] looks like this at *Dziennik Literackie*: your article, already submitted, was to be printed, but due to tactical considerations . . . it was held back. For the time being. (Sometime I will tell you about these "tactical considerations"; they were real—that's no fib.) But in November the essay will certainly appear.

It is not difficult to guess just what these tactical considerations were. The period of "errors and deviations" had begun in Polish cultural politics, and for many subsequent years one could only write inaccurately about Schulz or keep silent.[5] I chose silence, although I did not stop gathering scattered Schulzian materials for the book which I was determined to write. Only in 1948, however, did I succeed in getting into *Odrodzenie* (Renaissance) a photograph of the portrait of Schulz done by Stanisław Ignacy Witkiewicz,[6] together with a one-sentence notation that "six years ago" Schulz had perished in Drohobycz, murdered by the Nazis.

Only at the beginning of 1956 was I able to publish an article entitled "A Reminder about Bruno Schulz," making the details of his life public for the first time. In addition to a series of articles that I published in the following years, I published the letters which I had collected along with an introduction and commentary in the 1964 edition of Bruno Schulz's *Prose* (Cracow: Wydawnictwo Literackie). Then in 1965 in *Twórczość* (Artistic Creation) I published a newly discovered cycle of letters from Schulz to Zenon Waśniewski,[7] together with an article about that correspondence, as well as letters to the Lwów journal *Sygnały* (Signals) and several other correspondents. In 1975 I published the majority of Schulz's preserved letters then available, together with an extensive biographical and bibliographical appendix, in *Księga listów* (Cracow: Wydawnictwo Literackie).[8] I have continued to publish more recently discovered letters in journals and in two subsequent books: *Bruno Schulz: Listy, fragmenty, wspomnienia o pisarzu* (Cracow: Wydawnictwo Literacki, 1984) and *Okolice sklepów cynamonowych* (Cracow: Wydawnictwo Literacki, 1986).

To see the setting of Schulz's entire life with my own eyes, I traveled in 1965 to his native region, now in western Ukraine. I visited

Lwów, Borysław, Sambor, and other locations, and above all his native city, Drohobycz. My findings were meager, but my Drohobycz walks were like a pilgrim's visit to a sacred site—to the cradle of Schulzian myth.

What I have gathered in *Regions of the Great Heresy* is biographical information combined with the comments of a fascinated reader along the margins of a great work. The peculiarity of my own perceptions means that the choice of materials considered and their proportion may seem subjective. Perhaps. I have written about *my* Schulz, about what I found in him and how I understand him. It was not my intent, however, to undertake the kind of analysis that would reduce Schulz's work to its lowest common denominators. As Schulz wrote to his friend Witkiewicz:

> I think that the rationalization of the vision of things rooted in the work of art is like the demasking of actors. It is the end of the game, it is the impoverishment of the question of the work. Not because art is an anagram with a hidden key; philosophy is this same anagram—solved. The difference is more profound. In the work of art the umbilical cord is not yet cut that joins it to the whole of the problem. The blood of the mystery is still circulating; the ends of the vessels escape into the surrounding night and return full of a dark fluid. In a philosophical interpretation we now have only extracted an anatomical specimen for an entire problem.

In this sense an analysis of a work of art may be a destructive activity, but fortunately it accomplishes its devastation—even when it is most ambitious—only partially. The essence of the work remains unattainable, always happily eluding the critics' scalpels and microscopes. I do not desire to dissect Bruno Schulz's *living* work. The purpose of *Regions of the Great Heresy* is to sketch the story of Schulz's life and to highlight several aspects of his work within the context of his biography, showing correlations between the man and the writer, the life and the work, the actual events and the artistic creation.

I would like to thank all those who shared information, papers, and recollections with me about Bruno Schulz. Their kind and generous assistance enabled me to collect abundant materials and recreate the outline of a great writer's biography, fragments of which were preserved in the memory of those close to him. I profited enormously from oral information and letters, from cooperation in searching, from manuscripts, letters, drawings, and photographs made available to me, from help in photocopying and microfilming Schulz's works and correspondence. I thank the editors of many newspapers and weeklies, both Polish and foreign, for their kind advertising for data needed for my research during the years 1948–1992, as well as the following people: M. Ambros, R. Auerbach, J. Backenroth, T. Breza, M. Chajes, M. Chazen, A. Chciuk, K. Czajka, S. Dretler-Flin, H. Drohocka, J. Flaszen, L. Fries, J. Garbicz, T. Głębocki, E. Górski, E. Hoffman, K. Hoffman, M. Holzman, L. Horoszowski, P. Horoszowski, S. Howard, E. Iwanciw, Iwanowski, M. Jachimowicz, Z. Janicki, O. Karliner, H. Kaufman, W. Kiecuń, A. Klinghoffer, A. Klügler, J. Kosowski, M. Krawczyszyn, A. Kuszczak, St. J. Lec, K. Leibler, E. Lewandowski, T. Lubowiecki (I. Friedman), J. Łoziński, G. R. Marshak (G. Rosenberg), M. Mirski, B. Moroń, Z. Moroń, A. Pawlikowski, J. Pinette, J. Pollak-Jasińska, A. Procki, S. Shrayer, R. Stiller, J. Susman, J. Szelińska, T. Szturm de Sztrem, K. Truchanowski, M. Waśniewska, E. Werner, P. Zieliński, and many others.

2

Bruno, Son of Jacob

The younger son in the Schulz mercantile family, their third and last child, the frailest of the children, was born on July 12, 1892. He was named Bruno, a name perhaps determined by the day of his birth: Bruno (Brunon in Polish) was the saint's name on that date in the calendar.

Drohobycz, Bruno Schulz's native town and the setting for almost his entire life from birth to death, was one of the provincial towns of eastern Małopolska. As a result of the eighteenth-century partitions of Poland it had become part of the Austrian Empire, together with other southern Polish lands.[1] Less than a century after the fall of the Polish Commonwealth in 1795, these lands, then called Galicia, had finally been granted autonomy, a more independent status within the Austrian Empire that affected many aspects of life, including education. Since Bruno Schulz was born a quarter century after the establishment of autonomy, from his earliest school days he was educated in Polish, although the school was named for Emperor Franz Josef.

Bruno's childhood also coincided with the early growth of Galician industry, which brought about rapid changes in economic and social life. The turn of the twentieth century saw the development and operation of oil fields in the region. Drohobycz, soon to have a population of over ten thousand, together with the nearby town of Borysław, became a center for the oil industry. The life of small-town shopkeepers and impoverished artisans continued in the shadow of this enormous transformation, in old and long-inhabited quarters on the fringes of industrialization, and often verging upon poverty and bankruptcy. From just such a family of small Jewish merchants came the great heresiarch Bruno Schulz.

Bruno was born at night, and when in time he learned that July darkness had greeted the first moments of his existence, he included the July night as an important element in the individual mythology that he created as a writer. Schulz's mythology discarded the ordinary appearances of things, but at the same time it respected actual facts and places in his biography.

Bruno's parents, Jacob and Henrietta Schulz, lived with their family on the second floor of a small eighteenth-century apartment house on the market square of Drohobycz: number 12, on the northwest corner of the square, at the corner of Samborska (later Mickiewicz) Street. Below them was the family dry goods or haberdashery shop, run by Jacob Schulz and with a sign out front reading, "Henriette Schulz." At the time of Bruno's birth, Jacob had lived for several decades in Drohobycz. The son of Simon and Hinda Schulz, Jacob was born in 1846, the year of unrest in Galicia.[2] He was a bookkeeper and had come to Drohobycz from his home in Sądowa Wisznia[3] looking for work and a wife; finding both, he remained in Drohobycz to the end of his life. Miss Hendel-Henrietta Kuhmerker brought a dowry to the marriage, making it possible for them to open a modest store in her name and gradually build up a business.

Bruno's daily life was controlled by his anxious, pampering

mother. She was his everyday love, the incarnation of practicality, the guarantor of security. Bruno's father, devoted to the rites of commerce, was seen less often. Little Brunio (as he was called) made visits to the dry goods shop, which enabled him to sense the superiority of his father's mercantile rituals to his mother's domestic bustle.

Bruno never knew his father as a young man in the way his brother Izydor (called Lulu), more than ten years older, or the oldest of the three children, his sister, Hania, could recall him. In Bruno's earliest recollected images, his father appeared hunched over, ascetically thin, and with a gray beard that seemed to grow white in the dusky depths of the shop. This is how Schulz would later portray his father in drawings and tales, endowing him with the attributes of a magus and rendering him the central figure in Schulzian mythology. Only many years after the death of his father did Bruno's mythological consecration of him occur. The shop was already long gone when Bruno Schulz rendered it the setting for the many mythic peripeteia in his two cycles of stories.

In addition to Polish, the language used in the Schulz home, Schulz became fluent in German, which his mother taught him before he could read on his own. Fluency in German was common and even obligatory in Galicia of the time. Bruno's first reading experiences were the passages read to him by his mother—in both Polish and in German.

While the Schulzes belonged to the Jewish community and visited the Drohobycz house of prayer, they were not conservative in their religious practice. Closer to secular literature than to the Hebrew scriptures, the family was more connected with the abacus of the store than the menorah of the synagogue. Bruno was not taught Yiddish, the language of his forebears, a language he understood only to the extent that its words were similar to German. Nevertheless, Bruno was not indifferent to myths or sacred rites. Experiencing them, he lost himself in the aura of mythic beginnings, and in the magic of ritual he returned to the "depths of poetry," where he took part, as it were, in the creation of a cosmogony—a story of the creation. For this reason he liked to attend solemn religious ceremonies even after he had become a mature writer-mythologizer. To the amazement of his friends, Schulz, who was essentially distant from religious observance, liked to join the festive, noisy crowd on the solemn Jewish holy day Yom Kippur, silently experiencing his own silent return to mythic time so that it might pervade his own mythological genealogy. Likewise, as a teacher in the gymnasium, assisting pupils during the recitation of prayers before class, he was wont to cross himself just as the Catholic professors did. He took his class to Easter confession and related his fascination with the figure of Christ. This behavior inclined some to assume erroneously that Schulz had converted to Catholicism, something which he never did.

Bruno was not only sickly and physically frail. His hypersensitivity was evidenced in his fear of going out without his mother onto the balcony; his timidity with his playmates, whom he avoided and from whom he retreated into solitude; and the inexplicable tenderness he could show the last autumn flies that struck the window panes—by feeding them sugar.

Bruno's maladjustment to life with children his own age became more pronounced when he entered school in 1902. It was difficult for him to adapt to the company of other pupils. He was affable but mistrustful, and unable to compete with them physically. He was a capable student who learned his lessons very well, but along with the good marks on his report card, Bruno received poor grades in gymnastics. Although among his classmates he was sometimes disparagingly termed "the oaf," Bruno's teachers soon recognized his uncommon talents; with time other students came to respect him as well. Languages, history, mathematics, and natural sciences were the subjects in which he excelled. Beginning in the first class, or fifth grade, he demonstrated a particular liking for drawing and for Polish language, and his achievements in drawing amazed his professors in his early school years. But Bruno evidently had been conscious of these talents even before he entered school at the Emperor Franz Josef "modernized classical gymnasium." Many years later he wrote to Stanisław Ignacy Witkiewicz:

> The beginnings of my drawing are lost in a mythological mist. Before I could even speak, when I covered any piece of paper and the edges of newpapers with scribbles that caught the attention of

those around me. . . . Around the age of six or seven, there constantly recurred in my drawings the image of a carriage with its top up and lanterns lit coming out the night forest.[4]

A fascination with the image of a horse and carriage never left Schulz, and it found expression in numerous drawings and stories even in his mature artistic period. In childhood Schulz had already made hesitant attempts to express this earliest and most long-lasting fascination. His first drawing teacher in 1902, Adolf Arendt (whom years later Schulz mentioned by name in the story "Cinnamon Shops"), and Arendt's successor, Franciszek Chrząstowski, admired Schulz's work, which often, when he had his own choice of theme, would return to the horse and carriage, to the motif whose genesis and influence upon him Schulz himself could never fully explain. One might say that the carriage horse was a kind of Pegasus created by Schulz's world—a wingless Pegasus wandering the roads of Schulzian mythology. Its very ordinariness contained a hidden symbolism for Schulz, a metaphysical vehicle enticing him to mythological investigations and discoveries.

Once, in the second or third class,[5] when given a homework assignment in which the pupils were free to choose their topic, Schulz filled up an entire notebook with a kind of fairy-tale story about a horse. Amazed at the extraordinary composition, the Polish instructor showed the notebook to Joseph Staromiejski, director of the gymnasium. Realizing the value of the composition, Staromiejski shared it with his colleagues. It was widely commented upon in school and gained Schulz the respect of his class. Moreover, because he helped weaker students with their lessons, sometimes doing their drawings for them and correcting their homework, Schulz won over those who otherwise might have been inclined to slight him.

Schulz's unusual personality distanced him from his surroundings. As if unable to confine itself in his frail body, Schulz's extraordinary inner life radiated outward. On the one hand, it filled his classmates with a kind of superstitious awe that blocked normal familiarity, while on the other, Schulz kept himself apart from others, not out of superiority or disdain, but because he felt himself entirely unworthy as a companion and envied his schoolmates their elemental vitality. He was ashamed of his physical weakness and the illnesses to which he was frequently prey. A profound inferiority complex accompanied him all his life, for which his artistic creativity later became a partial remedy, but never a complete liberation.

Despite his unprepossessing outward appearance, Bruno's personality was intensified by the phenomenon of an unaffected demonic aspect which was sensed by everyone with whom he came into contact. His manner of speaking, sometimes hushed almost to a whisper, combined softness with a compelling but unobtrusive, even self-deprecating, strength of conviction. The shyness or embarrassment which rarely left him precluded closeness with others and intensified the growing sense of isolation that tormented him from childhood: his increasingly hermetic solitude. With the passage of years, these feelings, although at times suppressed, became more pronounced. He remained physically frail, somewhat hunched over, very thin, and draped with overly long arms, so that even in childhood he differed from his contemporaries in outward appearance. Consumed by fears and complexes, Schulz nevertheless did not hide his knowledge and intelligence from those close to him. What he did conceal, however, was the literary and artistic fruit of his spiritual entanglements and complications.

In his school years he was already frank in his drawings, not camouflaging even the most embarrassing content. Here intimate matters emerged without guise, and in this early period the subject matter of his drawings was already marked by an unambiguous masochism. Domineering women appear, sometimes with whips in their hands, surrounded by dwarfed men who crawl on all fours at their feet. Sometimes, especially in the early period of his art, such scenes were still quite conventional: figures were clothed and the masochistic element could be discerned only in the very reverential bow being made by a man upon whom a woman gazes from above. Soon the expressiveness became sharper and the protective masks disappeared. Women seduced men with their long legs, trampled them and enticed them to masochistic humiliations. As a rule, one of the male dwarfs resembled Schulz himself. Schulz was reluctant to discuss the content of his drawings. When questioned about the recurring masochistic theme, he replied characteristically that precisely this kind of drawing best suited him, that he did not choose the theme, but rather the theme chose him, and that even when one is free to choose a theme, one is a prisoner of one's self. And it cannot be helped what that self is like.

Thus Bruno was the cause of great concern and of many anxious domestic debates about his physical and mental state. His mother, sincerely devoted to him it seems, did not understand him very well, so different was he from her own sunny disposition and predilection for the practical. Considerably closer to Schulz was the father he adored, the father known in town as the merchant-dreamer, a man of unusual wit and intelligence. Like Bruno, Jacob was sickly and thin. Continually unwell, he contracted tuberculosis and then developed cancer. With time the Schulz household increasingly became absorbed in worry about Jacob's return to health. As long as Bruno's father had sufficient strength, the shop prospered and the family lived well. As disease took its toll, the business failed to such a degree that finally the shop had to be closed, reducing the family to the indigence that would accompany Bruno the rest of his life. His father's lengthy illness and the anxieties it wrought cast a shadow upon Bruno's childhood and early youth.

Schulz's mother, sturdy and plump Henrietta, not only differed from her wiry husband in size; at home her happy temperament and equanimity eased the atmosphere of anxiety. Her presence was Bruno's guarantee of safety, of stability in a family tending toward collapse from his father's illness. She devoted many years to nursing not only her husband, but also Bruno himself, whose frail health demanded constant care. He suffered all his life from a heart defect. Knowing his sensitivity, and not wanting to hurt him, Bruno's mother never punished him severely. Bruno always recalled her as the one from whom he never had to fear loud reprimands, as the one who was the guardian of domestic peace. Later she appears in this protective role several times in Schulz's stories, but always as a marginal character and in the background. Spiritually distant and providentially levelheaded, she did not qualify for a place equal to Father in Schulzian mythology. "That was long ago," writes Schulz in his story "The Book." "At that time mother did not exist yet." And further: "Then mother came and that bright early idyll ended. Beguiled by mother's caresses, I forgot about father; my life went along on a new, different track, without holidays and without miracles. . . ."

Spared by his mother, who never raised a hand to him, Bruno was often punished by his nanny when his parents were not at home. He never complained about this, and only many years later did he confide to someone close to him that probably those dim and apparently minor incidents were the cause of his masochistic tendencies, which with time developed and intensified.

Bruno Schulz spent the years 1902 to 1910 at the Drohobycz gymnasium, where from class I b to VII b until graduation, he remained one of the best students. At the end of the fifth class (ninth grade) he received an all-round perfect mark, something achieved by only two other students. When he finished the seventh class (eleventh grade), he found himself one of four students considered "commendably talented," an achievement he repeated the next year, his final one at the gymnasium. He easily passed his matriculation exam with a grade of Very Good, and the examination committee entered a note into his secondary school certificate: "passed with distinction to studies at the University."

In Bruno's last year at the gymnasium, the Schulz family had to leave their home on the market square where Bruno had lived all his life. They moved to a house on Bednarska Street, where the oldest Schulz child, the daughter, Hania Hoffman, now lived with her husband and small son, Ludwik. That year a second son named Zygmunt (called Zyguś) was born to the Hoffmans. Like many other moments in Bruno Schulz's life, this event was recorded in one of his stories, "A Night in July":

> During the long holiday of my last year in school I became acquainted for the first time with summer nights. Our house, through whose open windows the breezes, hum, and glares of the hot summer days entered, now put up a new lodger, a tiny, pouting, wailing creature, my sister's small son.

Bruno's depression, driven by the illness that increasingly weakened his father and sadness at leaving his childhood home, was soon overshadowed by a new tragedy: Bruno's brother-in-law, Hoffman, under the strain of an incurable disease, committed suicide by slitting his throat with a razor.

Immediately after summer vacation in 1910, Bruno left Drohobycz for the first time for an extended period (although frequently making return visits home) in order to study architecture in nearby Lwów. He felt uncomfortable there, bereft of familiar people and places. His studies were not altogether satisfying; he had chosen architecture as a compromise between his real love for art and the practical advice of his older brother, who had suggested that architecture would be more profitable than painting.

He traveled back and forth to Drohobycz during semester breaks and more frequently when worried about his seriously ill, beloved father. Bruno himself was also sick. In the summer of 1911, after finishing his first year of his studies, he returned home and was confined to bed with pneumonia and a heart condition. He subsequently took treatments at the local health resort, Truskawiec.[6] Only at the beginning of the 1913–14 academic year, and thus after a two-year interval, did Schulz return to Lwów to resume his studies at the polytechnic. Although continuation seemed impossible after another year of study, his poor health, worsening financial situation, worry about his father and longing for Drohobycz, and even an increasing desire to change his course of study would not have forced Schulz to abandon his classes in the "Department of Land Building," as architectural studies were officially termed. The approaching summer vacation coincided with the outbreak of World War I.

Fearing the advance of the Russian front, part of the Schulz family went to Vienna, but Father's deteriorating health forced them to return immediately, and Bruno was also unwell. Once back in Drohobycz, Bruno's indefatigible mother began to care for both her sick charges. The home was again transformed into a hospital, just as it had been a few years earlier. This was probably one of the longest periods of uninterrupted contact between Bruno and Jacob. When better himself, Bruno helped tend his dying father. The image of Father's emaciated head, resting helplessly on pillows, would later recur in many of Schulz's drawings. Jacob's death on June 23, 1915, was the most painful blow the twenty-three-year-old Bruno had ever suffered. It slammed the door shut forever upon the "happy epoch" of his life, a period irrevocably lost "on the other side" of the war, but later resurrected in Bruno Schulz's writing. Together with Jacob, the shop and house on the market square disappeared as well; the business had been liquidated earlier, but the destruction caused by the war erased any physical traces of it. The Schulz home burned in a fire along with the rooms of their former shop. The life work of Jacob, the deposed ruler of a dry goods business, was reduced to ashes. Even before a new apartment building stood on the site of the old Schulz house, Bruno Schulz began his own reconstruction of it— in a literary mythology. In his writing, he would return to what in reality was irrevocable, and in myth document the imperishability of what had passed.

One of Bruno's first secret attempts at writing was a mythical resurrection of his father, the patron saint of his youth. In almost biblical dimensions, on the scale of a newly created mythology, the character of Father from *Cinnamon Shops* and *Sanatorium Under the Sign of the Hourglass* is repeatedly recovered through a life in the world of things around him: a stuffed bird, a fur pulsating with his breathing, a cooked crab that is still capable of a successful escape. Father's spirit switches masks and goes through various incarnations that allow him to continue to exist despite his apparent absence. The forms of objects that had lived with him preserve him within themselves; he becomes their essence. By means of every device of poetic magic, Schulz returns his dead father to existence, undoing in myth what occurred in life, and posthumously rendering his father a spiritual alter ego, to some extent the enunciator of Bruno's own views, the major mythologue of his childhood, whose best times became inseparably fused with the ascetic image of Father, embroiled in mysterious merchant rituals. In this way, Schulz commands time to turn back at the sanatorium "under the the sign of the hourglass"—to return to the moment when Father still lived, together with all the qualities of time so regained, and hence with the possibility of recovered health. Here, somewhere in mythic time, on the fringe of time that flows only one way, Schulz guarantees his father this partial, relative existence—in art.

Lean years came upon the Bednarska Street home after the

deaths of Bruno's father and brother-in-law. Bruno's mother, always protective and responsible for the fate of the family, now took upon herself the care of her widowed daughter and two grandsons. Bruno reflected bitterly upon his orphanhood: without his father, without his childhood home, and without the recent aspirations of his architecture studies. He attempted to continue them once more, taking classes in architecture in Vienna just before the end of the war, in 1917 and 1918. But the imminent collapse of the monarchy combined with revolutionary unrest in Vienna, wartime confusion, and the prospect of a new independent Poland caused Bruno to stop again—this time for good—and he returned home. Vienna's art galleries, where he could see original European masterpieces, and the Vienna Academy of Fine Arts, where he could audit lectures as a guest, had convinced Bruno that painting was the only art to which he wanted to devote himself. All this, however, now had to be consigned to the realm of dreams, and he had to return to Drohobycz. Later he described this difficult and critical moment in his life: "A new era had begun, empty, sober, joyless—white as paper" ("Father's Last Escape"). Only after the "new era" would come the period of creative accomplishment, the period of return through art to the "paradise lost."

Many years later, walking with friends through the changed Drohobycz market square, Schulz pointed out the spot where his childhood home had stood at number 12 and, describing it as it had been, he reached into an even more distant past than his own childhood, as if in that shadowy era he discovered his own prehistory, the root of his personal mythic origins. So, too, all the peripeteia of the characters in his tales never enter present time, the time of Schulz's maturity, but exist—mythologically—everywhere and always, or perhaps anywhere and anytime, together with Drohobycz and the childhood of the narrator-author.

3

Return to School

In the story entitled "The Old Age Pensioner" from *Sanatorium Under the Sign of the Hourglass*, Schulz tells of a city councillor who at an advanced age decided to return to his school days and begin his education once again, from the first grade. It is just one more version, the most grotesque one, of the Schulzian "return to childhood."

In reality Schulz was condemned to another return, distressingly similar in its details: he returned as a teacher of drawing and handicrafts to the same Drohobycz gymnasium which he had left after graduation in 1910. On September 3, 1924, after a fourteen-year interval, he again crossed the threshold of the King Władysław Jagiełło State Gymnasium, this time as a beginning teacher. Bruno Schulz's return to school occurred after bad luck had interrupted his studies and after years of unemployment, but this period had also been one of prodigious reading, solitary contemplation, and secret study. Schulz's economic situation was hardly favorable; he was unable to buy the books that interested him. He spent long hours sitting in the cramped little office in the back of Pilpel's bookshop, engrossed in the books that the old Drohobycz bookseller, the father of his friend and schoolmate Mundek Pilpel, had on his shelves. It was then that the writer in Schulz matured and the graphic artist in him emerged. Although much later Schulz described this period as a "lost, stupidly wasted youth," these were not years fruitlessly squandered.

Thus, after a long interval Schulz undertook work as a teacher, an occupation which would be his sole actual support almost until the end of his life. Although the job was in some ways a curse, he clung to it with all his might, trembling lest he lose it. In the beginning, before Schulz's position was regularized, his situation was particularly precarious. This was primarily because of his lack of formal training to teach drawing in school. He was self-taught and without professional qualifications. The school authorities hired him on probation, on the condition that within a specified time he pass a special examination and submit his work for a qualified evaluation. The date was finally set for April 1926, and beginning March 16, Schulz interrupted his work at the gymnasium to prepare himself. On April 19 he took the exam administered by the State Examination Commission at the Academy of Fine Arts in Cracow for candidates in the teaching of secondary school drawing. Schulz's exam work received very good mark as the signatures of outstanding artists such as Wojciech Weiss, Konstanty Laszczka, and Teodor Axentowicz testify.[1] It turned out, however, that the exam alone was insufficient; still other formalities were necessary for full certification to teach in a secondary school. In the meantime, however, Schulz continued to teach on the condition that he fulfill the qualifications within four years of beginning work.

Four years elapsed; the legal deadline passed, and Schulz came to school on the last day of the academic year in June 1928, planning not to return to work after summer vacation. He had neglected his own affairs, but this is hardly surprising. This was only the official side of his life; precisely at this time he had secretly begun to develop his literary work, the most crucial matter of all, which with time would overshadow even painting, graphic art, and drawing. He had already been sketching out his literary works for several years, but only now, having freed himself for a period of time from the drudgery of teaching, could he devote himself to their completion. Hardly had the school year ended when in July 1928 Schulz wrote "A Night in July," one of his first tales, which only years later in 1934 would at last appear in book form in *Cinnamon Shops*.

Schulz's secret writing—which had no chance of publication, and he made no efforts in this direction—provided no means of support. Schulz could not forget the school, which, although it robbed him of writing time, did provide a modest income. In October 1928, he took the necessary examination, and having attained professional qualification in this way, was rehired by the school in November. On January 1,1929, he was transferred to a regular position, although he was still referred to as a "temporary teacher." Only a decree of the Curatorium of the Lwów School District (March 8, 1932) enabled him to be transferred to the category of permanent instructor—after nearly eight years of teaching. Schulz worked thirty or more hours per week. Soon classes in handicrafts were added; to his teaching in the state gymnasium were added lessons in a private gymnasium and in a public school. In addition to classes, he was entrusted with the duties of a "superintendent of the department of drawing and practical classes." At times he even taught mathematics.

His duties were excessive; in addition there were trips for courses and teachers' conferences—to Stryj, to Lwów, to Żywiec, to Augustów. It was difficult for Schulz to continue his writing in these circumstances, and yet he did not give it up, even when on top of it all conditions at home disturbed his peace. He lived with his mother until her death in 1931; with his older sister, Hania, and her two sons, Ludwik and Zygmunt Hoffman; and with a crochety old female cousin. Hania, seriously ill with a nervous disorder, caused much anxiety and difficulties. Often during the night when Hania would fall into a serious nervous state combined with convulsions, an alarmed Schulz would have to go for a friend, a doctor related to Schulz's sister by marriage. Schulz's nephew Zygmunt was also a source of concern in the family. He suffered from prolonged melancholic disorders and needed to be supported by his uncle until the end. The elder nephew, Ludwik, married Dora Kipień, an actress from Lwów, and moved away from home. The entire household was permeated by a strange and gloomy aura: three old women pacing like cats its cluttered length and width in soft carpet slippers, appearing unexpectedly at any moment in every nook and corner of the large flat. The depressing atmosphere of this impoverished home impressed every visitor. Its silence was broken only by Hania's nervous attacks or the meowing of cats. It was a quiet without isolation, one threatened by continual anxiety.

Schulz was wont to describe how each person has in his brain a "quiet corner" which under the right conditions becomes a center for the creative process. His own "quiet corner" was especially fastidious, inclined toward quietude, enjoying the taste of life in calm. "I could not create, as Kafka did, in a climate of acute fear," said Schulz. Answering a letter from critic Andrzej Pleśniewicz in 1936, Schulz wrote:

> You overrate the advantages of my Drohobycz situation. What I miss even here—is quiet, my own musical quiet, a stilled pendulum, subject to its own gravitation, along a clear line of track, undistracted by any foreign influence. This substantial quiet, positive—full—is already itself almost creativity. Those things which I think want to express themselves through me take place above a certain threshold of quiet, they take form in a solution brought into perfect equilibrium.

In the meantime reality was immeasurably distant from such an ideal. Schulz's remarks about the torment of teaching are numerous and range from complaints tinged with irony to painful discontent. Equally frequent in his letters is the question of leave time: efforts to get leave, worry whether it will be granted to him, despair that leave has been denied, hope that he will receive it at long last. As Schulz's single possible way to regain personal freedom, leave time takes on particular significance, becoming the *conditio sine qua non* of creativity, of the fulfillment of his most important desires. In a 1934 letter to Julian Tuwim[2] Schulz wrote:

I am very downcast: the leave time upon which I had so counted was not granted to me. I will remain in Drohobycz, in school, where the mob will continue to cut capers on my nerves. You have to know that my nerves are spread like a network throughout the entire handicraft workroom, stretched out across the floor, papering the walls and wrapped around the worktable and anvil in a thick braid. It is a phenomenon known in science as *telekinetics*, through which everything that happens on the workbenches takes place to some degree on my skin. Thanks to such a finely developed signal network I am destined to be a teacher of handicrafts.

Elsewhere Schulz thanks an acquaintance for advice concerning "tactics regarding the boys in school." He had complained that the pupils "are impossible showoffs" and that after vacation he was unable to deal with them. Schulz writes: "No, it's not that bad. I don't observe any malice in them, only the temperament that is natural at this age." Despite Schulz's sense of ill-treatment and a distaste for his increasing school duties, he was fair and kind toward students, and graduates of the gymnasium have the best possible recollections of him.

When Schulz wanted to win over the class and inject some variety into the lessons, he customarily used a foolproof method, especially in the lower grades: the telling of fairy tales. These were fantastic stories which he improvised and illustrated on the blackboard. There is no one among the former students of the Drohobycz gymnasium who does not recall these extraordinary classes during which one forgot about school, about everything, and listened with bated breath to the strange tales told by Professor Schulz. No one is able to repeat these tales, but they left an impression of a singular, unrepeatable atmosphere, a magic—the memory of a beautiful and colorful narration. One of the students recalls: "One motif recurred frequently: a child, his adventures, his sometimes strange fate. If during the whole time there was quiet in the room, [Schulz] would end the tale with a good and very sad smile. He left the room quickly, stooped over."

Schulz was well known as an unusual storyteller in all the schools where he taught, and "everywhere they waited for his tales." Another former pupil writes:

He told us, old fellows from the fourth class, the most wonderful tales. Today when I think about it I regret that no one noted down these marvelous Schulzian tales. Illustrating them with a few strokes of chalk on the blackboard, Schulz recounted these extraordinarily beautiful and unique stories in an exquisite Polish with a fluency that no one would have suspected of this melancholiac. We all loved these tales and didn't even realize how time flew during them. . . . Those tales in which a pencil, an inconspicuous water jug, or a tile stove had their own histories and lived in a manner close to us and so much like human beings; always in the background was the sad smile of a sick little girl who longed to be out in the sunshine.

A female pupil from the coeducational gymnasium writes:

He sat down on the chair as if astride a horse and began to tell us a story. It was about a wandering knight who was cut in half along with his horse by the unexpected closing of a gate. From that time on, the rider wandered throughout the world on half his horse, "half and half."

We would be mistaken to assume that Schulz told these tales during his classes only for the pleasure of his students. It was a surrogate creation for him, an escape from the boredom and routine of school: only while telling stories was he really himself, in his own element. During the war years of 1939 to 1941, while Drohobycz was still under Soviet control and before the German occupation, Schulz was unable to count on having his works printed, and he continued to find an outlet in improvised tales. A colleague from school at that time notes that Schulz's "linguistic mastery together with the richness of his imagination found expression in his tales. He told them to our daughter, then seven years old, during the evenings, seated by her bedside." The half-real, elflike aura that radiated from his person, his expression, and his voice made the magic of his fairy-tale improvisation even more charming to the listener. That unusual aura struck everyone who encountered Schulz. Stefan Jaracz, then a popular actor and director, met Schulz in 1934 when he visited the Atheneum Theater in Warsaw.[3] Later the great actor recalled that Schulz made an extraordinarily fascinating impression on him. Here, to a great extent, lay the source of the respect and esteem which young people, despite everything, accorded this shy teacher, so defenseless against the pranks of a group of children. Sitting before a rapt group of students in the drawing classroom on the second floor and inventing his fantastic stories, Schulz must have seen himself alone among his young listeners. Here, after all, in this very same place years before, he himself had come as a schoolboy for drawing lessons. Here an old professor had taken out plaster of Paris models to be drawn by the students. In 1932 some of the plaster models were removed from the cabinet because, in the opinion of the directors, they were too old and no longer usable. Precisely then—perhaps connected with their reduction in rank—Schulz immortalized them in "Cinnamon Shops," as the professor

> quickly locked the door of his study behind him: through it for a brief moment we could see crowding behind his head a throng of plaster shadows, the classical fragments of pained Niobides, Danaides, and Tantalides, the whole sad and sterile Olympus, wilting for years on end in that plaster-cast museum. The light in his room was opaque even in daytime, and shed sleepily from the dreams of plaster-cast heads, from empty looks, fading profiles, and meditations dissolving into nothingness. We liked to listen sometimes at the door—listen to the silence laden with the sighs and whispers of the crumbling cobwebbed rubble, decomposing in the boredom and monotony of a twilight of the gods.

For an eccentric, Schulz enjoyed a considerable degree of respect. This respect was not, however, far-reaching: the small-town philistines did not regard him with esteem, nor did some of the members of his family. This lack of recognition sometimes showed up in their slightly disdainful attitude toward his uncommon personality, his lack of resourcefulness in practical matters, and his inability to climb the ladder of success in teaching. This disdain diminished after Schulz's literary debut in 1934, but more as a result of snobism than of an understanding of his work. Up until then, he alone knew about his carefully concealed literary work. Only as an artist did Schulz—hesitantly—reveal himself. He bound a series of his graphics in a portfolio entitled *Xięga bałwochwalcza* (*The Booke of Idolatry*) and sold them through bookstores, such as that of Jacob Mortkowicz in Warsaw. He also made attempts to organize showings of his artwork. In March 1922 the first exhibit of Schulz's graphics was held in Warsaw at the Society to Promote Fine Arts, and in June he participated in a group showing at the Society of the Friends of Fine Arts in Lwów. During the following years Schulz exhibited his works several times in Wilno, Lwów, and Cracow.

In the summer of 1928, Schulz went to Truskawiec, a nearby health resort. He took some of his pictures and drawings. There he turned to an acquaintance, a professor of chemistry, asking him for his opinion of his work—primarily graphics and drawings as well as a few oil paintings, distinctive in their dominant colors of clear violet and azure. The acquaintance reacted very positively and advised Schulz to set up an exhibit in the hall of the Dom Zdrojowy (Health Resort Club). Raymond Jarosz, then the owner of Truskawiec and mayor of Drohobycz, made space available to Schulz free of charge. Crowds of resort visitors began to attend the exhibit, but unexpectedly an amusing incident occurred that nearly closed it down and robbed Schulz of the hope of earning some money. Taking the cure at Truskawiec at the time was the nearly eighty-year-old senator Maximilian Thullie. Thullie was the leader of Chadecja, the popular name of the interwar Christian Democratic Party in Poland, taken from its initials in Polish, "Ch D," and a professor at the Lwów Polytechnic. Thullie gave orders for the immediate closing of the exhibit, which in his opinion amounted to "hideous pornography." He presented his complaint to the *starosta*, or head of the district authorities, demanding prompt intervention. Cued by Jarosz and several persons friendly with Schulz, the *starosta* refused, explaining that it was beyond his power to close the exhibit, and he advised the indignant senator to submit the matter to the Sejm, the Polish parliament, which at this time was in recess. The matter was forgotten. Schulz sold almost all his pictures—for very low prices, because he was afraid to ask more and considered the very sale of his work a sufficient reward. In this way he succeeded for one of the few times in his life in earning some money to supplement his modest teacher's salary. In a letter to his former fellow student the painter and drawing teacher Zenon Waśniewski, Schulz wrote: "So much mechanical, soulless work for someone who could do other things—that is after all a great injustice. Done to both of us."

Summer vacation passed quickly; its Schulzian relative time raced by, only to resume its unbearable snaillike pace during the school year. Teaching absorbed Schulz's time mercilessly; even after returning home it was sometimes necessary for him to check students' homework. Added to this was Schulz's own great kindness, his inability to refuse anyone's request. He was commonly considered to be a person who was good "to the point of being ridiculous." An egotist, Schulz nevertheless did not know how to be neutral toward human injustice. Himself sunk in poverty, he never refused alms to a beggar. He once even gave a beggar five zlotys.[4] He was naive, and more than once others took advantage of his charitable sensibility. Perhaps when giving to others he saw himself in them, in some mysterious but always ominous future whose obsessive specter, irresistible premonition, constantly followed him.

Schulz invited his more talented students home. He corrected their drawings. He made drawings for the cover of the students' paper, Młodzież (Youth), and did the graphic design for the so-called tableaux or school portrait of the graduates of the gymnasium. He decorated the school hall for festivities, and he drew borders and posters advertising school dances and holidays. He projected the school banner of Jagiełło gymnasium, honoring the twentieth anniversary of Poland's independence. Above and beyond these voluntary activities, he had—in addition to his classes—numerous obligations of the most boring kind. He gritted his teeth in hopeless despair when he was overloaded with many hours of handicraft work classes, and at the same time had to prepare and give specialized lectures, such as the one he gave in Stryj in 1932 entitled "Artistic Formation in Cardboard and Its Application in School." What remained of his time was his own: his "scraps and leftovers," which he did not know how to utilize. The prospect of leave time or vacation provided his sole hope—often illusory—of undertaking creative work. And after vacation, again lessons and meetings, like the training sessions led by "Professor Schulz" entitled "The Organization of Work on the Basis of a Working Drawing."

With the publication of Cinnamon Shops in 1934, Schulz became a known and respected writer, but his literary achievement was a complete surprise and shock for the Drohobycz community. Certain school honors ensued. Bureaucratic procedure moves slowly, but finally in April 1936 Schulz was given the title "professor" by a special decree granted during the midterm break "in order to make his literary work possible." In 1938, Schulz attained a still higher position in the ranks of Drohobycz teachers: "Schulz, Bruno, professor, honored with the golden academic laurel PAL [Polish Academy of Literature]." The splendor of being a distinguished writer also affected Schulz's status as a professor of drawing and manual work. And so, after his literary debut, Schulz enjoyed greater respect at school. A colleague, who at that time was beginning work at the gymnasium, recalls:

> The young people knew him as a drawing teacher. And in this subject he was extraordinary. He taught drawing differently than was ordinarily done in school. His unusual, uncommon, inspired and delicate character elicited respect—the young people experienced his lessons, they sensed that they were dealing with an extraordinary person. Moreover, he did not confine himself exclusively to drawing—he taught art history; he would fall into a kind of trance, talking about art, and not only the plastic arts. . . . He was an extremely subtle person, highly cultured and tolerant. He had no conflicts with people.

In the upper classes Schulz conveyed to older students a profound passion for the history of art. These were not lectures in the popular sense of the term, but stories in which Schulz suggestively presented the history of the fine arts to the imagination of his listeners, arousing their interest through an associative approximation of distant things to elements of everyday experience. They were skillfully spoken essays which became the basis for lively discussion in which even students uninterested in art participated. Once, when Schulz was speaking about the Renaissance, about a period rich in great men and works, one of his students vehemently opposed its glorification, declaring that the masses were not allowed to participate in the creation of these cultural treasures or to take advantage of them. With a forbearing smile, Schulz expressed the conviction that there has not been and cannot be a period which would have "a recipe for the production and propagation of great men."

Schulz had labored for fifteen years in the teaching profession, up until the outbreak of World War II in 1939; and then he had to spend the next two years as a teacher in Soviet Drohobycz.[5] School swallowed up Schulz's most productive artistic years—he could create only in stolen moments. He remained in continual poverty: in 1937 he earned around three hundred zlotys a month and had to support a family on it. The publisher of *Cinnamon Shops* paid Schulz no royalty. This left Schulz with only dreams of winning the state lottery and of obtaining leave from teaching. Schulz's one real trip abroad— a three-week trip to Paris in 1938—was preceded by vacillations: should he go, or should he buy a couch? The dilemma was resolved in favor of Paris. To the end of his life Schulz never managed to buy the couch. Neither was he ever able to give up teaching. Still, in 1939, two months before the outbreak of the war, he wrote to a woman friend: "For some time I was bolstered by the thought that I would take my retirement next year (at 40% salary). Now I have moved away from that idea because I would be unable to support my family."

School was servitude for Schulz—and yet he was a good and valued teacher. From among the masses of students he chose the talented, those cherishing the hope of being artists, those showing a love for the subject. On his own initiative he took them kindly under his own care, invited them home, taught them for free, and bestowed his friendship on them. This gave meaning to his teaching duties. He could not bear coercion; he valued spontaneity. He allowed one of the students from the public school, in whom he'd discovered a talent for art, to come to his home often. He talked to him about art and gave him reproductions to look at. I think that Schulz was touched to perceive in this student and those like him his own childhood, the first enchanting travels into the realm of art. When the boy asked why Schulz painted things "differently from the way they really are," Schulz responded by explaining the most complex artistic matters visually, in the manner easiest to understand. He spoke of artistic creation as a great compensation and as an act of personal freedom. "We can turn day into night and night into day," he said. "We may cover snow-capped mountains with luxuriant foliage. That is our, the artist's, freedom, and such is artistic truth, which we can demonstrate through our works." Although decades had passed since these conversations, that former student remained able to recite the words of his most beloved professor.

4

⊙━━◆━━⊙

The Prehistory and Origin of
Cinnamon Shops

Precisely when Bruno Schulz began to write is difficult to determine. While he may have made earlier attempts, concrete evidence points to the years 1925–26. The solitary Schulz needed an exchange of thoughts and ideas; he longed for an interlocutor to enliven and crystalize his own speculations and intuitions. As Schulz said of himself, he was by nature reactive and in need of outside stimulation. He expressed this desire in a letter to Tadeusz Breza in 1934:

> I need a companion. I need the closeness of a kindred person. I long for some affirmation of the inner world whose existence I postulate. To persistently cling to it by my own faith alone, heave it despite everything with the strength of its resistance—it is the

labor and torment of Atlas. Sometimes it seems to me that with this strained gesture of lifting I hold nothing on my shoulders. I would like the power for a moment to set this weight down upon someone's arms, straighten up my neck and look at what I have been carrying.

I need a partner for undertakings of discovery. What for one person is a risk, an impossibility, a caprice stood on its head— when reflected in two pairs of eyes becomes a reality. The world waits as it were for this partnership: until now closed, confined, without further plans—to begin to mature with the colors of a dahlia, burst and open up inside. Painted panoramas deepen and open into actual perspectives, the wall lets us into a dimension formerly unattainable, frescoes painted on the horizon come to life like a pantomime.[1]

During the 1920s, Władysław Riff became just such a confidant for Schulz, a "partner for exploratory undertakings." Ten years younger than Schulz, Riff had been a student of Polish philology at the Jagiellonian University in Cracow, but he was forced to interrupt his studies when he contracted rapidly progressing consumption. He moved to the Tatra Mountain resort Zakopane, south of Cracow. There Schulz sometimes met him during his own vacations, and the two maintained a correspondence. Riff, a highly talented prose writer, had also tried his hand at poetry. He undoubtedly exerted an essential influence upon Schulz. The close contact between the two friends over several years and their correspondence must have caused the Schulzian world of the imagination to crystallize and prompted Schulz to try writing by the mid-1920s.

In any case, the influences were doubtless mutual: Schulz's outstanding individuality influenced Riff and created a positive climate that fostered creative attempts and discussions. After Riff's death, recollection of him or even hearing his name was painful for Schulz. Schulz remained alone in the regions they had once explored together. A few years later, when a mutual friend wrote to Schulz, she received in reply two letters full of fantastic plots without any personal comment at all. In the next letter she mentioned Riff. Schulz did not write back a word. When she met him later, he apologized and explained with embarrassment: "Please don't be angry. I couldn't write back—I didn't want you to write me about this. . . ." When Schulz began to write he felt somehow guilty that he alone had profited from their common speculations, that it was given to him alone to accomplish the plans they both had made. He feared remembrance of his dead partner: it pulled him, as it were, into the nonexistence which was now the lot of his friend. Riff described his ambitious and innovative novel as a "novel of psychic adventures." Many years later, the Polish poet Adam Ważyk[2] tried to recall the impression that a passage from Riff's novel made upon him:

> I was startled by the long, complex sentences—reasoned, devoid of stylistic effects. It was first-person narration. The narrator told of his home during his school years, about his mother, about the coming of a renter to whom his mother let out a room. Over the course of chance meetings the narrator grew accustomed to this new personality introduced into the family circle. He attempted to define this person, supplementing his limited observations with his own inventions; he mythologized the new individual.

Schulz and Riff devoted little space in their letters to daily affairs. Theirs was a long discussion, conducted in installments, on the topic of art; any scattered references to ordinary reality were artistic transpositions bearing signs of literary treatment. Undoubtedly their correspondence must have been advantageous to both writers, but we cannot know for certain. On December 25, 1927, the twenty-six-year-old Riff died of tuberculosis at his mother's pension in Zakopane, and the fumigators who disinfected his room burned, among other things, the manuscripts of Riff's unpublished works and all of Schulz's letters.

Schulz's lush prose, with its cascades of exotic words and rich colors, is evidently unlike Riff's lost work. Riff's letters, however, were more extreme in their style and grotesque mythologization. Whether he took those qualities from Schulz or whether in the end they were common to both writers we do not know. Ważyk writes:

> Bruno Schulz sent me some letters written to him from Zakopane to Drohobycz. [Riff's] boardinghouse had been transformed into a

ship in these letters, and a crew recruited from among the board-
ers under the command of a fictional captain. The ship was
bizarre, the prose supple and thickly sown with metaphors; it was
all in a humorous tone and did not convey an impression of Riff's
lost novel. . . .

If even the ship-pension arose from Schulzian inspiration, it would signify a reverse influence as well. In "Night of the Great Season," a story
from the collection *Cinnamon Shops*, we find the following passage:

> Father was listening. In the silence of the night his ear seemed to
> grow larger and to reach out beyond the window: a fantastic coral,
> a red polypus watching the chaos of the night.

Untypical of Schulzian metaphor and imagery, this passage is—
according to the testimony of people acquainted with both Riff
and Schulz—a metaphor taken from one of Riff's letters to Schulz.
Contact with Riff may have led to the identification of classical,
mythological figures dear to Schulz with persons from his own
biography: the character of father, of the maid Adela, of cousins,
or of the town madwoman, Tłuja. During the years 1920 to 1921,
when Schulz was giving titles to the graphics in his cycle *The Booke
of Idolatry*, he borrowed generously from the terminology of ancient
myth, from plots of fairy tales and legends like those of Hestia,
Circe, and The Infanta and her dwarfs. In Schulz's works, however,
the bearers of these classical names became different characters,
ones born of his imagination. For Schulz, the goddess of the
hearth, Hestia, is a maid with a broom in her hand; theytholog-
ical Circe, who turned men into pigs, becomes "Mademoiselle
Circe," a circus rider enticing men to delightful humiliation. The
Infanta with her dwarfs becomes another typical Schulzian composition with masochistic content.

Although Schulz's literary creation began during the time of his
friendship with Riff, and grew out of correspondence, their letters
were not its only source. Schulz continued to write after Riff's death.
Having lost his sole reader, Schulz wrote in isolation and confided in
practically no one. He put his works in a drawer alongside his scrap-
book. Sometimes he would smuggle, as it were, snatches of his writing

into letters to other acquaintances—to the Cracow artist Stefania Dretler,[3] for example—and then anxiously await a response.

Schulz's works from this period are not dated, and because those which he did not destroy were included only in his second volume of tales, *Sanatorium Under the Sign of the Hourglass*, they were received by both critics and readers as stories written after those in *Cinnamon Shops*. We know from one of Schulz's letters that "A Night in July"—published only in 1937—had been written almost ten years earlier, in 1928. We should date the composition of other tales from *Sanatorium Under the Sign of the Houseglass*, such as "A Second Fall," "Eddie," "The Old-Age Pensioner," "Loneliness," "Dodo," and also very likely "My Father Joins the Fire Brigade" and the title story, "Sanatorium Under the Sign of the Hourglass," to the same earlier period. "Did you happen to see my story 'Dodo' in one of the January issues of *Tygodnik Ilustrowany* [Illustrated Weekly]? . . . Did you read the excerpt about father-the fireman in *Wiadomości Literackie* [Literary News]? Those are all older pieces," wrote Schulz to Zenon Waśniewski in 1935. "My little pieces that you read were all dashed off—some time ago; I've hunted them up now as a kind of 'paralipomena,'" Schulz wrote again in 1935 to Tadeusz Breza. ". . . I am, however, having a volume of earlier stories published by Rój," Schulz wrote to Tadeusz Breza in 1937. During this same period—between Riff's death in 1927 and beginning *Cinnamon Shops* in 1928—Schulz probably composed the story entitled "My Father Joins the Fire Brigade." An anecdote connected with this tale demonstrates how a minor plot element became the stimulus for fiction.

An older colleague, a fellow teacher at Schulz's gymnasium, recalled that he had once told Schulz about his father, a fireman:

> One day Bruno confided to me that under the influence of my childhood story he had composed a new role for his father, namely, "My Father Joins the Fire Brigade." I had once mentioned to Schulz that sometimes at night, when I was already asleep, I would be awakened by light and movement and in the light of the table lamp would see my father hurriedly dressing in his fireman's uniform, putting on his shiny helmet, a wide belt with a hatchet hanging at his side that had two blades, a wide one and a narrow one, and then rushing off into the night. Out in the streets there

were unusual lights and wagons racing along. I heard words and I guessed people were saying "it's burning." I would try to get up too and go with my father, because a struggle with the element of fire was irresistibly attractive to me—but I was held back. One time, however, I did succeed in outwitting them and then I saw the fire up close. And especially my father. He directed the activity—everyone listened to him. In his fireman's uniform he seemed to me the embodiment of daring, energy, and devotion.

Schulz's artistic version of this motif was perceived by his colleague as a grotesque transposition, the deprecation of a cherished recollection that he had shared with Schulz.

The year 1930 arrived, and Schulz visited the writer and painter Stanisław Ignacy Witkiewicz ("Witkacy") in Zakopane several times. He had known Witkacy for five years, and it was through him that Schulz met a woman from Lwów named Debora Vogel. Debora Vogel had a doctorate and was the author of a volume of poetry as well as an enthusiast of modern painting.[4] Schulz discovered an intellectual affinity in her and their casual acquaintance turned into a lasting friendship. From that time on, he visited Debora—called Dozia—in Lwów and spent long hours in walks and discussions with her. They began to exchange letters, and over the course of a year Schulz's letters began to contain startling mythological stories developed in lengthy postscripts. Set against the background of a magically transformed Drohobycz and occurring in time without continuity, liberated from its irreversible flow, there emerged from the letters the peripeteia of the Father Jacob and the son, Joseph—all to enchant a single reader. As had happened earlier with Władysław Riff, the discovery of a new "partner for exploratory undertakings" acted as a creative stimulus for Schulz. From the postscripts, originally written for Debora Vogel alone, the book *Cinnamon Shops* was composed.

Debora received these extraordinary letters with increasing delight; she encouraged the continuation of the mythical history and even showed them to a friend, a Jewish journalist named Rachel Auerbach, who began to press for their publication. This was not an easy matter. Both Schulz's timidity and the fact that the prose was so different from everything known to publishers and critics rendered the first attempts to publish the stories from the letters unsuccessful.[5] Only Debora Vogel's continued efforts and the intervention of the sculptor Magdalena Gross finally brought the matter of publication to the attention of the writer Zofia Nałkowska, who agreed to meet Schulz.[6]

From the account of an old friend of Magdalena Gross, Alicja Giangrande, we know the circumstances of this fateful encounter. It began in Warsaw in the private pension of Miss Róza Gross, Magdalena's mother, at 33 Nowy Świat Street, on Easter Sunday in 1933. Bruno Schulz showed up there, having just arrived from Drohobycz, carrying the manuscript of his book in order to present it to Zofia Nałkowska. Turning to Magdalena, Schulz said:

"The fate of my book depends upon you. I know that you are a friend of Zofia Nałkowska and if you phoned her and asked her to meet with me, she would not refuse you. Please do it; I have only this afternoon—the return train leaves tonight and I've no time to lose."

There was a pleading tone in his voice, but at the same time it was very forceful.

. . . Magdalena rose from the table and went to telephone to Zofia Nałkowska.

. . . Nałkowska protected herself as best she could from unknown geniuses who piled her desk with manuscripts, which in their opinion deserved immediate publication. I don't know what arguments Magda used to persuade Nałkowska to see Schulz, but a few minutes later she returned and announced triumphantly: "Grab a taxi right away and go to this address." Schulz left, practically pushed out the door by Magda and myself, but when we were already on the stairs, he stammered out: "My briefcase!" The three of us returned to the apartment to look for the briefcase that contained the manuscript. Poor Bruno was pale, his hands trembling. The taxi took off and after about an hour later Bruno returned, calmer, . . . [saying,] "Nałkowska asked me to read a few of the first pages; then she interrupted me and sent me out, asking me to leave the manuscript with her. She wanted to read it through herself. It was an encounter between a comet and the sun. The comet burned up. . . ." Schulz paced back and forth across the room, refusing even some tea. . . . Finally, around seven in the evening the longed-for call came: "This is the most sensational discovery in our literature!" Nałkowska exclaimed to Magda. "I'll run tomorrow to Rój so that this book can be published as quickly as possible!" When Magda repeated Nałkowska's words to Schulz, he stood as if rooted to the floor, paralyzed. We started to shake him, to hug him in order to revive him.

This fragment of a recollection (from a letter to me) dramatically records a turning point in Bruno Schulz's life and in the history of Polish literature as well. After long delay, the *Cinammon Shops* "opened"; toward the end of December that same year, 1933, *Cinnamon Shops* was published by Rój.[7]

One other incident connected with Schulz's efforts to find "fellow-believers" in art and to get his works published is worth noting. Prior to 1934, Schulz had also made contact with the literary group Przedmieście ("Outskirts") and as a member had published part of *Cinnamon Shops* in one of their collective volumes.[8] But his participation in this circle of writers had ended there. On the map of literary geography he remained alone, both personally and with regard to his art.

Cinnamon Shops was, of course, not simply an epistolary improvisation. Schulz utilized some earlier works and fragments saved "in the drawer," while other stories and literary motifs were the fruits of his correspondence and the ideas contained in letters. This is particularly true of the three stories entitled "Treatise on Tailors' Dummies." The motif of the tailors' dummies or mannequins was common to both Schulz and Debora Vogel, although it signified different philosophical meanings for each of them. In 1934, Debora Vogel published a small volume of poems entitled *Manekiny* (Mannequins). In 1936, Rój published a collection of her prose writings, entitled *Akacje kwitną* (The Acacias Are Blooming) and containing various selections with such titles as "The Demasking of the Mannequins," "New Raw Materials Are Necessary," "New Mannequins Are Coming," "A Chapter on Mannequins: Continuation," "A Few More Categories of Dolls, or Rubbish Is Overflowing the World."

Schulz also was fascinated with the substance of things, with the texture of matter, and wrote: "This is . . . our love for matter as it is, for its emptiness and porosity, for its unique mystical consistency . . . we love its roughness, its resistance, its haglike awkwardness." Debora Vogel, on the other hand, formulated the problem more dramatically: "Here we see that the haglike and boring matter of the world entered its most perfect stage of life: in the epoch of artificial forms, decisive for its fate."

When comparing such passages from Vogel's work and *Cinnamon Shops*, it is as if we are still participating in the long-ago epistolary debate between Debora and Bruno. Artificial forms of matter? Boring matter? Schulz proposes the opposite: "Do you sense the pain, the mute suffering, constrained, etched in matter, the suffering of that hag who does not know who she is, why she must continue to exist in this form, this parody, thrust upon her?" Debora responded:

> Rubbish pours over the earth. Percales . . . stiff and dry, without pulp. Sometimes they awkwardly attempt something else: they try to liken themselves to soft silks or plush velvet, but even their sheen is flat and artificial, lifeless.

Schulz replied:

> The demiurge fell in love with dry, perfect, and complex materials—we give preference to trash. It simply enraptures us; we are enchanted by the cheapness, shoddiness, and trashiness of material.

If this is elemental, raw material, Debora is prepared to agree: "But the soul of raw material is very delicate and fantastic. It is only necessary to release the hidden soul of matter." She complained, however, that "finished things and ended matters ring with glass and melancholy. Everything that has permanent outlines and a right-angled or cubic shape is gray from sadness since it is that way once and for all." Schulz countered:

> There are no dead, hard, limited objects. Everything diffuses beyond its limitations, and lasts only for a moment in a particular shape in order to leave it at the first opportunity.

And so nothing exists once and for all:

The root of furniture, its substance, must now be relaxed, degen-
erated, and subject to illicit temptations; then upon that sick, tired,
and wild ground a fantastic deposit will flower like a beautiful
pockmark, a colorful, blooming mold.

I have randomly juxtaposed their statements, of course, but
what is important here is the shared motifs despite the disparity of
interpretation. Although almost all their correspondence has been
lost, we may at least in part reconstruct their debate from the few
extracts above, comparing their writings, and the few later letters
from Debora which by strange accident did survive. In these later
letters Debora sometimes returns to the time of the genesis of *Cinnamon Shops*. Significantly, in the realm of art and creativity Schulz
found optimistic solutions; the key of myth opened all the doors
locked for Debora. In everyday life, however, he was more helpless,
more defeatist, and sought intellectual support and consolation from
the more "sober" Debora.

For her part, Debora Vogel realized the stimulating role played
by their dialogue and spiritual communion, but at the same time she
understood the value of isolation in which the creative stimuli could
mature and bear fruit. On September 1, 1938, she wrote:

> Bruno,
>   Your letter today recalled an image of an autumnal landau[9] in
> which we used to travel together into the land of colorfulness. The
> smell of the trip has irresistible charm and by some curious custom
> is associated with the image of someone else, of a comrade. Then
> it turns out that it is good to be alone, it's quite good to be more
> than alone—even lonely, bereft, hopelessly given over to being
> deserted and homeless. Then one "sees" well.

At one point Schulz even wanted to marry Debora, but the idea
was abandoned because of opposition from the Vogel family. Then,
just before the publication of *Cinnamon Shops*, Debora Vogel married
an architect from Lwów named Barenblüth. Perhaps she did not trust
Bruno's feelings, considering them—on the basis of her knowledge
of his nature—to be a tangle of illusions. Years later, during Schulz's
four-year engagement to Józefina Szelińska, Schulz's meetings and

correspondence with Debora resumed. After his engagement to Józefina was broken off, Schulz and Debora returned in their letters to the question of their unfulfilled marriage plans. Bereft after the departure of his fiancée, Schulz again longed for close intellectual contact with Debora, for a renewal of their former association. He wrote suggesting it, undisturbed by the warnings of acquaintances who feared that the writings of Bruno and Debora were too similar, resulting from their conscious borrowing from one another. Aware of such talk, Debora wrote after a meeting on November 21, 1938:

> Bruno,
> Yesterday, which I was so happy about, wanting through it to revive and begin a new series of Sundays as in the past, left me with a residue of dissatisfaction: you and I hardly talked at all, and those superficial, intellectual conversations with others are exactly what I avoid. So much deceit, so many artificial, mechanical feelings and false but enticing interest, making pretense necessary! But maybe we are avoiding one another subconsciously, and hence this surrounding ourselves with others for some time now, no matter how often we meet? Perhaps all these voices have had an effect and done their damage and we now do not want to open ourselves up to one another too much? Such meanness is so sad and unproductive. How much harm human foolishness can do and how regrettable that such foolishness has so much power despite man's most essential need and deepest longing. After all, our past conversations and contact was one of those rare, marvelous things that occur once in a lifetime, and maybe even only once out of several or a small number of hopeless, colorless lives.

In response, Schulz immediately proposed a return to their former relationship, recalling that for years he had wanted to extend it to include their personal lives as well and that he regretted that this had never come about. Schulz's suggestion prompted Debora's reflections about the past, indicating her understanding of Schulz's psyche and her assent to creative exchanges. This was confirmed in a passage from Debora's reply of December 7, 1938:

> . . . concerning your last letter. I would like to go over it with you line by line—in conversation. Not only because you so seriously

demand a serious response—"not just anything"—but because it warrants debate. But when we read this letter—maybe next Sunday?—we will read one other one: the one which you wrote when you had learned of the engagement, and my letter at that time, evidently not sent, or perhaps not sent in that form. . . . Is there some connection? I have a kind of peculiar, irrational association of thoughts; the letter I refer to, having been read accidentally just before the last one, prompted the following thoughts: was it because I did not draw the right conclusion from that first letter that I did not believe it literally? That I treated it, even though I myself then felt in those categories and so despairingly, as if poetry were more to the point than a literal declaration, that I did not believe that you truly knew how to desire life and happiness, but instead transposed longing into a pure, sublimated experience and are satisfied somewhat with that poetry of life, that extract of the miraculous, not wanting or not knowing how to taste the thick, gray raw material, full of boredom and work? Probably I sensed that, having at hand what seemed to me (perhaps incorrectly) certain proof. Then we matured. The center of gravity in our life shifted to the putting of life into words and so today you write to me a letter about searching for happiness above all on that basis. About our searching together. I accept. . . .

Contact was renewed, but it was limited to letter-writing. In any case, little time was left. In less than nine months the war broke out. Their correspondence continued through the Soviet occupation, the coming of the Nazis, and up to the time when Debora, having fallen into extreme apathy and resignation, could no longer bring herself to write letters. Her literary output—inferior to that of Schulz—is not of primary importance. Above all, Debora Vogel was the best, the most intellectually stimulating and creative, muse for Bruno Schulz.

And so it is said that *Cinnamon Shops* was composed for a single reader, the addressee of letters sent from Drohobycz to Lwów. Letters preserved the intimacy of contact between the creator and the reader so necessary for Schulz. He referred only to the taste and opinion of a single trusted reader. Neither the demands of literary coteries nor fear of the caprices of official criticism oppressed him. Schulz experienced these pressures only later, after his début in print. He stated several times that this paralyzed him, changing the quiet intimacy of communication with *someone specific* into a threatening and anxious activity addressed to the unknown. Perhaps what was essential for Schulz was not so much a partner as a wise recipient, a trusted listener. Without such a sounding board he felt lonely, even though he had many readers and was exceptionally well able to evaluate his own work.

Bruno Schulz needed to be listened to and supported—not only by his muse, but by anyone willing and friendly toward him. Through his extensive correspondence, Schulz populated his solitary life in Drohobycz. "I once lived through writing letters; at the time that was my only creativity," he confided in a letter in 1936. He added emphatically that this period of epistolary creativity seemed to him particularly rich, full, and blooming—the period of the gradual emergence of a literary masterpiece, sealed piece by piece in envelopes and dropped in a mailbox. Few other works of literature were born in such a peculiar and, at the same time, natural way.

5

The Book, or Childhood Regained

hildhood is the time of our most intense communion with the world around us; our creative imagination is stimulated by every impression and experience. We experience reality without prior knowledge or awareness of its rules or structure; it submits to new associations suggested by our consciousness. Myths about causality are born at each stage in the child's growth and development. The individual's biography recapitulates the primordial beginning: the creation of the world. This myth-creating sphere of childhood is both the wellspring and object of Bruno Schulz's writing and artistic creed.

Schulz's art finds distant precedents, primitive prototypes in myth, in the ancient cosmogonies and beliefs of humankind. Using the model of mythologies from the "childhood" of humanity, Schulz creates his own individual mythology. In accordance with its mythic model, Schulz describes his own childhood as an "age of genius," a time when no barrier existed between the inner psyche and the outer world, between dream and reality, between desire and fulfillment, between the intellectual and the sensual—the time of the origins of poetry.

Longing for the fullness of childhood is as old as art itself, but Bruno Schulz turned this longing into the primary focus of his literary art. He unlocked the door to an enchanted realm which artists had only glimpsed previously. His approach is exceptional and unrepeatable and his key cannot be duplicated; mere fantasy about childhood is no substitute. Schulz does not recreate by means of memories, rather he fulfills longing; he does not enshrine the past but returns it to us; he does not observe childhood from the distance of age but instead reenters childhood itself.

Schulz's consistently developed program emerged intuitively in his writing, but from time to time he expressed it discursively with full awareness of its artistic significance. In a 1936 letter to the literary critic and essayist Andrzej Pleśniewicz,[1] Schulz wrote:

> What you say about our artificially prolonged childhood—about immaturity—bewilders me somewhat. Rather, it seems to me that this kind of art, the kind which is so dear to my heart, is precisely a regression, a returned childhood. Were it possible to turn back development, achieve a second childhood by some circuitous road, once again have its fullness and immensity—that would be the incarnation of an "age of genius," "messianic times" which are promised and pledged to us by all mythologies. My ideal goal is to "mature" into childhood. This would really be a true maturity.

Schulz's own childhood disappeared along with the last vestiges of the era of traditional merchants that he himself had witnessed, but the destruction of his "land of childhood's years" did not signify a catastrophe for him as a writer. Not only could his fiction revive what had disappeared, along with the emotional value of objects and processes. His artistic program of "returned childhood" postulated the activity and dynamism of experience of childhood. Schulz's recovery of that ability to *see*, an intensified receptivity, could, after all, include other spheres and penetrate them with equal precision. The real reason why Schulz's art accepts new forms of reality seems deeper; it concerns Schulz's understanding of myth.

The acceptance of new forms of reality occurs because of Schulz's myth, which might be termed the myth of the fallen angels and the descent of the Messiah. It is a particular degression of myths from noble forms in eternal systems to the mundane, a descent into incarnations which seem to contradict their original grandeur. For Schulz, this descent of myth is really an advance, because it enlivens the prose of everyday life. The contrast between the remote genealogy of myth and its un-Olympian, earthly accessibility becomes a source of new value and fascination.

In *Cinnamon Shops*, exalted myth descends to the depths of the mundane, where it encompasses even the grotesque. New consequences ensue from the mythologizing of the ordinary. Myth becomes humanized, and mythologized reality may also become inhuman. Speculation is easily transformed into certainty, clarity into delusion, possibility into fulfillment. Living and omnipresent matter molds itself into countless shapes, generating or destroying individual existences according to its whims. Every object contains a hidden joke or design of myth. Myth roams Drohobycz, transforming ragamuffins playing with buttons into magical soothsayers foretelling the future from the shapes of holes in a wall; a merchant becomes a prophet or dwarf.

As Father says in "Treatise on Tailors' Dummies, or the Second Book of Genesis," "there is no dead matter. Lifelessness is only a facade concealing forms of life unknown to us." This is the attitude of primitive man, but also of the child and of the poet. To exist in childhood means to find oneself in the land of fairy tale, and Schulzian fairy tale is ruled by the same laws as mythology. Like any scientific theory or religious system, it reflects a coherence to which even the most peculiar events and metamorphoses in *Cinnamon Shops* and *Sanatorium Under the Sign of the Hourglass* conform. As a whole, Schulz's stories are really reconstructions of a mythic "book of childhood," and he terms its symbolic prototypes the Book and the Authentic.

In Schulz's second volume of stories, *Sanatorium Under the Sign of the Hourglass,* the "descent of myth" creates an ennobled reality in his story "The Book." Its pages show accordions, zithers, and harps advertised in newspapers, where "once instruments of angelic choirs—thanks to industrial progress—[were] available today at popular prices for the ordinary person, for the lifting of the hearts and suitable enjoyment of pious folk." Similarly, Caspar and Balthazar become wandering organ grinders, while in "My Father Joins the Fire Brigade," loony firemen descend from a "once noble order," the "unhappy race of the salamander," to a caste of "poor, disinherited fiery beings." The domain of degenerating myth and its faulty realizations reveal another fundamental Schulzian concept: the charm of *tandeta,* or trash. Pedestrian actvities become ritual, and, as the narrator in "A Second Fall" explains, a reversal occurs—the mythological ascension of the commonplace: "For beauty is a disease, as my father taught; it is the result of a mysterious infection, a dark forerunner of decomposition, which rises from the depth of perfection and is saluted by perfection with signs of the deepest bliss."

The Book is primary and fundamental; it is the foundation of Schulz's imagination and thus his world. It need not necessarily possess objective value and may be even odds and ends, scraps, or trash. For its believer, however, even the great edition of the Bible illustrated by Gustave Doré would seem in comparison merely an "imperfect apocrypha, a thousandth copy, a poor imitation." The Book is the bible of one's own lost childhood, and its words and signs evoke a vast mythology-poetry extending far beyond any verbal text. The Book stimulates our earliest childish transports of imagination, which in turn add their lines to its text, not omitting "our suppositions with which we fill in gaps." In Schulz's story "The Book," the narrator finds the back pages of an old weekly, pages of advertisements considered rubbish by the household. Despite their vestigial, slighted form, it seems that these pages' power has not faded, and a kind of electric charge of former experiences emanates from them. The return of myths ensues: the reconstruction of the Book in all its illimitable content. In addition to its artistic value, the story "The Book" might be termed programmatic. It contains, as it were, the birth and proclamation of the Schulzian mythology of childhood. Having found bits of the myth-creating Book, the young

Joseph now contradicts the sober rationalism of the adults around him. He cannot accept Father's explanation that "as a matter of fact, there are only books. The Book is a myth in which we believe when young, but we cease to take seriously as we get older." Joseph thinks to himself: "At that time I already held quite a different opinion. I knew then that the Book is a postulate, that it is a task. I felt the burden of a great mission on my shoulders."

The Authentic turns out to be really bits of an old weekly containing a section of advertisements: a collection of fetishes, magic signs, evocative slogans of myth. Ordinary ads take on a magic power and poetic content. In comparison, the "master of black magic," Bosco of Milan, who claims extraordinary magical gifts (the subject of one of the ads), does not impress the reader of the Book at all. For Schulz, creative magic, myth-making substance, is contained only in tangible things that our senses can test. The true miracle arises from the bedrock of the everyday, from things that do not suspect their mythic potential. Ordinary signs which manifest nothing esoteric come to life in the Book. By means of life-giving myth, each random faded ad gives birth to a story that runs far beyond the literal text of the Book. In such a transcendent history, Anna Csillag promotes a concoction for hair growth and promises to provide hosts of followers with monstrous beards; she is an emissary of happiness to a balding world. Further along, characters from different advertisements meet and combine as parts of one universal mythology. Anna Csillag's bearded disciples carry barrel organs found in another advertisement and form a wandering group of organ grinders. Swarms of Harz mountain canaries from still another ad in the Book flutter out of the melodies of their instruments. All mingle, losing their separate content, just as in Schulz's story "A Second Fall," Don Quixote turns up at the manor house of Adam Mickiewicz's Pan Tadeusz[2] or Robinson Crusoe reaches the Drohobycz area of Bolechów. The characters who appear in Schulz's world form a great community controlled by the unity of the consciousness who experiences it.

Schulz was a mythologizer not only in the sense that myth was the basic principle of his artistic creation, but also because he was skeptical regarding scientific knowledge. In his 1936 essay entitled

"The Mythologizing of Reality," Schulz states his theoretical views that the limitations of human knowledge, our epistemological helplessness, decreases the distance between the power of knowledge and art. Bergsonian intuitionism was not foreign to Schulz's views and psychological make up. Despite their different means, poetry and knowledge even share the same goal. Schulz writes:

> Thus all poetry is mythologizing and strives to reconstitute myths about the world. The mythologizing of the world is not over yet; the process was only halted by the development of knowledge, diverted into a side channel where it exists on without comprehending its true meaning. But knowledge is nothing more than the construction of a myth about the world, since myth lies in the very elements themselves, and there is no way of going beyond myth. Poetry reaches the meaning of the world intuitively, deductively, with large, daring shortcuts and approximations. Knowledge seeks the same meaning inductively, methodically, taking into account all the materials of experience. Fundamentally, one and the other are bound for the same goal.

Sometimes the consequences of Schulz's mythologizing the world appear deceptively similar to the conclusions of contemporary science. Guided by poetry and based upon subjective, intuitive reactions, they seem to lead independently into the area of scientific theory about the nature of reality. Einsteinian, relativized time also contradicts common sense, but not subjective emotional experience. These parallels intensify the verisimilitude of Schulzian mythology, which often utilizes its own quasi-scientific terminology.

There is no return to childhood "in general," however; Schulz returns to his own particular childhood and it is there that he finds the elements of his poetic constructions. His own childhood supplied what he termed the "iron capital" of his imagination and his "archetypes." A fundamental motif at the heart of Schulz's imaginative world, like the image of the droshky taken from Goethe's ballad "Erlkönig," the image of the child carried at night in the arms of his father, was an image acquired in his own childhood.[3] The meaning of such images is definitive, as Schulz explains in his 1935 interview with Stanisław Ignacy Witkiewicz:

. . . such images constitute an agenda, establish an iron capital of the soul, proffered to us very early in the form of intuitions and half-conscious experiences. It seems to me that all the rest of one's life unfolds on the premise of interpreting these insights, breaking open their entire content as best we can manage, moving across the entire extent of intellect of which we are capable. These early images mark out for artists the boundaries of their creative powers. Their creative work is a deduction upon given assumptions. They do not discover anything new after that, they only learn how to understand better and better the secret entrusted to them at the outset; their creative effort is an unending exegesis, a commentary on that one verse assigned to them.

While Schulz's analysis may not apply to all creative work, it is extraordinarily accurate for his own writing. It accounts for its monothematism—the countless variations on particular themes that appear in all his fiction. Along with the motif from Goethe's "Erlkönig," the horse and coach pervade Schulz's tales and graphics. When Bruno was eight years old his mother had read to him, "Wer reitet so spät durch Nach und Wind? . . ." Many years later he recalled how he "received Goethe's ballad with all its metaphysics at age eight": "Through the half-understood German I caught, or divined, the meaning, and cried, shaken to the bottom of my soul, when my mother read it to me. . . ." This image became a formula to express danger, for it symbolized both flight and its impossibility:

The father hugs the child, folds him in his arms, shields him from the natural element that chatters on and on, but to the child these arms are transparent; the night reaches into him, and through the father's soothing words he continually hears its frightening seductions. And oppressed, full of fatalism, he answers the night's importunities with tragic readiness, given over wholly to the mighty element from which there is no escape. . . .

In the story "Spring," written in 1936, we find one Schulzian interpretation of the emotional content of Goethe's ballad, its motif having returned after many years, in a different version but with the same power, aura, and significance:

Among all the stories that crowd entangled at the root of spring, there is one that long ago passed into the ownership of the night and settled down forever at the bottom of the firmament—an eternal accompaniment and background to the starry spaces. During every spring night, whatever might happen in it, that story passes in great strides above the thunderous croaking of frogs and the endless grinding of mills. A man walks under the starry grist spilling out of the mills of night; he walks hugging a child in the folds of his cloak; constantly on his way in his continual wandering through the endless spaces of night. . . . The distant worlds come quite close, frighteningly bright, they send violent signals through eternity in mute, unutterable statements—while he walks on and on and soothes the little girl endlessly, monotonously, and without hope, helpless against the whispers and sweet seductions of the night, against the one word formed on the lips of silence, when no one is listening to it. . . .

With development of his cult of childhood and his placement of faith in its demiurgical power, Schulz resembles an avid alchemist who has discovered an elixir that changes ordinary matter into the precious metal of poetry.

Schulz felt best in the world of the imagination, in his reconstructed childhood where the inferiority complex that haunted him in real life disappeared; he could believe in himself and his art. This was the paradox of Schulz's life: while timid and lacking self-confidence in the everyday world to which he was condemned, he nevertheless was convinced of his value as a writer in the world most essential to him, that of art. Schulz's escape into childhood was at the same time an excursion into the realm of art and creation. Although he sometimes traveled from Drohobycz to nearby towns such as Lwów, Cracow, Warsaw, and Zakopane, and ventured once to Sweden for a day, and even to Paris for three weeks, his longest and most daring trip was the one into childhood as a mythological genesis. In 1936, Schulz wrote to the critic Andrzej Pleśniewicz:

The quiet that I have here, although more perfect than in that happier era—has become insufficient for a more sensitive, more fastidious "vision." It is increasingly difficult for me to believe in it. But precisely these things require blind faith, to be taken on credit.

Only united with that faith, do they agree reluctantly to come into being—to exist to some extent.[4]

Schulz's frequent doubts and depressions were akin to loss of a faith that had to be continually rekindled. Skeptical of intellectual knowledge, he was at the same time a passionate believer in the power of emotional impressions. The sensualism that governs his fictional world is consistent to the extreme: experiences shape reality and dictate its laws, finding in it "divine elements." As an artist and writer he gathered strands of the mythic tradition in an effort to be the child-inheritor of his own prehistory. Out of the emotional chaos which he ordered and shaped, out of things which he said "wanted to express themselves through him," emerged the laws of his aesthetics, philosophical concepts deduced from his own feelings and experiences as a writer. His creation was hovering over an impenetrable secret, a means to approach it. In Schulz's view, artistic creation penetrates deeper and farther into that secret. In this sense, writing was not only an entertainment of the demiurge, but also a unique cognitive process. The love of matter in all forms so typical of Schulz did not contradict the metaphysical principle of Schulzian biologism. Witkiewicz writes:

> Schulz loves matter which is for him the highest substance, not in the physical sense (and this renders him philosophically close to me); for him there is no division between matter and spirit. They are a unity for him: "there is no dead matter—lifelessness is only an appearance which conceals unknown forms of life." This is the conviction of a monadologue (or rather a monadist) or hylozoist. But that would be merely a rather obscure general philosophical view were it not integrated into the entire continuity of actual being in which the word "becomes flesh."[5]

The renowned scholar of religion Mircea Eliade states that myth is not merely a part of one phase of human development, but rather a fundamental and constant feature of it. In searching for meaning and significance, man strives to make reality accessible to the intellect by means of language, the word. Schulz conveys precisely the same idea: "The human spirit tirelessly expresses life through the power of myth, toward a making sense of reality. The word itself left on its own gravitates, presses toward sense." In Eliade's view, sacral rites actualize myth by destroying ordinary chronological time and substituting mythic time. Schulz arrived at similar conclusions in his writing, in which not religion but artistic creation is the "sacral rite," the "short circuit between words, a sudden regeneration of the primeval myths." Thus, in the words of Schulz's essay, "all poetry is mythologizing and strives to restore myths about the world."

Eternally repeating schemas, stories returning in different variants, from antiquity to the present, appear in the plot of Thomas Mann's *Joseph and His Brothers,* a work beloved by Schulz. Whereas Mann presents the biblical story on a monumental scale, Schulz confines mythic archetypes to his own biography, connecting that biography with ancient myth and ennobling it by an affiliation with fairy-tale time. Most likely, Schulz's major work would have been the now lost novel *Messiah,* in which the myth of the messianic coming was to symbolize a return to the happiness of perfection that existed at the beginning of time.

Longing for childhood's Age of Genius and disgusted with ordinary, profaned time, Schulz proclaimed a mythic time in art. In the unthreatened realm of art, offshoots of time might sprout, hidden currents break loose whose course he could direct. It was then that Bruno Schulz could write, a victorious rebel artist defying the rigors of the daily, one-way flow of hours.

6

Schulzian Time

Fate tied Bruno Schulz for his entire life to Drohobycz, the town of his birth and childhood, his "promised land." There he had to travel, not in space, but through time; the time of clocks and calendars which was the distance to be conquered. The passage of actual time both increased the distance and impeded Schulz's creative moments of mythical communion. Awareness of time's mundane cares constantly disturbed Schulz's inner peace and blocked his writing, a frustration he expressed in a letter in 1934 to the younger novelist Tadeusz Breza:[1]

> Since we are sharing with one another the secret failings that plague us, I'll confide to you a particular ailment that persecutes me and which also is connected with time, although it is different

from the symptoms of gastric diarrhea that you described about yourself. Your alimentary canal lets time through too easily, incapable of holding it in—mine is distinguished by a paradoxical fastidiousness controlled by the idée fixe of the *virginity of time*. Just as for some Rajah of a melancholic and unsatisfied spirit each woman who is grazed by the glance of a man is already defiled and worth only a silk noose, so for me time to which someone else has laid claim, to which someone made the slightest allusion—is already tainted, ruined, inedible. I can't tolerate any rival to time. For me, the scrap that they have touched is made repugnant. I don't know how to share time, I don't know how to live on someone else's leftovers. (Jealous lovers use this same vocabulary.) When I have to prepare a lesson for the next day, buy materials at the lumberyard—the entire afternoon and evening are ruined for me already. I renounce the remaining time with noble pride. All—or nothing—is my motto. And because every school day is profaned this way—I live in proud abstinence and—I do not write.

Schulz introduces a subjective, psychological time in his fiction; he makes it real, objectifies it, making events submit to its laws. What in fairy tales may be caused by the external force of magic powers occurs in Schulz's world as a logical consequence of the inner structure of created reality, of its accumulating internal tensions, or in the processes of the "fermentation" of its matter. The new Schulzian time obeys the precise rules of psychology, while in questioning ordinarily accepted principles, it is a mythic refuge in the face of the unavoidable passage of time.

Time was one of the major obsessions in Schulz's real life. He feared its all-consuming but finite capacity. In Schulz's writing, time is vast, ready to absorb everything that wants to exist. Ordinary present time is impregnated and ennobled by the past: the time of myth. In her reminiscences of Bruno Schulz, Isabella Czermakowa writes:

With shining eyes he would point out to us a riot of weeds behind little hovels held together by mud and a bit of imagination. He initiated us into the "dead bays" of alleys which stimulated his imagination and nurtured his musings. We walked as if enchanted. Bruno enticed us into the world of his poetic vision. He transformed the dullness and provincialism of small-town life far from modern civilization. His painterly eye perceived the play of light and color and discovered beauty in ugliness. He would point out specimens of medieval Talmudist-mystics, hermetically sealed in the walls of the nonexistent ghetto. Schulz would describe his own town as a "marvel and mystery of anachronism, a reserve of Time." "Can Time stand still?" we would ask. "It's not permitted," he would reply tersely. "And for evolution there is already no time— do you understand?" And Bruno Schulz's eyes shone with terror.[2]

Schulz shielded himself with mythic time in the face of this terror; in art, he surmounted what he feared in life. In art, he not only allowed time to stop without penalty, but he allowed it to coexist harmoniously with the past. Writing became a great compensation, as Schulz wrote to Witkiewicz:

What the meaning of this universal disillusioning of reality is I am not able to say. I contend only that it would be unbearable unless it was compensated for in some other dimension. In some way we derive a profound satisfaction from the loosening of the web of reality; we feel an interest in this bankruptcy of the real.

The burdensome inescapabability of the rules of reality ceases in the regions of the great heresy; in these regions a new reality is an objectified projection of dreams, and hence their fulfillment. The freedom that flows from this creative power is fuller and heightened by danger, which cannot destroy it. Danger increases its value and intensifies the feeling of asylum, as in the story "The Gale" in *Cinnamon Shops*, where a storm is experienced in a snug kitchen, protected from the violent forces of nature.

"Yes, such offshoots of time do exist, somewhat illegal and problematic, it's true, but when one carries such contraband as we do, supernumerary and unclassifiable events, one cannot be excessively fastidious . . ." Schulz writes in "The Age of Genius." His mythical time, obedient and submissive to man, a kind of emanation of emotion, compensates for the mundane time that relentlessly dominates everything, bearing people and events along in an inexorable flow of change. Referring to "double-track time," or the "offshoots" of time,

Schulz describes it as "illegal" or "problematic." He terms the events that take place in its dimension "illegal happenings" and the process of shifting to that realm of time an "impure manipulation." No debasement exists in this terminology; nor is there, as some critics have attempted to prove, a sense of "sinfulness" that is supposedly an element in Schulz's creativity. Expressions such as the "great heresy," the adjective "illegal," or Schulz's description of Father as a "heresiarch" do not signify some sinful feeling of deviation or betrayal. They are ironic, a purposeful manipulation of language by a writer who regularly condemned hackneyed dogmas and conducted revelatory attacks upon accepted truths. In "Spring," the beauty and variety of the world emanating from a stamp album is opposed to the bureaucratized version of the world of the Habsburg monarchy, where everything was known from the start and no room was left for surprises. Thus,

> . . . the prison seemed to be irrevocably shut, when the opening was bricked up, when everything had conspired to keep silent about You, Oh God, when Franz Josef had barred and sealed even the last chink so that one should not have been able to see You, then You arose in a roaring of seas and continents and gave him the lie. You, God, took upon Yourself the odium of heresy and exploded upon the world with this enormous, magnificent, colorful blasphemy. Oh magnificent Heresiarch!

Schulz addresses God as a "heresiarch" in the sense of a rebel against the boredom prevailing in religion; an outburst of divine "blasphemy" means daring to proclaim the truth of poetry, so unpopular among adherents of the "gospel of prose." Schulzian time is "heretical" because it inventively departs from conventional conceptions. Past time returns and exists in the present, elements of dream coexist with reality and possess its same density in a fluid, changing chronology. Disparate elements of dream and consciousness weave a reality existing in an expanded time subject to man. The imagination can halt or even turn back time's flow like a river rerouted from its delta back to its spring. This is not a reverse flow, but rather the possibility of revisiting portions of the past and giving them new and different content. Events over and done with may return to their own genesis, to a stage of incompletion.

Time is one of the major characters in Schulz's fiction, and the story "Sanatorium Under the Sign of the Hourglass" is particularly monothematic in this sense. For Schulz, time is one of the elements of the world, as in an Orphic cosmogony, but its power is limited; in "Sanatorium Under the Sign of the Hourglass," it submits to the human desire to struggle with the transitory. The hourglass in Schulz's title is deliberately ambiguous, referring to both the hourglass symbol of death used in obituary notices and to a time-keeping instrument.[3] Its double meaning is easily explained: at the sanatorium, time is perversely enlisted to counteract death. In a discussion of the books announced for the 1938 *Wiadomości Literackie* award, the famous Polish novelist Maria Dąbrowska declared that "Schulz's book, with the exception of its pretentious title, is a manifestation of true art."[4] Despite her admiration for Schulz's work, she did not grasp the almost definitive precision of his title story for his second volume of tales.

Father, long since deceased, resides at the sanatorium, where its peculiar time conditions allow his return to life. The head of the sanatorium, Dr. Gotard, explains:

> . . . we have put back the clock. Here we are always late by a certain interval of time whose length cannot be defined. The whole thing comes down to a matter of simple relativity. Here your father's death, the death that has already overtaken him in your country, has not materialized yet. . . . Here we reactivate time past, with all its possibilities, therefore also including the possibility of recovery.

The sanatorium is both a Hades transferred from the far side of the river Styx to the side of the living and a metaphoric parable about Schulzian art that revives the past. In place of the boat there is a train; Charon is now an old railway conductor afflicted with a toothache. Even the dog-man appears, both a terrifying figure from dreams and a new version of the classical Cerberus. Schulz's transposition of ancient mythology stresses the commonality of all myths, although these similarities are not the most important elements here. Schulz creates a new Hades, somewhat modernized in its externals and yet still eternal in its mythological essence. Events "stripped of the mold of time" reveal their "ancient formulas," recurring in ever new forms.

Schulz's particular sensitivity to real time, this threatening and all-consuming monster, led to an antidote: the mythical time that prevails in his fiction. Writing became a remedy for Schulz's own fears, and although in at least one of his letters he notes that "creative expression is the better half of control," he prefers to remain silent about his own terrors or he disarms them in his writing. His fear of space, experienced since childhood, found liberating relief in *Cinnamon Shops* in the image of being carried off by the wind, as in "The Old Age Pensioner" or Father's bravura leap out the window as a fireman in "My Father Joins the Fire Brigade." The sense of being hemmed in by time stimulated the creation of "Schulzian time," while an acute inferiority complex dictated the work of a demiurge or a mission in creative art. In his tales Schulz becomes Joseph, the son of Jacob, and even tries to establish a real basis for this transformation. Like his biblical prototype, he is an "interpreter of dreams" and dreams biblical dreams. He is the youngest child of his old father—just as was the biblical Joseph in the Book of Moses. Elements of biographical time merge with biblical time; the resurrected past freely intersects with the present. Only the future may not enter here, a nonexistent category in Schulz's capacious present. There is only the present and time past returned to the present.

In Schulz's world, things are just as we see them. Our sensations determine the appearance and structure of reality. The change of the customs of time is the same as our changed attitude toward it. The hackneyed expression "time hangs heavy on one's hands" becomes an objective fact: "time became heavy" in Schulzian reality. The quality of human perception becomes a quality of its object. In the story "Sanatorium Under the Sign of the Hourglass," the hourglass eliminates time from the patients' minds, which means that its flow is effectively halted by their psyches. Dream comes to the rescue: no respecter of chronology, it doesn't have to deal with time and slips into an atemporal domain: a "rapid disintegration of time ensues, unsupervised by constant attention." The patients' continual dozing off and wakening contributes to the loss of chronological order and sense of the continual outflow of time. As the narrator comments:

> We all know that this undisciplined element [time] holds itself within bounds but precariously, thanks to unceasing cultivation, tender concern, and a careful regulation and correction of its excesses. Free of this vigilance, it immediately begins to do tricks, run wild, play irresponsible practical jokes, and indulge in undisciplined clowning. The incongruity of our private times becomes increasingly evident. My father's time and my own no longer coincide.

The narrator is only partially safe, for an undercurrent of anxiety remains: the fear of the restitution of ordinary time. While he escapes from the sanatorium, he cannot elude the boatlike train of Charon and ends up wandering through its cars, begging as an old railway man in rags. As Schulz remarked in a letter, the narrator becomes a character "already lost . . . a victim of a barren fantasy of Hades." Usually a compensation for the failings of everyday life, fantasy becomes strangely threatening when it begins to lose *all* links with reality. Only the security of such links allowed Schulz to feel free to explore the offshoots of time. During his years-long engagement to Józefina Szelińska,[5] Schulz himself feared the fate of the railwayman begging for alms. Schulz saw in his fiancée a guarantee of some connection with the world, but without her? Without her, he wrote, he visualized himself as a beggar in tatters, extending his hand to strangers among whom he sees his former fiancée. She passed by disdainfully, leaving him empty-handed. The realm of fantasy and imagination is the region of Schulz's true biography; his connections with the real world were slight and increasingly tenuous. Fearing this disproportion, Schulz longed—helplessly—to strengthen his links with the world.

In Schulz's longest story, "Spring," past and present time exist on a single plane; the hero is at once a child and an adult. The time that prevails in this story is neither past nor present; it is the time of discovery and creation: springtime in which nature renews herself, an eternal resurrection of past events, an unconscious repetition of ancient patterns. In his essay "The Mythologizing of Reality," Schulz writes:

> As we manipulate everyday words, we forget that they are frag-
> ments of ancient and eternal stories, that we are building our
> houses with broken pieces of sculptures and ruined statues of gods
> as the barbarians did.

In "Spring," eternal myths lie at the root of existence; each year spring derives sap for her life-giving greenness from past history. This imagery is not a formal device, but the expression of Schulz's belief that "in the beginning there was myth" which ceaselessly repeats itself in ever new versions. These returns of myth, its continually renewed incarnations, interweave the indissoluble ancient model with later reconstructions, the past with the current moment.

Schulz's imagination did not favor epic forms or a dramatic sequence of events in its construction of great metaphor-metamorphoses. When Schulz does create such a sequence, it is only as a pretext, as a frame for nonfabular "events." As he often said, "biographical memory," or the tendency toward narration, was foreign to him. His raw material did not lend itself to narration or to the elaboration of a chain of events occurring in the logical order of time. Instead, time itself became the actor of a drama, and not simply its background. Schulzian storytelling does not run parallel to chronology; it renounces continuity in favor of a deeper penetration, a "descent into the essence." Digging into the root of things, pursuing an actualized metaphor inevitably leads into a multileveled time that adapts to the needs of the creative imagination; instead of a dictator, time becomes a submissive servant. One could say that Schulzian reality is "beyond time," beyond the reach of its autocratic power.

The memory of facts, a lack which Schulz felt in himself, is not the memory of time in the Schulzian understanding of the word. Facts occur forever, and they may fit anywhere. They do not determine the coloration of time, or its distinct morphology. Past time is the realm of our transspatial travels, the dimension in which the broad changes of the psyche are acted out, its whole revivifying archaeology.

The semblance of an objective phenomenon of contracting and expanding of time is Schulz's magic trick, making the influence of the psyche upon the external world believable. Time is an individual and subjective psychological phenomenon. In "August," the opening story of *Cinnamon Shops*, foolish Maryśka, mother of Tłuja, sleeps in the morning in her room to the sound of the loud ticking of a clock while

> the silence, as it were, took advantage of her sleep and chattered, a yellow, bright, evil silence; it carried on, argued, loudly talking its vulgar and maniacal monologue. Maryśka's time, the time imprisoned in her soul, came out from her frighteningly real and walked alone across the room noisily, buzzing, hellish, growing in the bright silence of the morning from the mill-clock like bad flour, powdered flour, the silly flour of the insane.

Not only do such psychic phenomena gain their independence in Schulz's magic world. In "Night of the Great Season," calendar time is questioned as well. "Everyone knows that in the course of ordinary normal years whimsical Time now and again begets other peculiar years, unnatural years which—like a sixth little finger—grow a thirteenth fake month." Schulz's "apocrypha, slipped secretly between the chapters of the great book of the year," are his mythological appendix to the calendar his magic palimpsest seeks to rival. When he writes of his wish that Father's story, smuggled into the pages of an old calendar, would grow inside it to equal the real text, he is expressing his both artistic and human desire to fulfill the longing of his imagination, to endow it with the power to create reality, to erase the barrier between fact and fantasy.[6]

Schulz's mythic road to freedom transforms helplessness into demiurgic power. Overcoming all limitations, a new creation of the world occurs, one based upon faith in the omnipotence of dreams. As the narrator of "Loneliness" confides,

> Should I reveal that my room is walled-up . . . How could that be? How could I get out of it? Walled up. That's just it: for goodwill there are no barriers, nothing can obstruct strong desire. I must only imagine the door, a good old door as in the kitchen of my

childhood, with a metal handle and lock. There is no room so walled up that such trusted doors could not open it if there were only strength enough to imagine them.

On one side of the door is limited life, on the other—art. The door leads from the captivity of Bruno to the freedom of Joseph.

Herein lies the credo of Bruno Schulz, the Great Heresiarch insinuating new dimensions into time and thus taking revenge upon everyday life, so implacable, so immune to magic and destructive of hope. Thus, from behind the mythological faith of Schulz the writer the sardonic smirk of reality peeps out time and again, revealing the transitoriness of art which tries to compete with it.

7

Phantoms and Reality

The obsessively erotic scenes transposed to dimensions of
mythology that dominate Bruno Schulz's drawings and graphics compel the viewer to consider the recurrence of the same faces
and external features in so many pictures. Schulz himself appears
regularly as one of the hunched men groveling before women,
together with others who were close to him, such as his bulbous-
headed friend Mundek Pilpel, and his brother-in-law, the engineer
Hoffman. Among the powerful female temptresses the men idolize
one can recognize some of the Drohobycz ladies of whom Schulz
was fond: Mila Lustig, Tynka Kupferberg, and Frederika Wegner,
along with many others. In Schulz's drawings, they are fantastic creatures and their garb is much scantier than Schulz would have had
occasion to observe—only their faces remained the same. Schulz's

hallucinatory art ordered them to exist in a demonic realm, trans-forming them into phantoms without denying them proof of their identities in their faces.

Schulz's likenesses are so accurate that one Drohobycz resident, recognizing a long-legged naked nymph as his wife, remonstrated with Schulz, groundlessly accusing his spouse of having posed for the picture of a nude. As in Schulz's art, so too in his fiction: aspects of his own life had merged with elements of his imaginative cos-mogony. Writing in a 1935 essay addressed to his friend and fellow artist, Witkiewicz, Schulz explained:

> Just as the ancients traced their ancestors back to mythological unions with the gods, so I have attempted to establish for myself a mythic generation of forebears, a fictional family from which I derive my real origins. In some sense such "histories" are real; they represent my way of life, my particular fate.

These "real fictions" are grounded in details taken from a con-crete time and place. The childhood experiences of the young Bruno who became Joseph in *Cinnamon Shops* are elevated to cosmic signifi-cance, while traces of the authentic topography of Drohobycz—the breeding ground for the magic of childhood—remain. Knowlege of the autobiographical elements in Schulz's writing is not essential in order to appreciate it; his autonomous world is self-referential and does not require recourse to psychological origins, since what was personal became universal and what was provincial became a world in itself.

Nevertheless, the discovery of real elements located in actual time and space in Schulz's mythological events is both fascinating and relevant. Schulz scrupulously preserved the rudimentary details that endowed his own artistic creation with a kind of verisimilitude. Their traces scattered throughout his works were significant for his creative process: they were the guarantee of authenticity for his imagined world, in some measure certifying his vision, the vision of a reconstructed mythology of childhood. While the very symbiosis of authentic elements with myth and phantom is one of the secrets of Bruno Schulz's originality, dealing with this material is difficult because of the destruction of World War II and the deaths of most of those connected to the town's prewar life. Drohobycz no longer lies within Poland's borders, and the town and its environs are now inhabited by other residents. In a 1934 letter to Tadeusz Breza, Bruno Schulz wrote:

> First I would like to show you Drohobycz and its surroundings, to see anew through your eyes the scenery of my youth. To introduce you into unwritten chapters of *Cinnamon Shops*. Please come.[1]

In 1964, with Schulz's fiction as my guide and along with several Drohobyczans who had known Schulz, I took advantage of his 1934 invitation. The house where he was born and in which he spent his childhood no longer exists; another building has stood for decades on that corner site, where the dawn sunlight streams through its front windows. Here on the northwest side of the market square the sun comes earliest, creeping over the roofs of the apartment buildings opposite, and reaching the upper stories before it penetrates the street—just as we read in two of Schulz's stories, "Visitation" and "Dead Season":

> We lived on the market square, in one of those dark buildings with empty blind facades, so difficult to distinguish one from another. . . . At five o'clock in the morning, an hour glaring with early sunshine, our house was already bathed in an ardent but quiet brightness.

Late in the afternoon when the sun had left the deep interiors of the rooms in the buildings on that side of the market square and had begun to set, I retraced Schulz's footsteps along the two still-sunny sides of the market square toward the apothecary shop on the opposite corner where once Stryjska Street entered the square. Again Schulz's fiction was my faithful guide, this time in his story "August":

> On Saturday afternoons I used to go for a walk with my mother. From the dusk of the hallway, one stepped immediately into the sunny flood of the day. . . . Thus my mother and I ambled along the two sunny sides of the market square, leading our jagged shadows along the houses as over a keyboard. . . . And finally on the corner of Stryjska Street we passed within the shadow of the

chemist's shop. A large jar of raspberry juice in the wide window symbolized the coolness of the balms inside for the relief of all kinds of pain.

The glass jars displayed in the shop that once belonged to the pharmacist Gorgoniusz Tobiaszek are long gone. Only the sun, rising and setting precisely as Schulz described, still illumines the facades of the various buildings. Such details occur throughout Schulz's writing; they are elements of reality upon which his immanent poetic world hinges. Even the most extreme metaphor or the most peculiar myth in *Cinnamon Shops* has roots in the real world; its link to reality confirms Schulzian phantasmagoria and lends it an aura of authenticity. Precisely when Schulz's dynamic hyperbole ventures into "those suspect, risky, and ambiguous regions that we will call for short the regions of the great heresy" the authenticity of his fiction appears. Only Drohobycz and its environs inspired Schulz to recreate the charm of myths encountered in childhood. Only there was he able to undertake exotic and enchanted journeys to the colorful Hajderabad or Tasmania via a Drohobycz stamp album in his story "Spring," with its "money orders on empires and republics, on archipelagoes and continents."

When the narrator and hero of the story "Cinnamon Shops" decides to return along "the road to the Saltworks," he traverses not only a mythologized town, but also an actual Drohobycz street; when lost during his night wandering he compares a view of the outskirts of town to "Lesznianska Street with its lower and seldom-visited neighborhood," he has in mind the actual street that led to the village of Lisznia (misspelled in a printing error in the first edition). When, entering the building of the gymnasium, the narrator decides to peek into the room where Professor Arendt conducts drawing classes, he is in the Emperor Franz Josef Gymnasium where Schulz himself studied with the art professor, Adolf Arendt. The Basilian Hills also preserved their real name, as did Holy Trinity Orthodox Church, which still stands in the center of Drohobycz. Its great white baroque facade is described in "Age of Genius" as

an enormous divine shift fallen from heaven, [which] folded itself into pilasters, projections, and embrasures and puffed out with the

pathos of volutes and archvolutes before hurriedly straightening
its great billowing garment.

Also wending its way through Drohobycz was the "parasitical
quarter" which Schulz termed "the Street of Crocodiles," a mythological transposition of Stryjska Street—a tawdry provincial thoroughfare with grotesque big-city aspirations. In Schulz's stories it
became the symbol of the bewitching and pathological beauty of
imitation which conceals seeds of a magical metamorphosis. From
the rise in the Street of Crocodiles one could see "almost the entire
length of this broad thoroughfare to the distant . . . buildings of the
railroad station"—the very same view still visible from the highest
point along Stryjska Street. For Schulz, drawing upon his imagination was at the same time a process of drawing upon memory—not
what he termed "biographical" memory, whose lack he felt in himself, but an emotional "memory of climates."

In Bruno's childhood the Schulz family vacationed in the nearby
health resort Truskawiec. When the narrator of "Autumn"[2] bids
farewell to summer speaking as a fifteen-year-old boy, Schulz is
describing a specific spot in Truskawiec, although he does not call it
by name:

> But at the little round plaza in the park, empty now and bright in
> the afternoon sun, at the Mickiewicz monument, the truth about
> the crisis of summer dawns in my soul. In the euphoria of this rev-
> elation I climb up the two steps of the pedestal and, tracing an
> impassioned arc with my eyes and outstretched arms as if address-
> ing the entire resort, I say: "Farewell, Season!"

The small plaza in the park with the Mickiewicz monument still
exists, surrounded by the landscape of Schulz's story "Republic of
Dreams." Traveling from Drohobycz to Truskawiec, I recalled
Schulz's description:

> On such days, Mother would hire a cab and, jammed together in
> its black box, the shop assistants up on the driver's seat with the
> bundles or clutching onto the springs, we would all ride out of
> town to Little Hill. We rode into the rolling, hill-studded land-

scape. The vehicle toiled its long, lonesome way among humped fields, rooting through the hot golden dust of the highway.

This passage and subsequent ones evoke the undulating countryside which unfolded before us. The range of hills in the shadowy distance enclosed the great expanse difficult to take in a single view. I inquired and was told, yes, just where we were was what's called "Little Hill." The building to the left had been the old inn of Putz on the outskirts of Truskawiec mentioned in "The Republic of Dreams":

> We came to a halt at last on Little Hill, next to the squat masonwork tavern. It stood alone on the watershed, its roof spread out against the sky, at the rise between two tracts of sloping land. The horses strained to reach the high edge, then stopped on their own, as if to ponder the tollgate dividing two worlds. Beyond this gate spread out the landscape seamed by highways, pale and opalescent like faded tapestry, wrapped in the vast air, sky-blue and vacant. . . . that landscape extensive as a map . . .

The mythic events of Schulz's fiction had their roots in the countryside near Drohobycz; here were harnessed the wingless pegasuses—two carriage nags; here the god Pan, a tramp, went off into the high weeds to relieve himself; the pagan sun worshippers were passersby squinting their eyes against the glare of the August sun; here the shingled roof of a merchant's house became an avian Noah's ark; and back-page ads of an old illustrated weekly became a Holy Scripture full of magic passages.

Schulz's tales ennobled not only himself, the boy-narrator Joseph, and his father, Jacob the merchant, the inspired magus and semidivine heresiarch. More characters from Drohobycz daily life earned a place in mythology: the eerie madwoman Tłuja from the story "August" and later recalled in "The Comet" was the retarded Awrumke, known in Drohobycz also as Tłuja or Tłoja, a sad, demented beggar woman. The simpleton Dodo was actually Schulz's cousin David Heimberg, the son of Schulz's aunt Regina. Schulz had observed David's extraordinarily large head and often sketched it. Even the little dog in the Schulz household carried the name Nemrod. Tłuja, Dodo, Uncle Jerome, and Father are all touched with a

Drohobycz Market Square, color postcard, about 1913. First corner house on the right from the church—burned in the course of the First World War—until 1910, the shop and home of the Schulzes where Bruno was born (from the collection of Jerzy Ficowski).

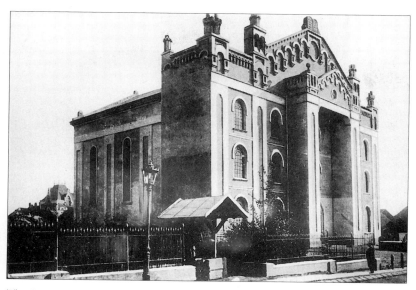

The Great Synagogue in Drohobycz, postcard about 1905 (from the collection of Jerzy Ficowski).

*Portrait of Bruno's mother,
Henrietta Schulz*, pencil,
from about 1930 (from
the collections of the
Museum of Literature in
Warsaw).

*Bruno Schulz after passing
secondary school examina-
tion*, photograph from
around 1910 (from the
collection of Jerzy
Ficowski).

Self-portrait of Bruno Schulz, pencil, crayon, 1919 (from the collections of the Jewish Historical Institute in Warsaw).

Portrait of Maria Budratzka, an eighteen-year-old woman from Drohobycz (later an Austrian opera singer), pencil, black crayon, 1919. Photograph from the owner of the portrait, Maria Budratzka-Tempele (deceased), made for Jerzy Ficowski around 1982.

Schulz's house at 10 Floriańska Street in Drohobycz. The third window from the right (glass doors) is the entrance to Schulz's room. Photograph from 1965 by Jerzy Ficowski (from the collection of Jerzy Ficowski).

Two windows of the corner room in the Schulz house, photographed in 1965 by Jerzy Ficowski (from the collection of Jerzy Ficowski).

The old stove—no longer in existence—in Schulz's room at 10 Floriańska Street in Drohobycz, photograph from 1965 by Jerzy Ficowski (from the collection of Jerzy Ficowski).

Bruno Schulz on the steps of his house in Drohobycz. Stairway no longer exists, photograph from around 1936 (from the collection of Jerzy Ficowski).

SPRAWOZDANIE
DYREKCJI GIMNAZJUM PAŃSTWOWEGO
IM. KRÓLA WŁADYSŁAWA JAGIEŁŁY
W DROHOBYCZU
za rok szkolny 1933|34.

Budynek gimnazjalny.

Treść :

WIADOMOŚCI URZĘDOWE,
podane przez Dyrektora zakładu.

NAKŁADEM DYREKCJI GIMNAZJUM PAŃSTWOWEGO
IM. KRÓLA WŁADYSŁAWA JAGIEŁŁY W DROHOBYCZU.
1934.

Title page of the annual report of the Gymnasium in Drohobycz for the year 1934 (from the collection of Jerzy Ficowski).

Portrait of Schulz's fiancée, Józefina Szelińska, pastel, photograph done in 1988 by Jerzy Ficowski (private collection).

Teachers and students from "Blatt's school" in Drohobycz. The graduating class on the day of their examination (*matura*) in 1940, under the first Soviet occupation. Schulz is standing on the left with his head lowered: on the wall are portraits of Karl Marx and Josef Stalin (from the collection of Jerzy Ficowski).

Little house in the Drohobycz ghetto at 18 Stolarska Street (no longer in existence) to which the Germans expelled Schulz. Photograph by Jerzy Ficowski in 1965 (from the collection of Jerzy Ficowski).

Felix (Richard) Landau, "Gestapo *Hauptscharführer,*" coordinator and perpetrator of the extermination of the Jews in Drohobycz (original photograph in Yad Vashem, Jerusalem; copy in the collection of Jerzy Ficowski).

Linen cover for the portfolio **Xięga bałwochwalcza** (*The Booke of Idolatry*) with a title headpiece by Bruno Schulz, India ink, from the 1920s (from a private collection).

Title page from one of Schulz's portfolios containing the graphics entitled *Xięga bałwochwalcza* (*The Booke of Idolatry*), drawing in pencil and India ink, as well as a list of the graphics (from the National Museum in Poland).

"The Pilgrims II," a graphic from the cycle *Xięga bałwochwalcza* (*The Booke of Idolatry*), around 1920 (from the collection of Jerzy Ficowski)

"Revolution in the town" (or, *"The Enchanted City – II"*). *Cliché-verre* graphic from the cycle *Xięga bałwochwalcza* (*The Booke of Idolatry*), done about 1920 (from the collection of Jerzy Ficowski).

Ex libris of Stanisław Weingarten, original design by Bruno Schulz; after reduction in size made into plates to be inserted into books. Black crayon, India ink, 1919 (from the collection of Jerzy Ficowski).

Ex libris of Stanisław Weingarten, printed from a 1920 design by Bruno Schulz (from the collection of Jerzy Ficowski).

Temptresses and boys from the Talmudic school, from the 1920s, printed in 1930 in the Jewish journal *Cusztajer* (*Contribution*) in Lwów (the original is lost) (photograph from the collection of Jerzy Ficowski).

Two gentlemen (Bruno Schulz and Stanisław Weingarten) and *two ladies*, black crayon, India ink, from before 1930 (from the collections of the Gallery of Paintings in Lwów where it was lost after 1965; photocopy from the collection of Jerzy Ficowski).

Fitting at the tailor, pencil, drawing on cardboard, before 1930 (from the collection of Jerzy Ficowski).

kind of madness; Edzio or Eddie is crippled, his broad shoulders and energy at odds with his useless legs. Such characters reflect Schulz's predilection for deformity, his deep fascination with curiosities that depart from the rigid norms of reality, a "teratophilia" reminiscent of surrealism.

The phrase "fantastic realism" has been suggested for Schulz's art. It is an imprecise description, although it possesses some validity in its vague suggestion of a symbiosis of phantom with realistic observation. Perhaps surrealism? But where surrealism seeks shocking juxtapositions and utilizes the alogicality of the dream vision, Schulz is a master of the visual world: he sees and observes accurately and precisely. These perceptions suggest connections and consequences to Schulz, and upon them he builds myth—distant from the ordinary vision of the world, not surrealistically alogical, but in some way obvious, and, to use a neologism, ruled by Schulzian mythologic.

This means that individual images in Schulz's writing, intensified by the mythicization of the object, are truer and more evocative than realistic description. The story of the puppy Nemrod uses neither naturalistic description nor the conventional device of anthropomorphism and yet is both accurate and convincing. The introverted Schulz, enmeshed in the depths of his own personality, was in fact an incomparable observer.

The story "The Age of Genius" provides two examples of Schulz's intensified or enhanced vision. The first concerns a deer. Were we to reduce Schulz's image to simple external observation, we would have this description: deer have long, protruding, and branched antlers and are very timid. A more penetrating observation would be that deer cannot see their own antlers, which extend beyond their field of vision. Schulz's mythicization combines and completes the two levels of observation, not only rendering the image vivid but adding the sense of a cognitive process:

> I understood then why animals have horns. It was something incomprehensible that could not fit into their lives, a wild intrusive caprice, an unreasonable and blind obstinacy. Some idée fixe, growing outside the limits of their being, high above their heads and emerging suddenly into light, frozen into matter palpable and

hard. It then acquired a wild, incredible, and unpredictable shape, twisted into a fantastic arabesque, invisible to their eyes yet frightening, an unknown number under the threat of which they are forced to live. I grasped why these animals are given to irrational and wild panic, to a startled frenzy: gripped by their madness, they are unable to extricate themselves from the tangle of these horns, between which—when they lower their heads—they peer sadly and wildly, as if seeking a passageway between their branches.

The second example in the story concerns a cat. Externally, one might note several qualities: lazy feline immobility, elegant shape and movement, and mysterious and expressionless oval eyes. Schulz, however, writes:

> Their perfection was frightening. Enclosed in the precision and meticulousness of their bodies, they knew neither fault nor deviation. They would descend for a moment into the depths of their being, then immobile within their soft fur, they became seriously threatening and solemn, while their eyes became round like moons, drinking the visible into their fiery funnels. But a moment later, cast ashore onto the surface, they would yawn away their vacuity, disenchanted and without illusions.

He seems to grasp the actual detail in its most elusive manifestation—only the conclusion, the generalization, the extension becomes myth and transformation, entering the sphere of Schulzian fairy tale. Likewise, one need only once see an acacia tree in the wind to remember the supple bend of its branches, the almost exaggerated bow produced not so much by the wind but by the qualities of its affected foliage, to realize the truth of Schulz's description:

> It seemed that these trees affected a strong wind, theatrically ruffling their crowns, in pathetic bending to show the refinement of their leafy fans with a silvery abdomen like the fur of noble vixens.

Schulz used the phrase "bankruptcy of reality" for *Cinnamon Shops*. Bankruptcy expresses the exhaustion of reality's claim to unequivocality, to hackneyed unchangeability. The poet-mythologist both recognizes reality's laws and opposes them, suggesting new relationships with new consequences. Schulz's creative fantasy does not invent a new parallel reality, independent of ordinary experience; rather, it enters the everyday, bypassing areas ignored by human experience, relieving its seriousness and competing with its well-worn roads. Here Schulz's metaphysics of an animate reality finally emerges. Reflecting a subtle familiarity with this principle, not only as an artist but in his full awareness of its means and mechanisms, Schulz wrote in a review:

> When the modern writer wants justification, verisimilitude for the transcendental world, locating it at points where our own knowledge has gaps, he achieves the opposite: he discredits fantasy. No bridge exists between the transcendental world and nature's reality.

Certain appearances of objective reality and certain external rudiments are respected, while simultaneously its basic laws are questioned: time, space, separation of individual existences. The fabric and structure of reality are weakened, its dogmas overthrown. With reality thus disarmed, myth can enter—with its quasi-rational appearance and antiheroic tone that sometimes perversely undercuts its own seriousness. Myth is then capable, as hesitant as reality that has been unsettled, of imperceptibly penetrating reality and merging with it. Myth blesses reality's new character, often with the smile of Schulz's sensitive and discreet humor, saving his world from pathos and grounding its high current of demiurgical power. Schulz's humor is subtle; it preserves his world from a serious attitude and it avoids gestures of exaltation. His humor has been interpreted by critics as an act degrading reality, whereas in essence it is an ally of myth, raising it to a higher level. This spice of the grotesque saves Schulz's creations from being esoteric, but it does not degrade them, it does not stem from parodic intentions, nor does it lead to the destruction of myth or its compromise.

Schulzian mythology was not simply an artistic game. It arose from the authentic depths of Bruno Schulz's personality, even though he had long been separated from the "age of genius" of myth-creating childhood. Once, during the 1930s, in the course of a lively conversation with a friend in a café in Łódź, Schulz suddenly turned gloomy. He finally admitted that a tall factory chimney glimpsed through the window so distressed him that he could not break free of it. From that moment the chimney had become a third person in their conversation. Its inescapable presence and the possibilities it contained "became, as it were, a reality for us both," explained Schulz's friend. As he was telling "me about the life of a postage stamp [the stamp album of Rudolf in "Spring," J.F.], a friend of mine unexpectedly stopped to greet me. She sat down at our table and Schulz continued to talk, ignoring her, simply not paying any attention to her."

To avoid the disturbing distraction of the chimney, Schulz had escaped into the land of the colorful, consoling stamp album. It became his mythic homeland where he found asylum from fear; the phantoms that pursued him were disarmed, domesticated by humor and the grotesque. When the element of fear is minor or absent in Schulz's writing, the grotesque derision diminishes or even disappears. It grows like an antidote, however, in proportion to the increase of terrifying elements. And so at the end of "Treatise on Tailors' Dummies: Conclusion," for example, we read:

> Am I to conceal from you, [Father] said in a low tone, that my own brother, as a result of a long and incurable illness, has been gradually transformed into a roll of rubber hoses, and that my poor cousin had to carry him day and night in cushions, singing to the luckless creature endless lullabies on winter nights?

Suddenly the tone and atmosphere of the description changes; humor, even on the stylistic level, relieves the horror: "What disappointment for his parents, what confusion for their feelings, what shattering of all hopes centered round the promising youth!"

When, however, within the safe range of Father, the colorful world is not threatened, words may burst forth into emotional exclamations, untinged by irony, as in the opening paragraph of the story "The Book":

> Somewhere in the dawn of childhood, at the first daybreak of life, the horizon had brightened with its [the Book's] gentle glow. It lay in all its glory on my father's desk, and he, quietly engrossed in it,

patiently rubbed with a wet fingertip the ridge of decals, until the blind paper began to mist over, to cloud, to rave with blissful foreboding and, suddenly shedding bits of tissue paper, disclosed a lashed peacock-eyed edge; he turned his glance downward, swooning, to a virgin dawn of divine colors, toward a miraculous moistness of purest azure. Oh, that shedding of the film, oh, that invasion of brightness, o blissful spring, oh, Father. . . .

Schulz's writing is unlike that of Kafka. Only a superficial acquaintance with Schulz's writing would suggest a similarity. Their worlds are diametrically opposed, their artistic motifs quite different, and their philosophies distant from one another. In 1927, Schulz mentioned in conversation the "great writing" of Kafka, whom he was then reading in the original German. However, while Schulz valued Kafka highly, contrary to groundless suggestions, he never considered himself his follower. Schulz was a builder of a reality-asylum that was a marvelous "intensification of the taste of the world"; Kafka was an inhabitant and propagator of a world of terror, an ascetic hermit awaiting a miracle of justice that never came. Schulz was a metaphysician garbed in all the wealth of color; Kafka was a mystic in a hair shirt of worldly denials. Schulz was a creator and ruler of compensatory Myth; Kafka was the Sisyphean seeker of the Absolute. Schulz, the lavish creator of mundane Olympians, produced a metaphysics of an animate reality, while Kafka became the bookkeeper of the all-enveloping Abyss. The power and the authenticity of Schulz's writing do not depend upon a direct revelation of his own personal anxieties, nor an admission of his permanent sense of beleaguerment, his fears about existence. Such inner content expressed by Kafka, for example, is camouflaged and disarmed by Schulz. His concealment and control is not deceptive: it is the satisfying of a need, a compensation, a construction of a reality enabling him to escape the trap which in real life had none. Thus, in a certain sense, Schulz's literary creation is the reverse of actual experiences, a deliberate and instinctive defense against tormenting obsessions before which in the sphere of art he was not as defenseless as Kafka—a hapless victim.

Life, real existence, had profound significance for Schulz as the raw material of his art and was valuable to the degree that it could be "creatively utilized." Schulz understood art as a mission; it was the fulfillment of longings and a shield against lethal fears. Hence, he imbued his fiction with a kindly magic and his own variety of demonism, without ever descending to the depths of the metaphysical terror from which there could be no return. The real names of the actual persons and places, transferred into mythology, were more than just a pretext for fiction: having changed their inner content, their externals remained as a link between the real biography of the writer and his own invented mythic genealogy.

8

⚜

Excursions Abroad

The milieu in which Schulz lived was distant from the concerns of art. Neither within his family nor within his circle of gymnasium teachers did he find persons with whom he could share his thoughts or carry on discussions about what interested him most. He sought such spiritual partners, sometimes bestowing his confidence and intellectual trust upon persons unable to understand him fully. The need for an interlocutor was overpowering, and his susceptibility to feminine beauty was so great that most often it was women who became his correspondent-confidantes. Some of them, such as Debora Vogel, were far from average. Friendship and correspondence with her turned out to be factors that inspired Schulz's creativity and so brought him the desired results.

At the beginning of the 1930s, many of Bruno Schulz's acquaintances had long known that he was painting, but no one suspected that he was secretly attempting to write. Even those closest to him were completely taken by surprise when he made his debut in print in 1934; he had never mentioned his literary ambitions or attempts at writing in conversations with them.

The society in which Schulz matured and with which he was most closely connected was the Jewish society of Drohobycz, and in particular the circles which—far from orthodoxy—constituted an important element in the local intelligentsia and which were to varying degrees assimilated. Family ties were his most crucial connections. School and youthful friendships did not extend beyond this circle, restricted sometimes by Schulz's fears of rejection. Only in letters directed to select recipients could such a sensitive person be free of such fears, not always unfounded, and especially in periods of rising anti-Semitism. Only when he publicly became a writer did Schulz's circle of acquaintances widen, gaining him new "comrades of the pen." As to comrades in life, however, fellow participants in his provincial daily toil, he had only his fellow teachers alongside whom he worked. With few exceptions, he found no basis for spiritual exchanges in this accidental and often burdensome contact with fellow professors. Despite the conscientiousness with which he discharged his duties, Schulz considered teaching a sad necessity robbing him of time and energy for art.

Until 1934, Schulz's only readers had been those who received his letters, epistolary confidantes like Debora Vogel whose correspondence occasioned and stimulated his creativity. When publication of *Cinnamon Shops* dramatically widened his readership, Schulz began to experience not only artistic satisfaction but also a nervous trepidation; consciousness of his vast, unseen audience hampered his writing. His literature had been born of solitary experiences and reflections and was responsible only to its demanding creator. Through numerous soundings in letters it become bold enough to speak to several recipients: the reader was known and trusted; writing in letters was like whispering a secret to a trusted friend whose reactions could be anticipated. To such a reader, Schulz had entrusted both his literary attempts and his paraliterary ones, as the majority of his letters were.

Bruno Schulz may have been the last outstanding exponent of epistolary art in Poland. His letters were not only the genesis of his writing, because he continued them even when publication deprived them of their original function. The art of the letter also constitutes a particularly essential element in Schulz's literary art. Letters were such a gladly practiced form of writing that his essays even include quasi-letters, such as the "letter" to Stanisław Ignacy Witkiewicz or the famous polemical "letter" in response to the writer and reviewer Witold Gombrowicz. Both were pieces intended for publication, although formally addressed to a particular individual. Schulz dreamed of going beyond the charmed circle of letters and planned moving from Drohobycz. The first dream was fulfilled—bringing with it fears of the vast, unseen audience; plans to move were never realized. Schulz himself unconsciously opposed them. He needed the intimate quiet of his native Drohobycz, as well as epistolary creation. In the meantime, however, as a writer he began to travel to more distant destinations, away from Drohobycz and into the unknown world.

As Schulz made new acquaintances through his writing, his most intimate circle began to shrink. In 1931, almost three years prior to the publication of *Cinnamon Shops*, Schulz's aged mother, who had cared for him so tenderly, died. Soon after, Bruno's admired older brother, Izydor, financial mainstay of the family, suddenly succumbed to a heart attack. Life became lonelier and more difficult and Schulz became more isolated. Then in 1934 the literary success of *Cinnamon Shops* brought Schulz acceptance by Polish literary circles.

Valuable friendships deepened with Stanisław Ignacy Witkiewicz and Zofia Nałkowska, as if in compensation for his private losses. Although Schulz had met Witkiewicz in the 1920s, their initial acquaintance was now renewed. Witkiewicz expressed his enthusiasm for *Cinnamon Shops* in reviews of Schulz's writing. Instrumental in the publication of *Cinnamon Shops*, Zofia Nałkowska was both Schulz's earliest supporter and then his close friend. In the first printed review of *Cinnamon Shops* she wrote:

> The style of this book illumines and penetrates reality as if from its underside, revealing it deformed and true, like a cross section of

tissue under a microscope—a reality that is intensified and threatening. It is an immensely interesting book to which one returns for new surprises that can be read anew in different ways, at different depths.

Nałkowska and Witkiewicz were not alone in their enthusiasm. In 1935, Adolf Nowaczyński, Antoni Słonimski, and Julian Tuwim nominated *Cinnamon Shops* for the *Wiadomości Literackie* (Literary News) prize. Tadeusz Breza praised Schulz's *Cinnamon Shops* highly in a book review. Not all critics reacted so favorably, however. Along with recognition and praise, Schulz's stories also elicited incomprehension and even some malice from critics who saw them as the work of a presumptuous newcomer. One young critic wrote: "There is something childish in this older vision that is destructive," and added knowingly that "such an imagination . . . requires more forbearance than does aversion. . . . [Schulz] impoverishes the world . . . [his] sick loneliness is unjustified, and could be explained more by a diagnosis, an evaluation of the conditions, rather than need." Others characterized Schulz as a "writer of snobbish twists and turns," "a sham," "an epigone," or a "mawkish sentimentalist." His work was condemned as totally worthless, without value, "even burned." These negative voices appeared in print eight months before the outbreak of World War II. Those critics who came out on the side of appreciation and recognition of Schulz were among Poland's most distinguished writers; those who unleashed abusive attacks were considerably inferior and associated primarily with far-right-wing circles. Although these attacks did not shake Schulz's conviction about his own artistic path, they did deeply depress him. His private work, saved for years in a drawer, had become public property to be applauded or decried. Voices from the outside now disturbingly invaded his Drohobycz seclusion. It soon became clear that this was not a productive factor.

Nevertheless, the success of *Cinnamon Shops* remained indisputable, and Schulz wanted to capitalize on this wave of recognition by composing a new work without delay. He intended to participate in a novel-writing contest sponsored by the *Ilustrowany Kurier Codzienny* (Illustrated Daily Courier) of Cracow, but could not get beyond the planning stage. A few months after the publication of *Cinnamon Shops*, Schulz wrote to an old friend: "I should have many reasons now for satisfaction, I could allow myself a little joy, and instead of that I experience an indefinable fear. . . . I write nothing, even copying something causes an insurmountable repugnance in me." And again, several months later: "It's a great shame for me to waste the kind of success that I had with *Cinnamon Shops*, but I am wasting it if this year I don't publish some things that are at least on the same level."

Schulz's intentions were never carried out. His second collection of stories, *Sanatorium Under the Sign of the Hourglass*, finally published in 1937, was composed primarily of previously written stories. His work on the novel *Messiah* dragged on with difficulty.

Public acclaim for *Cinnamon Shops* also meant that Schulz felt the pressure of his teaching job more acutely. He began a long battle to obtain a leave of absence during which he might continue his writing. He was finally granted a paid leave from January 1 to June 30 of 1936. During these months he wrote several book reviews, primarily for *Wiadomości Literackie*, the novella "Spring," and two short stories ("Autumn" and "The Republic of Dreams") which he omitted from *Sanatorium Under the Sign of the Hourglass* when it was published in 1937. He compiled that collection, along with its illustrations, as well. Schulz deprecated his second book unjustifiably because it was made up primarily of writings simply pulled from a drawer and then filled out with only a few stories. He spent a great part of his leave in Warsaw, but his writing indicates that he felt like an exile longing for Drohobycz. Schulz's "Republic of Dreams" opens with the paragraph:

> Here on the Warsaw pavement in these turbulent, fiery, bewildering days, I transport myself in thought to the distant city of my dreams, I rise with my gaze above that low countryside, sprawling and voluminous like a cloak of God flung down as a mottled canvas at the threshold of heaven. For that entire country bows down to heaven, bearing on its shoulders the colorfully vaulted, cloistered, full of triforia, and rosettes, windows opening onto eternity. . . . There where the map of the country shifts far to the south, bleached white from the sun, bronzed and singed by the glow of summer like a ripe pear—there it stretches like a cat in the sun,

that chosen land, that peculiar province, that town unique in all the world.

Schulz's prose echoes the poetry of Polish romantic poet Adam Mickiewicz's poetry. Living in Paris and overcome with longing for his homeland, Mickiewicz wrote: "What is there to meditate upon here on the pavements of Paris? . . . Carry my longing spirit to those forest knolls, to those meadows. . ."[1]

The summer vacation beginning in June 1936 was the last phase of Schulz's long-sought freedom from teaching, and at the last moment he decided to use his savings to go abroad. On August 26 he sailed from the port of Gdynia on board the ship *Kościuszko* for a three-day excursion to Stockholm. Except for his visit years earlier to Vienna and Kudova, this was Schulz's first experience of foreign travel. The tour group spent one day in Stockholm. On board ship Schulz met Karolina and Stefania Beylin. Stefania, the Polish translator of Hans Christian Andersen, spent long hours with Schulz discussing the Danish fairy-tale writer and fairy tales in general, but the brief voyage had no creative consequences for Schulz; it seemed that only the locale of Drohobycz was poetically inspiring for him.

In his letters Schulz complained that in exploiting the past he was unable to find new material, to find experiences heretofore unknown, that in the abstraction of his life he hungered for the concrete. "Force your memory as you like," he wrote to Debora Vogel, "you will not find in your biography anything that could be the subject of narration." Debora replied:

> We also pass through everything "human"; in my opinion, the percentage that is stronger or weaker in external details doesn't matter here. . . . You will say that this is precisely the problem—that I want to live by means of "examples" of life, those minute specifics that "we fan into a fire," as you say. I don't believe that others did differently, that they did not experience the exemplary quality of life . . . . And we, like they, have beyond the human, gray, and centuries-old life, or rather before it—a certain dose of the romantic . . . and a certain percentage of the exotic, coming to us in the form of travel, visiting foreign and unknown cities and areas and in the form of unexpected encounters there. And that travel need

not necessarily last six months in time in order to experience—
exemplarily—its essence, since one always experiences exemplarily for no one has known *all* trips. . . .

Travels in the imagination, however, were indispensable for
Schulz—trips like those to the colorful countries of Joseph's postage
stamps or visiting distant eras and lands through the paintings from
the collection of the Basilian fathers in "A Second Fall." Now even
Warsaw was too distant; Schulz constantly got lost in its streets,
because he was devoid of a sense of direction when away from home.
A foreign city in a foreign country was even worse; there the feeling
of disorientation inhibited his ability to experience the beauties of
new locales. Nevertheless, Schulz was curious about the wider world
and in 1938 undertook his second and final trip abroad, this time to
Paris. For a hesitant and timid person, the very decision to make the
trip was difficult. A close friend, the pianist Maria Rey-Chasin [or
Chazen], encouraged him to go. After numerous predeparture
arrangements in which friends assisted the completely resourceless
Schulz, he left in the last days of July, worried that during the summer off season in the French capital the museums would be closed
and his contacts away on vacation.

   Once in Paris, despite the solicitousness of Maria Chasin's
brother, Georges Rosenberg, as well as Ludwik Lille, a painter and
old friend from Lwów who had settled in France, Schulz felt lost and
insecure about sightseeing alone. Despondent over his isolation
amid the Parisian crowds, Schulz characterized Paris as "the most
exclusive, self-sufficient, and closed city in the world." His inade-
quate knowledge of French was also a handicap, and the Polish
embassy declined any kind of assistance. Schulz complained to
Romana Halpern after his return:

> Apart from this, Paris was empty—all the better art salons were
> closed. I did however make contact with one art dealer on rue
> Faub[bourg]. St. Honoré, who wanted to do an exhibit, but then I
> withdrew from the project myself. Despite that I am pleased that
> I was in Paris, that I saw so many astounding things, and could
> look up close at the art of great eras, instead of through reproduc-
> tions—but, finally, that I have gotten rid of certain illusions about

a world career. I saw beautiful things, disturbing and terrible. The wonderful Parisian women made a great impression on me—both those of proper society and cocottes, their free manner, the tempo of life.

Only reluctantly and with trepidation did Schulz venture out alone, fearing that he would become hopelessly lost in the labyrinth of streets. So most of the time someone accompanied him. Schulz saw Georges Rosenberg only periodically, since the latter's own obligations at this time constantly took him outside Paris. During each visit, however, they returned to the topics of their previous talks and their relationship was close. Rosenberg recalled:

We spent one evening in a very fashionable, well-known Paris cabaret, the Casanova, on Montmartre. Schulz was much taken with the beauty, elegance, and dress of the women with their "stunning" decolletés and he did not always realize the "business" approach of some of the ladies. He asked me timidly whether he might caress the arm of the woman at the next table, who obviously had nothing against it. He was moved by the touch. I realized that he was a prisoner of his own fantasy and not a happy man. But he so dominated us all with the richness of his spirit, thought, and poetry. . . . He remained in my mind as an extraordinarily rich intellect and a magician with words who had led me to unknown heights of the human spirit and at the same time into the dark recesses of our emotions. He was timid, sometimes even frightened, and when he spoke about the "threatening chimneys in Łódź," full of feeling for the essence of the feminine and very, very delicate.

Schulz's fears were confirmed: after Bastille Day on July 14, Paris was empty and his longed-for meetings with writers or artists did not materialize. He was unable even to meet the novelist and poet Jules Romains, something that he had promised himself before the trip. Delight at seeing original works of art only combined with a depressing sense of his own inadequacy when he viewed the masterpieces of the Paris galleries for the first time in his life. And so Schulz took back his drawings from the art dealer in the rue St. Honoré and decided not to exhibit them. Only a visit to the studio of the sculp-

tor Naum Aronson revived his spirits slightly. Aronson was fascinated with Schulz's drawings, and the degree and sincerity of Aronson's delight was obvious even to Schulz, who was inclined to lack
faith in himself. In the end, however, of the one hundred drawings
Schulz had brought with him, twenty or so were given to Parisian
acquaintances and the rest were brought back home.

Despite some efforts, there were absolutely no possibilities for
publishing his writings in France; a sufficiently influential intermediary was lacking. Schulz's illusions about a world career, his long-
cherished dream of breaking through the language barrier and being
translated in Western Europe, evaporated. Publication in Germany,
of course, was out of the question. Full of fear and revulsion at
Nazism, Schulz would not even consider publication there. When
traveling to France, Schulz took a longer route in order to avoid
passing through the Reich. Although in 1937 he did write one story
in German—"Die Heimkehr" (The Return Home)—counting on an
Austrian translator who might become interested in his other Polish
works, this hope never materialized. He still had some hope for an
Italian translation of *Cinnamon Shops*. A cousin of Maria Chasin,
George Pinette, expressed his willingness to negotiate with Italian
publishers and requested that Schulz write a synopsis that could be
presented abroad. Schulz composed a succinct analysis in German,[2]
but nothing came of the effort; Italian publishers were not interested
either. During the spring of 1939 the well-known Italian writer Mas-
simo Bontempelli was in Poland primarily to meet with Witold Gombrowicz and Bruno Schulz. The meeting took place, but because of
difficulties in language communication and Schulz's timidity, it was
without result. The outbreak of war, moreover, thwarted all plans and
broke off the contacts that had been established.[3]

Schulz's excursions abroad were limited and their consequences
negligible; his attempts to enter the European literary scene came to
naught. He tried, however, to break out of his Drohobycz isolation
and join the current of real life in yet another way: he attempted
what he termed "an excursion into matrimony," as he phrased it in a
1936 letter to Romana Halpern. Schulz became engaged to a Miss
Józefina Szelińska.[4] Their acquaintance and close friendship began
in 1933, and in 1936 they became engaged. Until their engagement

was broken off in 1937, their relationship provided Schulz with a feeling of security, a link with life and its everyday human concerns. He needed this palpable, concrete "ground beneath his feet" which provided meaning for actual existence beyond the realm of the fantastic. The affection of someone who loved him was a shield against danger, a compass point in life, a guarantee of the longed-for peace that he could not achieve alone: "My fiancée constitutes my participation in life; through her I am a person, and not just a lemur and kobold.[5] . . . With her love, she has redeemed me, already almost lost and fallen victim to inhuman realms, of barren underworlds of fantasy. She has returned me to life and reality. She is the closest person to me on earth."

Schulz was profoundly grateful for this anchor in life and for his profound spiritual communion with this beloved and loving woman. It turned out, however, that responsibility for the couple's future involved both parties. He saw his fiancée as his representative in the real world where he himself was not a citizen, an emissary to ordinary reality. Schulz, the lifetime patron of the Cinnamon Shops, was unwilling or unable to cooperate with her in practical matters. Active and creative in the regions of the great heresy, he felt like a stranger, passive and helpless in the world of conventional social norms. It was difficult for him to function, inclined as he was to flights of imagination that carried him "higher and higher into the yellow, uncharted, autumnal air." He felt indebted to his fiancée and realized how little he was capable of doing for her in ordinary life, since his powers lay elsewhere. Beyond the world of art, he was helpless and superfluous. Nevertheless, Schulz did what he could. Since his name was known from the publication of *Cinnamon Shops*, he "loaned" it to his fiancée for her translation of Franz Kafka's *The Trial*, which she, unknown in literary circles, would not otherwise have been able to publish. He advised her on corrections in the text, and the book appeared in 1936 as a translation by Bruno Schulz. The belief that this was Schulz's own translation persisted because of Schulz's strict confidence, his never allowing the story behind the translation to be revealed. The secrecy was so successfully maintained that the translation was used to support the thesis of some affinity between these two radically different writers.

After his half-year leave combined with the following summer vacation, Schulz—contrary to vague plans of moving permanently to Warsaw—prepared to return to Drohobycz. His engagement was already close to being broken off. Despite his lack of resourcefulness in practical life, he had taken some of the necessary steps toward marriage. In numerous letters he pestered friends for advice and assistance in bureaucratic procedures connected with such a union:

> My fiancée is Catholic. . . . I don't care to accept baptism, however. I made only this concession for her to give up membership in the Jewish community. Under these circumstances it is possible only to get married under German law, which holds in the former Prussian-annexed territory, for example, in Katowice. I understand that a marriage license can be obtained only after three months of residence in the province of Silesia. It's possible to get around this rule by a *pro forma* registration at some Silesian town. . . . I must have Józefina's (this is my fiancée's name) closeness and connection with me assured in order to function at all. That is the zero level from which I rise on the scale of fantasy.

This problem totally preoccupied Schulz for some time; he sent off imploring letters and even made a once-in-his-lifetime three-day trip to Katowice to see one of his former students, a lawyer. All efforts were fruitless and the plans failed. In 1937, Schulz broke off the engagement. For a long time he felt terrible, internally devastated and without any support. Only two years later did these feelings subside and did Schulz begin to prepare for a new, more crucial excursion—this time into the world of his imagination. The solitude of Drohobycz gave rise to hopes for a return of the former "seven years of prosperity" in his writing. In 1939 Schulz wrote:

> Somehow it's happened that my really numerous and teaming swarm of friends has thinned out considerably, connections have weakened and once again I am headed as it were toward parts and zones of fate where loneliness reigns. As in the past. Sometimes this fills me with sadness and fear in the face of emptiness, then again it entices me with some confident, long familiar temptation.[6]

A world free of the pressure of passing time opened up before

Schulz; the elusive elements of experience, diffused until now in the thin solution of idle time, again demanded expression. A period of great and different travels approached, of heretical explorations of reality. Traversing physical distance was unnecessary; such movement only squandered the treasure hoarded by the Drohobycz recluse. All Schulz needed was a quiet room in the two-story house on Floriańska Street and a window that revealed the distant Carpathian horizon in the narrow space between the houses. This quiet would be short-lived; it was shattered with utter finality by the bombs and gunfire of war. In 1939 it was already too late for any kind of traveling, even for Schulz's longest excursion: his venture into the depths of himself.

9

Magic and Definition

"Dream and wisdom" was the phrase Bruno Schulz used to describe the "Tales of Jacob," the first volume of Thomas Mann's *Joseph and His Brothers*. One might characterize Schulz's own writing as emotionalism shaped by precision of expression. Without losing its nature, hazy abstraction becomes concrete; elusive content becomes tangible. Sensual sensitivity of such a degree combining with nearly mathematical exactness in words and images is rare. In Schulz's writing, the romantic disdain for what the Polish poet Adam Mickiewicz termed the "sage's glass and eye"[1] finds new application and undergoes a metamorphosis: it is transformed into the magical conjunction of the jeweler's glass with a kaleidoscope. Disregarding the romantics' "feeling and faith," the skeptic views the world through his own optical device and records his observations like a rationalist. He builds a logically constructed, immanent reality, often creating quasi-scientific terminology and employing foreign terms to bolster its power and clarity.

The union of such contradictory elements as the rich sensuality that Schulz termed the "marrow of childhood" and an extraordinary intellectual suppleness with scientific inclinations is an unusual symbiosis. We find it not only in Bruno Schulz's writing but in his own life as well, for Schulz was also an amateur mathematician, periodically teaching mathematics at the gymnasium. For amusement he even solved problems put to him by a math-teacher colleague. As Schulz wrote in "The Mythologizing of Reality," "Mathematical symbols are an extension of the word into new realms."

It is sometimes said that Bruno Schulz's fiction rendered reality strange, but the actual world around him was incontrovertibly strange to him; he had only to give that feeling expression. Literature allows creative mystifications, the expression of an idea dictated by the needs of a specific work and valid only within its confines. Perception of the mainspring of reality as metaphysical was not simply an artistic device or premise for Schulz; it was his own deep conviction. He expressed it in a 1941 letter to his last regular correspondent, his friend Anna Płockier:

> I am continually under the spell of your charming metamorphoses. I think that they are so moving because they are so independent of your will, so automatic and unconscious. It is as if someone surreptitiously moved another person forward, replaced you, and you, as it were, accepted this new person and took her for yourself, and played your part further on a new instrument, unaware that someone else is now acting on stage. Of course, I am exaggerating the matter and stretching it to the point of paradox. Please don't take me for someone naive. I know that this is not entirely unwitting, but you don't realize how much of this is the work of more profound powers, how much is some metaphysical puppetry. At the same time, you are unusually reactive, conforming immediately to a complimentary shape, in wonderful accompaniment. . . . All this goes on as if beyond intellect, along some shorter and more direct road than that of thought, simply like a physical reflex. It's the first time that I have encountered such rich-

ness of nature not confined, you might say, to the range of a single person and therefore activating auxilliary personalities, improvising pseudopersonalities initiated ad hoc for the duration of the brief role which you must play. This is how I explain your protean nature to myself. You may think that I've allowed myself to be taken in, that I am suggesting deep interpretations in the guise of an ordinary flirtation. I assure you that coquetry is something very profound and mysterious, and incomprehensible even for you yourself. Of course, you cannot see this mysteriousness and that on your side it must appear unproblematic and ordinary. But that is a delusion.[2]

Virtually all of Schulz's philosophy is contained in this passage: his "extreme monism of matter for which individual objects are only masks," the "dark enveloping fluid of night" and the "blood of secrecy," and finally the form of pseudopersonality proposed in the "Treatise on Tailors' Dummies, or Second Book of Genesis" about which Father says that "sometimes for one gesture, for one word alone, we shall make the effort to bring [it] to life." Schulz's world is a realm of continuous and sudden changes of living matter. The alogicality of dreams is uncommon in Schulz's fiction (appearing only in the story "Cinnamon Shops"), and it rarely appears in a purely oneiric form, that is, in surreal happenings with unfathomable causes and consequences. In Schulz's stories, dream undergoes a quasi-rationalization; it is objectified, transferred to a category of phenomena whose origins may be discovered, that can be experienced in the imagination, and that exhibit the magic signs of verisimilitude. No metamorphosis appears as a *deus ex machina*, as an abrupt and inexplicable decree of some unknown power as in the case of Kafka's student, Gregor Samsa. In Schulz's fiction every change is a consequence of some inner tension that has reached its culmination. At that point, a new quality emerges and new dynamics are revealed. Their hidden embryonic state is externalized which Schulz presents as an exposition of the origins of the new phenomenon.

Schulz's fiction usually terms this process the "fermentation" of matter which is the causative factor in mythological processes. The phenomenon of "A Second Fall" is nothing other than the result of our climate having been poisoned by the miasmas exuded and betrayed by degenerate specimens of baroque art crowded in our museums. That museum art, rotting boredom and oblivion and shut in without an outlet, ferments like old preserves, oversweetens our climate, causing this beautiful malarial fever, this colorful delirium to which our prolonged fall is so agonizingly prone.

Elsewhere Schulz writes that "darkness ferments and degenerates, and stillness goes bad in the course of years of silence, deteriorating fantastically like old forgotten empty wine barrels." Sometimes the very moment of transformation or shift to a higher level of existence is tangible. We see the culmination point, both the very moment of change and its cause. In "Spring,"

> The villa was asleep with its curtains drawn, and its chalky whiteness glimmering in the deadness of a gray aura. Suddenly, as if the stagnation had reached its critical point, the air shook with colored ferment, dissolved into colorful flakes. They were enormous, heavy butterflies coupling in amorous frolics.

Ordinary objects and common occurrences acquire new dimensions and meanings because of a new genetic exegesis that Schulz suggests for them. In "Cinnamon Shops," an azure stage curtain with painted pink masks conceals the performance to come:

> This artificial sky spread out, flowing in both directions, swelling with the huge breath of pathos and of great gestures. . . . The masks fluttered their red eyelids, their colored lips whispered something inaudibly, and I knew that the moment was imminent when the tension of mystery would reach its zenith and then the swollen skies of the curtain would really burst open to reveal incredible and dazzling events.

A gale that blows over the town is an eruption from the dark clutter of untidy attics which "began to degenerate and ferment wildly. . . ." And in old apartments "there degenerates . . . a silence totally corrupt and demoralized into a thousand thoughts, in lonely deliberations, blindly moving along the wall hangings with unlit lightning." These events typically acquire extraordinary genealogies; unforeseen causes and emotional connections produce them. A new manifestation is often explained as the result of a chemical process taking place in matter, or even an abstraction made concrete: a "poison," a "fermentation," or a "degeneration" becomes the direct mythological road to change. Gradual degeneration is always the mythological path for change, as well as the source of beauty, the mythic principle of Schulzian aesthetics. Decline is at the same time the birth of a new quality; decay accounts for new vegetation; infection stimulates generative processes. Beauty annexes areas conventionally considered ugly and ennobles them with myth. It is not for paradoxical effect that Father says in "A Second Fall" that "beauty is a disease . . . it is a certain kind of shiver from a mysterious infection, a dark forerunner of decomposition, arising from the depths of perfection. . . ."

Similarly fantastic metamorphoses—the changing of a human being into a heap of ashes or into a cockroach—are based on the same psychochemical principle. Inner tensions rise and swell up to produce sudden transformations: we are witnesses to growing dynamic potencies and then to their fruition as new forms and incarnations are born.

Things do not appear out of nothing: spiritual states materialize in physical form and then dissolve into thin air. Creatures emerge that exist on the borderline between imagination and reality, problematic beings of semi-reality. This applies to the pseudo-fauna and -flora described by Father which

> sometimes appeared in certain strictly defined environments. These environments are old apartments saturated with the emanations of numerous existences and events; used up atmospheres rich in the specific ingredients of human dreams; rubbish heaps, abounding in the humus of memories, of longing and of sterile boredom. On such a soil, this pseudo-vegetation sprouted rapidly yet superficially, brought forth short-lived generations which flourished suddenly and splendidly, only to wilt and perish.

Schulz is particular about the gradation of reality, the definition of its texture. He doesn't strip away the illusory quality in the description above, but shifts its contents to the borderline area of "dream-reality," adding that this was "a mystification, an accident of the strange simulation of matter which had impersonated life." Elsewhere we read that the cause of certain incomplete events and partial realizations is the imperfection of reality which cannot support them and so these events exist in a potential state, in a sense beyond reality, where they preserve their surreal nature:

There are things which cannot entirely or completely happen. They are too vast to be confined and too splendid. They only try to happen, test whether the ground of reality can support them. Then they withdraw, fearing to lose their wholeness in the imperfection of realization.

Just as in the story "Birds" Father's pseudo-fauna breeds luxuriantly in the medium of fermentation, so too the ambiguous reality of the district of the Street of Crocodiles where "nothing can ever reach a definite conclusion" is explained by being

nothing other than a fermentation of desires, swelling prematurely and therefore impotent and empty. In an atmosphere of excessive facility, every whim flies high, a passing excitement swells into an empty parasitic growth; a light gray vegetation of fluffy weeks, of colorless fuzzy poppies sprouts forth, made from a weightless fabric of nightmares and hashish.

Primitive feelings such as resentment or anger are, like "fermentation," transformative agents. Aunt Perazja punctuates the gale raging outside with her own anger, becoming "one small bundle of gestures and imprecations," after which "in her paroxysm of fury she . . . began suddenly to shrink and dwindle, still shaking and spitting curses" until at last "she became smaller and smaller, black and folded like a wilted, charred sheet of paper, oxydized into a petal of ash, crumbling into dust and nothingness."

In a game-shooting fury, Father hunts for cockroaches until at last his obsessive revulsion and disgust begin to activate, changing him into a cockroach. The transformation occurs gradually: black scales on his fingernails, then segmentation, and finally a prone position. Father's situation becomes all the more ambiguous because Mother does not actually deny the change, but assures the son

Joseph that Father has merely gone off for a while. Similarly, Father's anger in the shop leads to a sudden intensification of transformative factors and rapid change:

> My mother came running, alarmed: "What is the matter, Jacob?" she cried out breathlessly. In despair, she began to slap him on the back as one would a choking person. But it was too late. My father was bristling all over, his face was rapidly decomposing quickly into symmetrical parts of anger, changing before our eyes, under the weight of an incomprehensible calamity. Before we could understand what was happening, he shook himself violently, buzzed, and rose in flight before our eyes, as a monstrous, hairy, steel-blue horsefly, furiously circling and knocking blindly against all the walls of the shop.

Again the narrator's commentary, suspicious of the event, nevertheless does not negate it:

> Yet, looking at it dispassionately, one had to take my father's transformation with a grain of salt. It was much more the symbol of an inner protest, a violent and desperate demonstration from which, however, reality was not entirely absent.

Hedging with the qualification of "dementia" and partially accepting the truth of the fantastic phenomenon, the narrator tends to underscore its dubiousness and strengthens the suggestiveness of myth. In Schulz's multileveled writing, every image prompts various, equally justified interpretations that are not mutually exclusive. Schulz's mythologization of reality, returned childhood, and autothematism are the features which warrant particular attention.

Schulz's writing constitutes a personal exegesis; the laws of his fictional reality are simultaneously the principles of his own creative process. Schulz's artistic program lies both in the metaphoric transposition shared by the elements and power of *Cinnamon Shops* and also a self-defining formulation about the writer and his creation applied to the phenomena described. Hence the suggestive identity between the creator and his creation, the biology of living matter and the creative activity of the artist.

In a review of Zofia Nałkowska's work, Schulz—always inclined to emphasize his own concerns in the works of other writers—wrote: "Art has the tendency to materialize metaphors, to embody them and endow them with a real life. . . ." A radical tendency to materialize metaphors is actually a feature of Schulz's own writing. He ascribes similar tendencies and potential to the season of autumn: "When for inexplicable reasons metaphors, projects, human dreams begin to long for realization, the time of autumn comes." Schulz confided to his friends that he "lived only in *depth*, not in extent like other people." We find this same tendency in his fiction:

> How to express it? When other cities developed economically, increased statistically, in population—our town descended to its essence. Here nothing happens free, nothing takes place without deeper meaning or without premeditation. Here events are not an ephemeral phantom on the surface; they have their roots in the depth of things and reach to its essence.

Among Schulz's characters it is Father whose speeches and explanations most often voice Schulz's own authorial principles, positing a kind of equation between the rules of nature and those of artistic creation the goal of which is not so much to imitate nature as her creative power—demiurgy: "We intend . . . to once more create the world, on a small scale of course, for ourselves alone, but according to our taste and desires." In the Schulzian world thus constituted, reality continues to program and materialize the artistic philosophy of the author; it is a ceaseless exemplification, a vivid and enchanting exposition of the creative premises of the writer, a treatise on creation.

Language is Schulz's magic wand; we cannot imagine his world outside of verbal material. It is indissolubly and organically connected to his vision, which cannot be translated into the medium of any other art. As Schulz wrote: "The unnamed does not exist for us. To name something means to join it to some universal sense"—in other words, to create. In one of his letters he explained: "This is after all the postulate of humanism, the humanizing of the entirety of life so that fewer things would escape the light of thought and elude expression. . . . Poetry—that is a short clasp of sense between words, a sudden regeneration of primitive myths." The Schulzian word is not intensified, laconic, and clearly measured as in contemporary poetry; rather, it is a component in a definition, in elaborate verbal images, a living thing leading a gregarious mode of life. Carefully chosen for the greatest accuracy and precision, words combine into apparent redundancies, each contributing to the vividness of description, to an analysis of the appearance of some new element or point of view. Only the entire series of quasi-definitions yields the full picture, enriched with the bounty of hypotheses and propositions but without tautological superfluity or monotony. Schulz's word serves to concretize an abstract content, to rationalize the irrational. His poetic myths acquire the quality of treatises, ephemeral impressions take on the sanction of physical laws as Schulz's vocabulary draws generously from foreign languages, even mimicking objective scientific terminology.

Schulz's terms and coinages have no substitutes in the Schulzian context. The fruit and vegetables brought in from the market by Adela are not earthly produce for a meal, but "the vegetative and terrestrial ingredients of dinner with a wild, field aroma." His terms cannot be translated into native, Slavic words without harming the stories' content. Schulz's "topography of a July night" or "outline of a general systematics of Fall" likewise have no substitutes. Only rarely do his expressions seem exaggeratedly foreign, as in the case of half-wit Dodo who maintained "with his lively mimic expression a suggestion of a comprehending resonance." More often, Schulz's use of academic or scientific vocabulary is a stylistic device to confirm the existence of his fictional world. "Our language does not have the expression that would measure its degree of reality and define its texture," wrote Schulz in one of his works. Thus, at times Schulz resorts to conventional similes: as if, seemingly, as it were, or it would seem. Hence "the room filled up with shadow, buried as it were in the light of sea-depths," vegetables "like dead cephalopods and medusas." "It would seem that the trees imitated a gale." Similes indicate only the first level of Schulzian reality, barely signaling further possibilities. At the second level, magic begins to operate, impressions objectify and transfer onto their object: "Time invented by silence flows backward for a moment beyond itself and in those uncounted moments night grows in return night on the wavy fur of a cat," or "a great down comforter shaken out the window and the stuffing fluttered over the city, little stars of fluff, the lazy sowing of nightly dreams." Finally, at a third level, metaphor as it becomes metamorphosis leads to the most peculiar changes, which are motivated by their own inner dynamic.

Schulz's story "Sanatorium Under the Sign of the Hourglass" presents a civilized Hades; here his style intellectualizes myth, renders cosmogony contemporary: the gods are among us, ancient myths are reborn in our own age, and a miracle may occur at any moment. All this exists by virtue of the power of the creative imagination, not in some heavenly realm but just under the surface of ordinary everyday life and everyday things. The suggestiveness of this artistic revelation and its compelling clarity is so great that Witkiewicz, who was enthusiatic about Schulz's work, wrote:

> The unfathomable peculiarity of the everyday appears: there where one normally would feel like a prisoner, under Schulz's spell one feels as if on a perpetual journey. . . . through what he writes there glimmers the *hope that this most valuable peculiarity can be shared by everyone, though under what conditions we do not yet know. Perhaps Schulz will explain that to us in his future writings.*

Witkiewicz, who sought the "peculiarity of existence" through narcotic visions, ascribed to Schulz the possession of a formula that would enable all readers to follow Schulz himself and enter into the regions of the great heresy.[3] Witkiewicz's moving hope testifies to his enchantment with *Cinnamon Shops*, to his captivation by its inner autonomous truth, almost not the work of a writer but the result of some magical initiation or shared secrets.

Schulzian reality is not a happy Arcadia, however. Its magic opens the door to many marvels, but it also knows the beauty of sadness and the fascination of fear and defeat that is the price of the ubiquitous freedom of the imagination. In "Birds," Father's great aviary is destroyed by the personification of common sense, Adela; in "Night of the Great Season," the birds, stoned to the ground by the uncomprehending crowd, return to their master in wasted tatters. Desiring its own unique verisimilitude, Schulzian reality does not deny suffering, but eases it through ambivalence and a sense of revocability. Nothing is final in Schulz's fiction; what has happened can always be "undone." Neither defeat nor victory is ultimate, and even death is problematic and uncertain. The general fluctuation of the laws of nature also gives rise to an anxiety and ambiguity about all things and an anticipation of realizing dreams, a creative joy. No creation reaches the limit of possibility; beyond each one lies another in an endless perspective:

> The main thing was not to forget . . . that no Mexico is final, that it is a point of passage which the world will cross, that beyond each Mexico there opens another, even brighter one, a Mexico of super-colors and hyper-aromas. . . .

Schulz's reality and his writing are one and the same: an expression of creative revolt against the world which is the kingdom "of everydayness, the determination of all possibilities, the guarantee of impassible barriers within which now and forever is . . . closed." Such statements concerning the task of his art appear throughout Schulz's writing like a poetic commentary on his new mythology, a creation so alive that it allows self-irony and permits the intersection of romanticism with comedy, the noble with the foolish.

Schulz bores deeply into the wellspring of ideas and imagination, regressing into the subconscious, into childhood, into the preverbal archaeology of the spirit, the "hatchery of history." "Only beyond our words . . . does that dark, incomprehensible element hum." "Yes, a regression along an entire line takes place in us, a retreat into the depth, a return path to the root." The semantics of these depths, the formulation of the inexpressible—that is Schulz's task of poetic definition. This task was at the same time his heroic struggle with his own depression and with the recalcitrant matter around him. In his letters he called himself a liar who "convincingly presents as existing and real that which inside him is in truly wretched disintegration and chaos." Reading his favorite poet, Rilke, bolstered Schulz's spirit in his creative struggles. For Schulz, "The existence of [Rilke's] books is a guarantee that the tangled, deaf mass unformulated in us can still rise to the surface wonderfully distilled." Father's shop is the mythic archetype of Schulz's art; the shop which is "unfathomable and limitless stood beyond everything that happened, dark and universal." In the sorcery of Father's shop the interest-bearing "one hundredfold, dark, mature colorfulness of things," the magic of multicolored matter, combined with the rational forms of mercantile ritual: in the bills, the accounts, and ledgers. Here, transposed into the setting of patriarchal merchant life, is the principle of Schulz's art: the cooperation of myth with mathematical precision, of magic and definition.

10

A Settling of Accounts

Bruno Schulz's entire life was overshadowed by his intuition of imminent danger. Ordinary daily discomforts assumed the dimensions of catastrophes and potential dangers confirmed his worst fears. Schulz became lost in large groups, amid alien people and surroundings. He felt prey to a frightening strangeness that overwhelmed his very existence. He was said to be childishly timid. Mechanically stroking the edge of his jacket, he looked like a pupil suddenly called to go to the blackboard or a child frantically seeking someone his own age to whom he could cling. Artistic creation helped Schulz ward off and even conquer these overpowering states. The realm of the erotic where the agents of threat were female enabled him to experience some satisfaction through masochism. While such satisfaction permeated his artistic and literary work, it did not extend to everyday life, where suffering always inhibited his writing.

Schulz was superstitious in his own way and tried to dispel the paralyzing sense of danger primarily through literary creation, but in daily life he resorted to another device in which he had irrational confidence. This was the sign of a little house: a rectangle with a pointed roof and a chimney sticking up—a kind of primitive, childish drawing. Schulz would trace it with his finger on a wall, in the air, or with a pencil on a scrap of paper. With this naively superstitous gesture he recreated in himself the quiet that was disturbed when harbingers of strangeness pressed upon him.

The little house had to be retraced continually, but the time was approaching when the imaginary charmed outline would fail, when even the thickest walls of real houses would no longer provide security. He would feel homeless and isolated, deprived not only of walls, but of illusions. The glorifier of the quiet of the *human home* would now exist in an inhuman time. As Schulz himself once wrote: "Like the stable of Bethlehem, man's home becomes a core around which swarm all the demons of the air, all the spirits of the upper and lower regions." The demons of war were emerging and could no longer be chased away by either a magical sign or brilliant literary mythologizing.

Artistic creation had helped Schulz overcome paralyzing states; at times, it had been a remedy for them. Only the sphere of erotic masochism allowed him to gain some satisfaction from threat. The masochistic compensation that penetrated his visual and verbal art did not diffuse beyond art into daily life. Coercion, the pressure of ordinary life, or suffering always interfered with his writing.

Given a sensitivity of this degree, Schulz's very work as a teacher was not only physically exhausting, but increasingly the cause of uncreative periods connected with deep and prolonged states of depression. The freedom and security of the individual in the broad metaphysical sense is one of the key obsessions in Schulz's writings. In his fiction, mythic time—relative and obedient to human desires—is a refuge from change and from the universal nature of human fate. The figures of the wax museum panopticon, that "Calvary parody of mannequins" from "Treatise on Tailors' Dummies:

"Spotkanie" ("Encounter"), oil on cardboard, painting by Bruno Schulz dedicated to Stanisław Weingarten, 15 August 1920 (from the collections of the Museum of Literature in Warsaw).

A Block of thirty stamps issued in Poland in 1992 on the occasion of the centenary of Bruno Schulz's birth and the fiftieth anniversary of his death (from the collection of Jerzy Ficowski).

Wall paintings by Bruno Schulz in the Drohobycz quarters of Landau (photograph by
T. Tomaszewski, B. Geissler, P. Kowalczyk, Mutor, or others).

Continuation," embody spiritual bondage. They exemplify form that is not an expression but rather an imprisonment of what it contains by force.

A mythologue-artist in the role of an overworked secondary school teacher was the contradiction and violation inflicted upon Schulz's own identity—the image and likeness of the wax figures, those "carnival parodies" upon whom an external alien biography had been imposed. In this sense, when writing about the panopticon figures, "beating their fists against the walls of their prison," Schulz was writing about himself, and also about contemporary man in general, harnessed to the routine of a soulless totalitarian machine.

On the eve of World War II, Schulz still dreamed creative plans. In 1939 he wrote to an acquaintance that he would "most willingly retire with some one person into complete quiet and, like Proust, set about the ultimate formulation of my world." Whether this *opus magnum* was to be the novel entitled *Messiah* that Schulz longed to finish or whether it was something new is not known. While these plans were never completed, at this time Schulz was nearly finished with a new book composed of four larger tales upon which he had been working for several years. In 1939 he wrote: "I still do not know when these stories will be ready for print. The inability to utilize fragments and bits of time forces me to put off their final completion until vacation."

We can presume that the book was completed. With the German invasion of Poland on September 1, 1939, the war broke out. Schulz had just returned from summer vacation in Truskawiec to Drohobycz for the opening of school. On September 17, Hitler's armies entered the town, only to be supplanted by Soviet powers. Drohobycz then found itself outside the region of German occupation and annexed to the territory of the Ukrainian Soviet Republic. It was soon obvious that in the new political situation Schulz could not adapt to the rigid obligatory literary prescriptions dictated to writers. The cultural politics of the personality cult and the sharpened political reality would not tolerate Schulz's genre, which was both distant from the Soviet model of popular literature and useless for propaganda. Schulz realized his inadequacy in the new circumstances. In 1940 he wrote to a young student from the Warsaw Academy of Fine Arts named Anna Płockier:

I was invited by personal letter to associate myself with *New Horizons*, a journal in Polish edited by [Wanda] Wasilewska.[1] But what could I write for them? I grow more and more conscious of how remote I stand from real life and how little I understood the mood of the times. Somehow everybody else has found an assignment, but I am left out in the cold. It comes from a lack of elasticity and a refusal to compromise, of which I'm not proud.[2]

Nevertheless, Schulz sent the editorial board of *New Horizons* in Lwów a story about a shoemaker's deformed son who strikingly resembled a shoemaker's stool. The piece was rejected, and one of the editors remarked to Schulz when he visited the editorial office, "We don't need any more Prousts." Shocked and depressed by this verdict, Schulz repeated it to friends as proof that he could no longer count on writing for a living. Teaching continued to be his main source of income; until June 1941 he worked in both the state (formerly Jagiełło) gymnasium and the Sternbach gymnasium, a long-established private school headed by Jacob Blat.

In addition, Schulz now began to earn money as a "painter." It did not mean artistic activity at all. As he stressed in his letters, however, this was a kind of "craft painting" or drawing. It involved executing special drawings ordered by local officials and enormous canvases showing government personalities, including Stalin himself. To those close to him, Schulz complained about being reduced to such pseudo-artistic work. The painting of large portraits in a naturalistic style using a so-called "rub-in" method didn't come easily; his own artistic personality, which was impossible to conceal, interfered. By all accounts, some of his former students, amateur artists, fulfilled such commissions more skillfully. With an amused distaste, Schulz recounted his artisan-painting difficulties and adventures. Once the town newspaper offered to hire him to illustrate a border for a story about harvests. Schulz completed the assignment, but was immediately summoned to the editorial office, where he was ordered to do an ideological touch-up: shoes must be put on the barefoot girls working in the fields. He added the shoes without argument—since he invested none of his creative ambitions in such jobs. On another occasion, when a large painting of Stalin ordered by local officials for the town hall building was destroyed by jackdaws, Schulz remarked to friends that for once in his life the destruction of one of his own works caused him real satisfaction.

Illness now set in on the already depressed Schulz. He developed kidney stones and had to take the cure at Truskawiec. His literary art reverted to its original method of communication: the revelation of written works only to his closest friends. Formerly, creation within the confines of private letters had been an outgrowth of his peculiar personality. Now Schulz returned to this form because official decrees determined what was worth publishing and what was not.

In 1940, Anna Płockier became Schulz's correspondent, and the critical reader of works once again destined to remain in manucript. Her presence, her literary sensitivity to his work, her companionship in dialogues about art, all sustained Schulz's spirits and kindled his intellectual liveliness despite the threatening circumstances. Schulz had met her in the nearby town of Borysław, where Anna—a student at Warsaw's Academy of Fine Art—came to visit her friend the painter Marek Zwillich. Already an admirer of Schulz's writing, she traveled from occupied Warsaw to Borysław, sneaking across the border of the German-occupied territory, the General Government.[3] She stayed in the Zwillich household with her fiancé, Marek, and her friendship with Schulz deepened with the adoration he showed her. His surviving letters to her contain his last known written words.

Schulz probably wrote nothing new during this time, but simply organized his notes, in the process giving Anna access to the contents of his drawers. He took a second job as a drawing teacher at the Sternbach gymnasium, where before the war he had taught periodically, in addition to maintaining his permanent position at the state gymnasium. He also accepted public obligations to which he was summoned: for example, in 1940 he sat on the electoral commission during the general elections to the Supreme Soviet and also worked on the decoration of the voting hall. A ten-year grammar school was set up at the time with Polish as the language of instruction; Schulz was summoned to a commission that admitted teachers to the Professional Union. He continued to work despite serious illness and a painful treatment to eliminate his kidney stones (secretly

saving the stones he passed in a little box). He was defenseless and
passive. According to a friend, J. Kosowski, Schulz

> could not bear turmoil and noise. Politics is, after all, constant
> struggle, and Schulz, even had he been forced to fight for eter-
> nal life, would not have lifted a club. There was lavender water
> in him where there should have been bile. How it happened that
> at that time he got involved in politics, I don't know—perhaps
> by accident.

While his attempt to publish in *New Horizons* had ended in fiasco,
Schulz tried again with another story, this time his only tale in German, "Die Heimkehr" (The Return Home). Schulz sent it in 1940 to
the German editorial board of Inoizdat, a foreign literature publisher
in Moscow, but this piece was rejected as well.

In June 1941, with Hitler's abrogation of the 1939 pact with
Stalin, the German-Soviet war broke out; Drohobycz fell again
under German occupation, and the final tragic stage of Bruno
Schulz's life began. As yet no one could foresee the dimensions
that the Nazi extermination action against the Jews would take. For
the time being, Schulz remained together with his family in their
house on Floriańska Street, but was denied any means of earning a
living. While all Jews were forced to wear the Star of David armband, the Nazis initially tolerated and hired skilled Jewish work-
men. Following the advice of acquaintances, Schulz submitted
some of his artwork to the Judenrat requesting the status of a "necessary Jew" and along with it the privilege of a bread ration and the
slim hope of survival.

Schulz's drawings intrigued a Gestapo officer, Hauptscharführer
Felix Landau, a cabinetmaker from Vienna who called himself an
architect. Landau was an official in charge of Jewish affairs in the
Drohobycz Gestapo and one of the main murderers of the Jews of
Drohobycz.[4] Having failed to obtain help from the Judenrat, Schulz
saw his only chance for safety under the protection of Landau, his
Gestapo Maecenas.[5] Landau commissioned several jobs from Schulz,
and as a result Bruno was classified a skilled workman, a "necessary
Jew": he wore a *glejt* or safe-conduct band in celluloid on his sleeve

that protected him, a skilled worker, from roundups and transports to the camps.

Landau hired Schulz mainly for personal jobs such as portraits of himself, the painting of his house, and drawings that were done in exchange for food. One of the works Schulz did was a portrait of Landau executed in a combination of painting and Landau's own specialty, skilled woodwork. It was a mosaic, painstakingly composed of varicolored pieces of veneered wood, put together like marquetry. Schulz was also commissioned to paint the interior of the villa where Landau lived. Schulz decorated the walls of a child's room with colorful illustrations from fairy tales.[6] In return for this free labor, Landau assured Schulz of personal safety, sometimes inviting him to dinner or giving him a little extra food—crucial help, since Schulz also had to provide for his sister, his nephew Zygmunt, and a female cousin, none of whom had work anywhere. In addition to these private jobs for Landau, Schulz got commissions from the town Gestapo for frescoes in the building called the Reitschule, the riding school, as well as in the Gestapo office.

Once, years before, in a letter to a friend, Schulz declared with joy: "Is it not an unmerited and unjust happiness that a book brings us—among other wealth—friends in addition?" Now the same could be said of painting, to which for the time being Schulz owed his life. While at work on the wall paintings, he was buoyed by hope; he went about as if in a trance, believing that his artwork ensured his life but realizing that safety would last only as long as his jobs remained unfinished. Consequently, Schulz delayed and completed his commissions late, all the while consumed with fear expressed in conversations with his friends that his waiting game would be detected by those in the Gestapo who held the power of life and death.

In a building where the plaster had been stripped from the walls, scaffolding would be put up and Schulz would paint all day, holding tightly to the ladder for fear of falling. Female figures constituted the major motif of these paintings, perhaps making the pressure of his servile labor less bitter. Then, in 1942, the Gestapo hired him to catalog confiscated book collections housed in the Drohobycz Old Age Home. The centerpiece of these collections was the library of the Jesuits of Chyrów. The number of books grew as the Nazis began confiscating more public and private libraries, so that eventually the Old Age Home contained more than 100,000 volumes. One of Schulz's friends, a young lawyer named Izydor Friedman, worked with him cataloging the books. Their task lasted several months and was less arduous than physical labor, which Schulz would have been unable to sustain. Schulz was also spared the beatings that were the daily lot of Jews working under the supervision of the SS. Their catalog of the collections was to assist the Nazi authorities in sorting out which books would be shipped to the Reich and which would be destroyed. At Gestapo orders, Schulz also served as an expert on the evaluation of stolen artworks, primarily paintings. A Gestapo officer named Pauliszkis instructed him to write up a report on the books assembled at the Old Age Home. Schulz composed the document in perfect German; Pauliszkis had only to place his signature beneath the text and submit it to Berlin.

Meanwhile, literary friends from Warsaw attempted to come to Schulz's aid; they raised money and arranged false documents for him to use in an escape from Drohobycz. But Schulz was paralyzed by fear, terrified of being captured. He could not make up his mind to flee; he was reluctant to abandon his family to a hopeless fate. The dangers connected with such a flight were depicted in his imagination, just as they had been in his art. His fears found expression in terrifying scenarios that haunted him day and night. He confided to friends that he visualized himself riding on a train with windows darkened with blue paint. At some small station the train halts, there is the sound of the hobnailed boots of military policemen, the beam of a flashlight falls on his face, and the words are heard: "Komm du Jude, komm!" So painfully and tangibly did he experience the dangers of escape in his imagination that he was utterly unable to attempt it in reality.

Schulz's faith in Landau's protection as the surest guarantor of survival certainly encouraged him to remain in Drohobycz. He trusted that the Gestapo officer's snobbish pride in having an acquaintance with an artist meant that it would be in his own interest to protect Schulz. Any brief absence on Landau's part threw Schulz into a panic. Once, in September of 1942 when his Gestapo protector was away for one day, Schulz with his sister, nephew, and other Jews, including a rabbi named Awigdor, hid in the basement of an empty villa on St. Bartholomew Street. Its owners, the Moroń family, had been turned out by the Germans. Obtaining an extra key from the Morońs, Schulz and the others entered. They were nearly discovered when they made a fire in the stove at night while crouching in the corners of the basement. Schulz brought himself to leave after twenty-four hours, but his sister remained with the Awigdors.

Up until November 1941, Schulz had been hopeful: he continued to live in his house on Floriańska Street, maintaining contact with Anna Płockier, although now less often and only by letter. Their correspondence was crucial because it enabled Schulz to discuss art; he was not yet completely passive, reduced solely to the primitive feelings of hunger and fear. On September 23, 1941, he wrote to Anna: "The thought of you is a true bright spot for me, I fence it off from everyday thoughts and save it for the best moments, evenings. You are the partner of my interior dialogues about things that matter to me." And when Schulz remarked in a letter that "intuition tells me that we will meet soon . . ." he was cautiously alluding to his own desired escape to Warsaw, where the twenty-six-year-old Anna and her husband also were secretly planning to flee.

Perhaps longing for Anna overcame fear and resistance, encouraging Schulz in spite of himself to try to follow her to Warsaw. Events turned out otherwise: Anna and Marek did not leave in time. In the second mass pogrom of Jews in Borysław carried out by the Nazis, aided by the Ukrainian fascist militia, they were transported together with hundreds of others to the woods outside Truskawiec, executed, and buried in a mass forest grave. This slaughter took place in the setting of Schulz's "Republic of Dreams," a hallowed childhood spot in the woods near Truskawiec where beneficent powers ruled and any distant danger only heightened the brilliance of a secure existence.

This catastrophe shocked Schulz profoundly, and he never recovered from the blow. At approximately the same time, he was forced to move into the Drohobycz ghetto. He suddenly had to leave the house where he had lived for over thirty years and settle in a small one-story house at 18 Stolarska Street. Compelled to leave behind all those possessions that could not fit into his new cramped quarters, Schulz then decided to save what was most important, his literary and artistic work. He entrusted his drawings and manuscripts to people less endangered whom he described only as "Catholics outside the ghetto." Unfortunately, the identity of these recipients has remained unknown.

Schulz's health continued to deteriorate. From time to time he attempted to get outpatient care at the Drohobycz hospital. Eventually, to avoid being in the street unnecessarily, he gave up treatment altogether. A time of sudden, violent swings of emotion set in when periods of rising hopes of rescue were followed by states of total despair. One day a fellow teacher from the state gymnasium met Schulz on the street. Depressed but outwardly calm, Schulz suddenly remarked, "They are supposed to liquidate us by November [1942]." The teacher wrote:

> I didn't understand, but the tone of his words made me think and was disturbing. I asked, "Whom?" and "What do you mean—'liquidate'?" Schulz replied, "Us. Jews," and then repeated the word "liquidate." Then I understood. Later I remembered the term he had used and recalled rumors that frequently appeared and disappeared among the non-Jewish population. But at the time I either did not want to believe them or I was unable to comprehend how it could really happen—I considered it incredible, unreasonable, and I said so. Schulz looked at me as if at someone completely foreign and unknown. I then realized the difference between his situation and mine. He was to be made an outlaw.

The essential information from accounts of people who escaped the execution squads or transports to death camps is that Schulz kept notes during this last, most agonizing period of his life. He lived in the ghetto among the starving. There was only a little German soup and a meager, sparingly rationed portion of bread for Schulz's entire family. One acquaintaince, an engineer named Michał Mirski, was among those who visited Schulz. Mirski had been shot three times but each time escaped alive. At Schulz's request, Mirski recounted these events in grim detail while Schulz diligently noted down the story. When the two men met for the last time on November 9, 1942, Schulz already had about one hundred pages of notes and said

that he was collecting material for a work about the most awful mar-
tyrdom in history. Emaciated and weak, Schulz spoke in a barely
audible whisper; he had only ten days to live.

Each day brought a worsening of the situation and a diminishing
of hope. The gnawing hunger and totally absorbing struggle for bio-
logical survival meant that in periods of deepest depression Schulz
was able to talk with his friends only about food, the delight of satisfying his hunger, and the pleasure of various tastes. He sent helpless, confused letters to Warsaw asking what he should do. Offers of
help came from groups close to the Home Army[7] and from left-wing
circles. Everyone advised Schulz to get to Warsaw as quickly as possible. Dollars were sent, some money was given to him personally by
his colleague, Friedman; Schulz at last decided that he would go
when Friedman also received "Aryan papers," false documents
enabling escape from Drohobycz. Finally, old friends in Warsaw literary circles concluded that they could no longer count on Schulz's
own initiative, but would have to physically assist him to escape
from Drohobycz. Schulz set the date at November 19, 1942.

Schulz died, shot on the street of his town, around noon on the
day of his planned departure, a day called Black Thursday, during
a Gestapo "wild action"—a shooting spree different from the regular roundups and transports to the camps. The pretext for the wild
action involved an apothecary in the Drohobycz ghetto named
Kurtz-Reines who had planned to escape to Hungary and had
equipped himself with a gun. Stopped in the street by a Nazi named
Hübner, Kurtz-Reines fired a shot, evidently wounding the German
in the finger. A wild action was ordered in retaliation; SS men went
out on the hunt and shooting suddenly began. That particular
morning, Schulz and Friedman were not at work, but happened by
chance to be in the ghetto to get food. The shooting took them by
surprise. Other unsuspecting passersby panicked and began to flee
in the chaos. Some of the SS men, having singled out a chance victim, took off chasing the fleeing person, at times running up the
staircase of a building in order to catch up with their prey in some
hall and shoot him.

Not long before Black Thursday, Schulz's protector, Felix Landau, had shot a dentist from Drohobycz named Löw, a prisoner pro-

tected by another Gestapo officer, Scharführer Karl Günther. There had long been deep animosity between Günther and Landau. The killing of Löw prompted Günther to seek revenge on his Gestapo rival. Günther blustered out threats and then searched for Schulz in order to kill him. He took advantage of the Thursday action and shot Schulz at the intersection of Czacki and Mickiewicz streets. Izydor Friedman, who had been with Schulz just moments before and witnessed Schulz's death, described the shooting:

> When we heard the shots and saw the fleeing Jews, we too rushed to escape. The Gestapo officer Günther caught the physically weak Schulz and held him, then he placed the revolver to his head and shot twice. At night I returned for Schulz's body; I went through his pockets and found some documents and notes that I gave his nephew [Zygmunt] Hoffman, who perished a month later. Toward morning I buried him in the Jewish cemetery.[8]

More than one hundred Jews died that day on the streets of Drohobycz, and their bodies lay on the pavement the next morning. In his story "The Comet," Schulz himself had imagined a world coming to an end:

> So it is, so it happened, unprepared for and uncompleted, at an accidental point in time and space, without a settling of accounts, not arriving at any finish line, as if in the middle of a sentence, without a period or exclamation point, without judgment. . . .

So Bruno Schulz's world ended at the corner of Czacki and Mickiewicz streets, late in the morning of a November day in 1942. According to accounts of several Drohobycz residents, when meeting Landau, Günther annnounced triumphantly: "You killed my Jew—I killed yours." Their score was even.

No trace remains of Schulz's burial place, nor even of the old Jewish cemetery where his body rested near the graves of his mother and father, for which Schulz himself had designed the headstones years earlier. A new housing district stands today on the site of the former Jewish cemetery.

When the life of a great artist is suddenly cut off at the peak of his powers, one is tempted to ask what would have happened had he lived and continued his work. After all, only nine years elapsed between Bruno Schulz's literary debut and his death. There can be no answers to such questions, only suppositions. The war, with all its attendant destruction, turned out to be most savage for the people from whom Schulz came. The foreboding that had haunted Schulz his entire life was transformed into a state of actually being hunted down. Decades of preoccupation with solitude gave way to the unremitting terror of torture and death. News came daily of the tragic deaths of his loved ones. One after another, they perished: all the professors of the Blat gymnasium were murdered, and then in turn others died—thousands, tens of thousands of Drohobyczans.[9] Schulz was one.

Bruno Schulz, the mythologizer of childhood, was writing the story of the tragedy of an individual and of the extermination of a nation. Could he find in the arsenal of his magic a weapon against despair as he had always done before? Could the Newest Testament that he would add to his Bible ensure a mythic resurrection for the dead, as Schulzian relative time had once accomplished for Father in "Sanatorium Under the Sign of the Hourglass"?

Whatever the answer to these questions, one thing seems certain: the writer who knew how to be a creative artist only in his native surroundings, whose creativity was overcome by incapacitation elsewhere, could not work outside Drohobycz. Whatever happened, it seems that the year 1939 closed definitively the final page of his mythic Book: without the Apocalypse that his sensitive, delicate pen could not manage.

Bruno Schulz perished, only to reappear to the world nearly twenty years after the war as one of the outstanding European writers of our century, his stories translated into many languages. In this way, Schulz's art, faithful to the magic of his mythic time, survived the fleeting passage of days and years.

11

Works Preserved and Lost

When discussing the writings of Bruno Schulz we are dealing, unfortunately, only with that part of his work which has survived. Perhaps his surviving work will never be substantially augmented or completed. My own search over more than fifty years for Schulz's lost writings would seem to confirm this; while it has unearthed many of his letters, it did not turn up any more fiction. My visits to his native region—to Drohobycz, Borysław, Truskawiec, and Lwów—turned up nothing. The fate of Schulz's fiction was extraordinarily cruel. From the manuscripts of works published before the war only one survived; no manuscripts of unpublished works survived at all.

Schulz published primarily in the Warsaw publications *Wiadomości Literackie* (Literary News), *Skamander*, *Studio*, and *Tygodnik*

Ilustrowany (Illustrated Weekly). Both volumes of short stories were printed by Rój in Warsaw. The siege of the capital in 1939 and then the Warsaw Uprising in 1944 reduced the publisher's archive to ashes. Manuscripts of two works published in the Lwów journal *Sygnały* (Signals) completely disappeared. Schulz had also sent two works to the monthly journal *Kamena* in Chełm Lubelski. One of these works was the novella "Spring," a portion of which later was printed in *Skamander;* "Spring" then appeared in its entirety in the collection *Sanatorium Under the Sign of the Hourglass.* The *Kamena* version, however, included a passage containing a vision of the holy day of Passover subsequently cut by Schulz and so never printed elsewhere. The second work published in *Kamena* was the story "A Second Fall," known from a later book edition. Its manuscript survived in the personal papers of *Kamena's* coeditor Zenon Waśniewski, who died in a Nazi camp during the war. WaÊniewski had been a colleague of Schulz's from the time of his Lwów studies before 1914. The manuscript of "A Second Fall" comprises six single sides of notebook paper and today is in my collection; it was published in a separate facsimile edition in 1973.

The only remaining manuscripts of Bruno Schulz that have survived are letters. Those which I initially collected were published in the volume *Proza* (Prose) in 1964. Letters which I subsequently found were published in *Księga listów* (Book of Letters, 1975), in *Listy, fragmenty, wspomnienia o pisarzu* (Letters, Fragments, Recollections of the Writer, 1984), and in *Okolice sklepów cynamonowych* (Environs of Cinnamon Shops, 1986). This is certainly not all that has survived of Schulz's correspondence; there is still hope that other letters may turn up, for example, those to Thomas Mann, to whom Schulz wrote in 1938–39. The surviving letters, a small portion of Schulz's vast correspondence, were saved in various ways, invariably involving some extraordinary chance. Destruction was the rule in wartime; each letter preserved had its own exceptional, often unbelievable story. A few examples serve to illustrate their strange wanderings.

Schulz's letters to Tadeusz Breza remained in the latter's Warsaw apartment on Słoneczna Street until the end of the war. They survived there even during the Warsaw Uprising and the subsequent evacuation and burning of the city. The Breza apartment was one of the very few that was not either burned during the uprising itself or set on fire by the Nazis afterward. When after liberation in 1945 Tadeusz Breza returned to his empty, looted apartment, he found in the trash strewn about the floor the trampled but complete letters of his friend Bruno Schulz.

Schulz's letters to the literary critic Andrzej Pleśniewicz were still in the addressee's hands in Warsaw in 1943. That was at the beginning of my enthusiasm for Bruno Schulz, a passion that I shared with my closest friends. One of them, the actor Adam Pawlikowski, told me one spring day about Schulz's horrific death and handed me three letters borrowed from Pleśniewicz. Andrzej Pleśniewicz died outside Warsaw toward the end of the war; his apartment burned. But the letters survived with me in Włochy, near Warsaw, where I found them undamaged after my own return from a prisoner-of-war camp in 1945.

The largest group of personal letters to survive are those to Romana Halpern. I began to search for them in 1949, alternately losing and finding their trail, until finally they emerged fifteen years later in Los Angeles. Following the Nazi order for all Jews to move into the area of Warsaw designated for their concentration, Romana Halpern left her apartment on Jasna Street and moved into the ghetto. She escaped, however, together with her son, in July of 1942. She traveled to Cracow, placed her son in a boarding school, and then with false papers worked in the office of a German firm. In 1944 she was recognized by an agent on the street, arrested, transported to a prison in Montelupy, and finally shot. Her son survived the war, twice changing his name; during the 1940s he remained in Poland, but then went to Frankfurt and finally to the United States, taking with him mementoes of his mother, including her letters from Bruno Schulz. The letters had been found shortly after the liberation of Warsaw in Romana's empty and looted apartment, in the only building not burned on Jasna Street, number 17. When moving to the ghetto, Romana had turned her apartment over to a friend, who maintained it and all its contents until the uprising. In July 1945, Schulz's letters were found also, scattered on the apartment floor.

The next-largest surviving correspondence comprises twenty-four letters to Zenon Waśniewski, Schulz's friend from their student days in Lwów. These letters survived after Waśniewski's death in the papers of his wife, Michalina, in Chełm Lubelski.

The third-largest group of those surviving are Schulz's "official" letters to school and educational authorities, discovered in the 1980s in Lwów archives. These comprise eighteen letters from the years 1924 to 1938 and concern Schulz's teaching in the Drohobycz gymnasium. Valuable biographical documents were attached to them, such as a copy of his birth certificate, his *matura* or graduation certificate, and his exams from the Lwów Polytechnic and from the Academy of Fine Arts in Cracow which enabled him to teach drawing.

Finally there are eighteen letters to Anna Płockier. Anna received the last of these one week before her own tragic death in a bloody pogrom in November 1941. A friend of Zwillich's, Marian Jachimowicz, stopped at their home after the pogrom, unaware of the fate of its occupants. He found the place empty, demolished, and looted. On the floor he too found only a handful of discarded envelopes, which he gathered and saved: letters from Bruno Schulz.

Among the biographical documents of great importance that partially survived through accidents of fate were also letters to Bruno Schulz from various people, primarily in literary circles. These were discovered in 1946 in the attic of the Schulzes' house in Drohobycz by Feiwel Schreier, a student and friend of the murdered writer. Mr. Schreier held on to them in Drohobycz and in 1957 informed me of their existence through a representative of the Cracow publishing house Wydawnictwo Literackie. I never saw the letters, and their subsequent fate is uncertain. If we assume, despite the denials of Artur Sandauer, that the letters to Schulz published in 1976 in the Warsaw monthly *Kultura* belong to this group, and unaccountably fell into other hands twenty years before, it would be some consolation: another miraculous survival, and an example of the devotion with which Feiwel Schreier preserved them. Not all of them were published (only eighteen), and there is no account for two decades of delay in publication. Out of all the letters found by Schreier I have now received only a few letters from Debora Vogel and one letter from Egga van Haardt which Schreier had separated from the group.

Aside from *Cinnamon Shops* and *Sanatorium Under the Sign of the Hour-*

glass, which form the core of Schulz's surviving work, there also exist some stories, essays, criticism, and reviews published in various pre-war journals. Most of these pieces were printed together with Schulz's collected works in *Proza* (Prose, 1964). A few pieces that originally had been printed in *Wiadomości Literackie* (Literary News) and *Tygodnik Ilustrowany* (Illustrated Weekly) were not included: a long declaration about the subjective aspects of the creative process and the emotional origins of his writing; an essay entitled "Powstają legendy" (The Formation of Legends); an article on the poetry of Kazimierz Wierzyński; and several book reviews of works in foreign languages.

This is all that has survived; everything else—substantial and significant—was lost or destroyed, and after many years of searching I think that the chances of finding anything more are remote. The entire collection of Schulz's now lost works was located in his flat in Drohobycz at 10 Floriańska Street until the end of 1941 and the beginning of 1942. He then took these papers with him when he moved into the ghetto. Once there, having to share one room with two other strangers, he realized that he had to ensure the safety of his works. Thus, in the winter of early 1942 he asked Zbigniew Moroń, to whom Schulz had his mail addressed, if he would take care of all the manuscripts and drawings as well. Moroń was quite willing to do so, but convinced Schulz that to entrust everything to a single person was risky and that a better plan would be to divide the materials among several reliable people. Schulz agreed and gave Moroń only a large folder containing over fifty drawings and one pastel, *Królewna i paziowie* (The Queen and Her Pages). As Moroń recalled, Schulz gave his literary manuscripts, notes, and the remainder of his artwork to "someone else whom I did not know; he told me the name, but unfortunately I completely forgot it." Only one thing is certain: that recipient was a Pole or Ukrainian and a resident of Drohobycz, Borysław, or Stryj. This information was independently confirmed by a statement made to me by Izydor Friedman in 1948:

> As a Jew, I was assigned by the Drohobycz Judenrat to work in a library under Gestapo authority, and so was Schulz. . . . We spent

long hours in conversation. Schulz informed me at the time that he had deposited all his papers, notes, and correspondence with a Catholic outside the ghetto. Unfortunately he did not give me the person's name, or possibly I forgot it. . . . Over several months in 1944 and 1945 when I worked in Drohobycz, I searched for Schulz's papers, having realized that a monograph should be devoted to him. I had an announcement placed in a Ukrainian newspaper published in Drohobycz, requesting the depositary of Schulz's documents to come forward and give his whereabouts. This search, unfortunately, turned up nothing. . . .

In 1965 I began searching again in Ukraine, in archives and through newspaper advertisements in the Lwów press, but again to no avail. Based on the information that we do possess, however, let us tentatively reconstruct what Schulz must have entrusted to the unknown person outside the ghetto. First and foremost, the papers would have included the manuscript of a book composed of four long stories. The only information we have of its existence is Schulz's own response to an inquiry from *Wiadomości Literackie* in April of 1939:

My next book will be a volume composed of four stories. The subject, as always, is insignificant and difficult to summarize. For my own use I have several names that convey nothing. For example, the theme of one of the stories bears a title borrowed from Jokai's "Marsz za porte-épée"[1]—I really don't know how to describe the theme before the contents crystallize. The real subject matter, the ultimate raw material that I find in myself without any interference of will, is a certain dynamic state, completely "ineffabilis" and totally incommensurate with poetic means. Even so, it has a very definite atmosphere, indicating a specific kind of content that grows out of it and is layered upon it. The more this intangible nucleus is "ineffabilis" the greater is its capacity, the sharper its tropism and the stronger the temptation to inject it into matter in which it could be realized. For example, the first seed of my story "Birds" was a certain flickering of the wallpaper, pulsating in a dark field of vision—nothing more. That flickering had however great potential content, enormous possibilities for representation, a quality of ancientness, a demand or claim to express the world itself. The first germ of "Spring" was the image of a stamp album, radiating from the center of vision, winking with unheard-of power of allusion, attacking with a load of content one may conjecture. This state, however poor in content, gives me the feeling of inevitability, a sanction for imagining, certainty of the legality of the entire process. Without this basis, I would be given over to doubt, I would have the feeling it was all a bluff, that what I create is arbitrary and false. At the moment I am drawn to increasingly inexpressible themes. Paradox, the tension between their vagueness and their evanescence and their universal claim, their aspiration to represent "everything" is the most powerful creative stimulus. I don't know when these stories will be ready for print. An inability to take advantage of bits and scraps of time forces me to set aside their completion until vacation.

We can assume that the volume was finished and ready for publication. It would not have contained stories that appeared in journals two years before the outbreak of war, such as "The Comet" or "The Fatherland" (described by Schulz as part of a larger work), because, as the above quotation indicates, the four stories were new, unknown, and as yet even untitled. On the other hand, it is possible that among them was the tale about the shoemaker's misshapen son, rejected in 1940 by the editors of Lwów's *Nowe Widnokręgi* (New Horizons).

The lost deposit must also have contained the manuscript of the novel entitled *Messiah*. This work, doubtless unfinished, has its own history. Early work on it probably occurred soon after the completion of *Cinnamon Shops* but before its publication. In 1934, Schulz published in *Wiadomości Literackie* a work entitled "The Age of Genius" which carried a note describing it as "part of the novel *Messiah*." In response to questions from Kazimierz Truchanowski, Schulz replied in a letter in 1935 that "*Messiah* grows slowly—it will be a continuation of *Cinnamon Shops*." In 1936 he again wrote Truchanowski, "You touch a sensitive spot, asking about my *Messiah*. I'm getting nowhere with it." And a month later Schulz wrote again, "I'm not touching *Messiah*."[2]

Sanatorium Under the Sign of the Hourglass, published in 1937, contained "The Age of Genius" as a separate story and not as a part of

Messiah. It is immediately preceded by the compositionally and thematically related tale "The Book"—unquestionably originally intended as a chapter of *Messiah*. Schulz's interruption of work on *Messiah* and placing of its fragments in another volume might be construed as indicating his having given up work on the novel: to a 1935 query about his writing plans from *Wiadomości Literackie*, Schulz mentioned *Messiah*, while to a 1939 query he is silent on the topic. Yet he must not have given up the work completely, since after sending *Sanatorium* to print he wrote to Truchanowski that he was "not touching *Messiah*." There must have existed more than the two fragments taken from it and included in *Sanatorium Under the Sign of the Hourglass*. During the war Schulz read unpublished parts of *Messiah* aloud to friends. As one listener recalled, the passage referred to people excitedly passing on to one another news that the Messiah has come and is only some thirty kilometers from Drohobycz. . . . The novel was to be Schulz's major work about the central idea in his mythology of the "return to childhood," "messianic times."

The next item in the lost deposit was *Die Heimkehr* (The Return Home), Schulz's sole work in German. The novella was written in 1937 and consisted of thirty pages in typescript. "Given the fact that I keep thinking about being translated into a Western European language, it occurred to me to write something directly in German," Schulz wrote to Romana Halpern in 1937.[3] In 1940, another copy of this story (in addition to the one in the deposit) was sent to Moscow to the foreign literature publisher Inoizdat, but it was never printed. Still earlier, in 1938, Schulz wrote in a letter: "The mother of a friend [Jerzy Brodnicki, husband of the graphic artist Egga van Haardt] wants to take 'Heimkehr' to Thomas Mann in Zurich." In a letter to Schulz dated March 23, 1938, Egga reports: "Jerzy's mother is leaving around April 10 for Zurich in order to present your novel with my illustrations to Mann." In addition to *Messiah* and *Die Heimkehr*, the deposit contained various other tales, unfinished works, fragments of prose, drafts of letters, and diaries kept for many years in thick, bound notebooks, as well as letters from acquaintances, painters, and writers including Zofia Nałkowska, Debora Vogel, Tadeusz Breza, Thomas Mann, Witold Gombrowicz, Stanisław Ignacy Witkiewicz, Julian Tuwim, Emil Zegadłowicz, Maria Kuncewiczowa, and others.

Although this valuable deposit has not yet been found, I am not convinced that it was destroyed. After Schulz's death the war dragged on in his native region. Then came the "wandering of peoples," or great repatriation of populations. As a result of the change in Poland's boundaries, Drohobycz and its environs became part of the Soviet Union, where Schulz himself and his writing were unknown. This complicated, if not preventing altogether, searching for traces where they had the greatest chance of survival. Opportunities for destruction were numerous, while occasions for saving mementoes were few. Nevertheless, defenseless papers sometimes had a most peculiar ability to survive in private collections, and those to whom Schulz entrusted his most valuable materials may come forward. Perhaps increased access to archives in the former Soviet Union may unearth at least a portion of the enormous missing Schulz materials in the archives of Lwów, Sambor, Stryj, and Drohobycz, and even Kiev and Moscow. In such a wave, those who now hold items privately may be encouraged to release them and those once entrusted with a most valuable Schulzian legacy may come forward.

Schulz's collected letters now number 156. These and perhaps a few more remain from the writer's long and vast correspondence, which amounted to several thousand letters. Many perished together with their addressees, others were swept away by the war or its aftermath. In a few cases I was able to establish beyond doubt the fact that letters were destroyed. The first such sad evidence concerns Schulz's correspondence with Debora Vogel.

The letters to Debora were extraordinarily important and of unusual content. They included long postscripts which contained the first versions of *Cinnamon Shops*, composed between 1930 and 1932. Some years later in 1936 Schulz wrote to Romana Halpern:

> It's too bad that we didn't know one another a few years back. I still knew how to write beautiful letters then. *Cinnamon Shops* emerged gradually from my letters. The greatest number of those letters were to Debora Vogel, the author of *Akacje kwitną* [The Acacias Are Blooming]. Most of those letters got lost.[4]

The loss to which Schulz refers was probably connected with confusion during a move. In 1932 Debora married the architect

Barenblüth and moved from Zborowska Street to her husband's home on Leśna Street in Łyczków, Lwów. However, in 1938 she found the letters, and in December of that year she wrote to Schulz:

> While sorting things I came upon the packet of letters from you; I would ask you then to return to me those others, the borrowed ones, if you don't need them, and those that were for a time with Dr. Fr. [Friedman? J.F.], as I would like to arrange them in chronological order.[5]

Toward the end of 1941, Debora and her entire family were moved into the Lwów ghetto. There, after some nine months of torment, she was shot together with her husband and six-year-old son in a closed-up shop on Bernstein Street in which they were hiding during the so-called "great action" of August 1942.

All their papers had been left in Łyczków, in the house on Leśna Street. Not until 1965 did I have the opportunity to search there. The caretaker of the building, having lived there more than forty years, told me that the papers in the basement left by the "old residents" had been burned during a general cleaning several years earlier.

A second similar confirmation of loss concerns the letters from Schulz to Józefina Szelińska, to whom he dedicated *Sanatorium Under the Sign of the Hourglass*. These letters date from the 1930s, and there were about two hundred of them. In 1941 they were hidden in the attic of the Szeliński house in Janów near Lwów. Although Janów was not greatly damaged by the war, unfortunately the Szeliński house evidently burned toward the end of the war or just after.

Scattered surviving works have also included some of Schulz's art: graphics and drawings. Often a drawing had a greater chance of survival than a manuscript, which could be considered just a worthless piece of paper. Schulz's drawings are now in the Adam Mickiewicz Museum, the collection of the Jewish Historical Institute, as well as in private hands, primarily in Warsaw, Cracow, and Łódź.

Fearing he would not survive, Schulz gave the thick folder of drawings and one large picture to Zbigniew Moroń at the beginning of 1942. This was not all the artwork that he wanted to save. The remaining graphics, drawings, and pictures (both pastels and oils) he gave to another, unknown, person. In 1944 Moroń had left Drohobycz and moved to Maków Podhalański. There he put the folder and picture in a basket of linens. Just before the entrance of the Soviet army into Maków, the Germans evacuated part of the town population for three days. When Moroń returned after liberation, he found that his house had been completely looted. The basket of linens had disappeared; the picture was torn to bits and trampled beyond repair. Years later, in 1985, a folder of drawings unexpectedly turned up in Gdańsk among scraps of paper in an old suitcase belonging to Zbigniew Moroń's deceased brother, Bogusław. To the end of his life, Bogusław never knew that the lost drawings had not been stolen. The folder contained over eighty works, the majority of which are presently in the collection of the Museum of Literature in Warsaw through my efforts and those of another admirer of Bruno Schulz, Andrzej Kietowicz.

Schulz had given another folder containing over one hundred drawings and sketches (the latter including the illustrations for *Sanatorium Under the Sign of the Hourglass*) to his former student Emil Górski. I learned about this in 1948, and at that time I was able to view the works, and later, in 1964, together with Marek Holzman, I served as intermediary between their owner and the Adam Mickiewicz Museum in Warsaw, which purchased the entire group for its collection.

Only a single oil painting by Schulz seems to have survived. It is a composition titled *Encounter* by an antique dealer who put it on sale in an art auction in Łódź. It comes from the looted collections of Schulz's friend Stanisław Weingarten, who perished during the war, murdered by the Nazis in the Łódź ghetto. The painting was purchased by the Museum of Literature in Warsaw in 1992. A somewhat different version of the same subject matter as *Encounter* appears in a photograph of a similar work; the actual picture, however, is lost. All, or practically all, of Schulz's oils were lost in the territory of his home region, today Ukraine. And there were quite a number of them. One oil, *Zabicie smoka* (The Slaying of the Dragon), hung in Schulz's own room; two others, a landscape and a portrait, hung in the Lwów Municipal Art Gallery. *Bal wiariatów* (Ball of the Insane) and *Nadejście Mezjasza* (Coming of the Messiah) were owned by Bruno's brother in Lwów until 1939 and the outbreak of the war.

Numerous other works, in small part only known to us from oral testimony, disappeared along with their owners, victims of Nazi geno-
cide. Some are doubtless in existence today in unknown places and
await discovery.

Around 1922, Schulz began to compile *The Booke of Idolatry*, a
portfolio of graphics which he himself hand-bound in canvas. On
the cover was an ink drawing, a different one for each copy of the
volume. The title page inside, sometimes containing a table of contents, reads "The Booke of Idolatry: Original Graphics of Bruno
Schulz" and was decorated with a garland border. Glued on the
leaves were a dozen or so individual graphics, signed and dated, their
arrangement varying somewhat in each volume. The graphics were
completed between 1920 and 1921, when Schulz could devote all
his time to study, reading, and drawing. Schulz sold a number of the
volumes of *The Booke of Idolatry*, primarily in Warsaw, and he gave a
few to friends and acquaintances.

Witkiewicz coined his own term for Schulz's technique: "drapo-
graphic." Schulz himself wrote to Zenon Waśniewski that

> my technique is a laborious one. It isn't aquafortis etching but the
> so-called *cliché-verre* technique, using a glass plate. You draw with a
> stylus on a black gelatin layer covering the glass, and the translu-
> cent negative drawing obtained in this way is treated like a pho-
> tographic negative, i.e., it is printed in a photographic copying
> frame onto light-sensitive paper, developed, fixed, and rinsed. The
> procedure is like photo printing. The cost is considerable—so is
> the labor. I have an offer from Rój for ten to twenty folios; I am
> not taking the offer up, although I could make several hundred
> zlotys out of it.[6]

Individual copies of *The Booke of Idolatry* survived in the holdings of
Polish museums and in private collections, both in Poland and
abroad. The first Polish edition of *The Booke of Idolatry* prepared by me
for print appeared in Warsaw in 1988.

Even a cursory glance shows how enormous and lamentable is
the loss of so much of Bruno Schulz's work. The possible discovery
of some additional small fragments would not alter this state of

affairs. If no further discoveries of manuscripts are made, Bruno Schulz's literary heritage will consist only of two books and a handful of texts published in his lifetime in journals. Nevertheless, that surviving portion of the output of this gifted artist ensures him a prominent place in the literature of our century.

12

Awaiting Messiah—
a Postscript

For a half century I have lived in expectation, believing and not believing by turns that I will see it in the end. I have maintained a wavering faith since the time years ago when I became a disciple, the biographer, and a passionate researcher of the works of Bruno Schulz.

Since 1934, Bruno Schulz had been struggling with the novel entitled *Messiah*, which in his hopes and plans aspired to the level of his most important work, one worthy of the name *opus magnum*. Here and there in surviving statements, mainly in Schulz's letters to friends, we find references to the difficult process of the emergence of his novel:

"Recently I have undertaken certain designs and plans for a work of broader scope for which intermittent work at the margins of school duties is insufficient to complete." (1934)

"I am waiting for more free time in order to return to work on the novel *Messiah*."(1935)

"*Messiah* is growing a little at a time—it will be a continuation of *Cinnamon Shops*." (1935)

"My work progresses very slowly. I've not had good periods. Over vacation I couldn't write anything. Now when I could write—school."(1935)

"My subject is still in its infancy." (1937)

From various letters and recollections, we now believe that at the end of 1937 or the beginning of 1938, Schulz returned to work on his novel, believing that it could be completed. In 1938, full of hope, he returns to the reconstruction of his "messianic times." He begins to believe that this time the work is going well for him, and he shares this news with friends with whom he corresponds. They reply, bolstering his spirit, although as yet they know nothing of the concept of the work or even a portion of its prose. One such friend, Witold Gombrowicz, writes back cautiously to Schulz in 1938: "Regarding your *Messiah* it's difficult for me to say anything, since I don't know even the basics of the work—if it provides the possibility of refreshing yourself, so much the better!"

Also in 1938, emphatic exhortations came from Artur Sandauer, then just beginning his career as a literary critic. Sandauer writes: "I'm terribly interested in *Messiah*. May your inner God give you the greatest possible strength and genius in these great moments. I would advise you to go to Paris only if it would not be detrimental to the work on *Messiah*." We can imagine that there must have been a considerably greater number of responses, considering that those references which have miraculously survived come from the few fragments of Schulz's large correspondence which was almost completely destroyed along with his entire archive in Drohobycz.

Thus, in 1938 work on *Messiah* and the new aspect of Schulz's myth moves off dead center, pushes forward, and augurs hope in its speedy conclusion, although—as various testimonies seem to indicate—it was never finished. Meanwhile, paradoxically, the successful efforts of Schulz and his friends to arrange a trip to France became a handicap. Now, grievances and discontent about the anti-messianic disfavor of the Muses were supplanted by a series of epistolary pleas for advice, directed to family and closest friends: to go or not to go? Paris or *Messiah?*

Paris won out, and after Schulz's return to Drohobycz from his none too successful summer trip, he had to rest and pull himself together after disillusionment and failed hopes. Then the demands of school and drawing and woodworking classes triumphed. Barely a year remained, a time fraught with dark forebodings, until the outbreak of World War II. Little time or artistic inclination was left for *Messiah.*

Our information is very scant about Schulz's lost book. Those to whom Schulz had read an excerpt of the prose recalled many years later that its opening words or the beginning of one of its chapters was to go more or less like this: "Mother awakened me in the morning, saying, 'Joseph, the Messiah is near; people have seen him in Sambor" (or in Stryj, in Truskawiec, thirty kilometers from Drohobycz). In Schulz's words, *Messiah* was to be a continuation of *Cinnamon Shops*, and consequently a kind of mythic transformation of Jewish religious motifs, a transposition of universal myth into individual, biographical terms, into the childhood of the author-narrator. In one of his letters referring to *Messiah*, Schulz wrote:

> . . . this kind of art which is so dear to me is precisely a regression, it is a returned childhood. Were it possible to turn back development, achieve by some circuitous path a repeated childhood, one more time have its fullness and limitlessness—that would be the realization of an "age of genius," of "messianic times" which through all mythologies are promised and pledged to us. My ideal is "to mature" to childhood. That would be a real maturity at last.

Such is the Messiah who is the theme and title character of the lost novel, mythicized, and hence incarnated, descending from higher biblical-archetypal spheres to a small town, to children's alleyways, sanctifying the quotidian with myth.

Right after the war, a few surviving Drohobyczans expelled from their native area, annexed to the Soviet Union, now found themselves in the territory of postwar Poland. Through them, I could reach back to times and places of which no lasting trace remained. Still in my early searching for all traces of the life and creative work of Bruno Schulz, I found two persons among them who had been able to save the packets prepared by Schulz and entrusted to them and containing the artist's drawings. Unfortunately, the packets contained no manuscripts, and no one else to whom Schulz had entrusted his literary writings replied to my queries. *Messiah*—the idea born of legend, myth, and belief—returned to its prehistory: to the regions of myth and legend, to promises and hope. Its loss inspired the imagination of many, including Cynthia Ozick, who wrote a novel entitled *The Messiah of Stockholm*, whose phantasmagorical plot turns upon the search for Schulz's lost manuscript.

In the years from 1943 to 1945, Nazi terror did not abate; its genocidal action persisted. Prisons filled and transports to death camps were a daily routine. Fear haunted those who remained in the town, and they secretly burned "compromising" papers and scraps, erasing the traces of the past, just in case. Then new Soviet overlords arrived—and hence the NKVD, surveillance and searches, confiscations, deportations and death; the crowning goal of all these processes was the so-called repatriation of the local population, that is, mass deportations. Too much destruction, too many cataclysms for one to be able to believe in the preservation of defenseless Polish-language manuscripts, which in the best case might serve, as was the custom of those days, for smoking coarse tobacco or *machorka*.

Over forty years passed between my first Schulz studies and archival searches and the year 1987. That year a former Drohobyczan, a United States citizen, came to me in Warsaw: one Alex Schulz, a cousin of Bruno, he assured me. He showed me a photocopy of his birth certificate, from which one had to conclude that he was the illegitimate son of the writer's brother, Izydor (Israel Baruch) Schulz, although he used his mother's last name. He showed me letters as well, written to him by Izydor's daughter, Ella Schulz-Podstolska, thanking him for financial support and for assisting with the cost of a grave monument for her husband. My task and my desire, however, was not to verify his presumed familial relationship. Mr. Alex Schulz had come to inform me he had received a call at his home in California from someone in New York who was from Lwów (a diplomat? a functionary in the KGB?). The unknown person offered to sell him a package of manuscripts of Bruno Schulz, the contents of which he could not describe precisely. He communicated only that everything was written in Polish, that the packet also contained eight drawings by Schulz, and that the entire package weighed about two kilograms! He would sell it for ten thousand dollars. Alex Schulz expressed readiness to buy it, but the seller asked for patience and promised to telephone again in order to agree on specifics of the meeting and completion of the transaction. At the request of the future owner of the treasure and with the permission of the seller, I was to be present at the meeting as an expert to confirm whether or not the texts were written in Schulz's hand.[1]

Realizing that what was soon to take place would be the fulfillment of my bravest dreams and faltering hopes, a revelation of worldwide import, I abandoned my vacation, refusing even to leave my apartment. I stayed close to the telephone, assuming that the mysterious seller had a very limited amount of time and realized the illegality of his actions.

Summer passed. The seller telephoned California once again with the assurance that the entire matter would soon conclude successfully. Then an ever-lengthening silence ensued. Before long, I learned that Alex Schulz had experienced a cerebral hemorrhage, paralysis, and loss of speech. He died not long after, leaving no indication of how to contact the man from Lwów. The arrival of the *Messiah* faded into the unknown future, perhaps forever. I do not give up hope easily, but this time I had lost it almost completely.

A few years passed. In May of 1990 a telephone call announced the visit of the Warsaw ambassador of the Kingdom of Sweden, accompanied by a secretary. Ambassador Jean Christophe Öberg, a friend of Poland and admirer of the work of Bruno Schulz, knew nothing about my dwindling hopes of finding the writer's manuscripts. He could not have heard of my fruitless searching, about which I tried to say little publicly, lest I endanger the slight chance of discovery in which, despite all odds, I tried to continue to believe.

At that first meeting and in several successive ones, I learned that the ambassador had reliable information that amid millions of documents in one of the Soviet KGB archives was a bulging packet containing the manuscripts of Bruno Schulz, with the novel *Messiah* at the top. In addition to the manuscript of the novel there were other works, including more that were never published. Moreover, the archival "pouch" (as the ambassador termed the container of manuscripts) should still contain letters and various personal documents belonging to Schulz and perhaps to other persons.

This astounding news had come to light during some ceremonial meeting of diplomats in which Ambassador Öberg had participated. It had taken place at the Soviet embassy in Sweden or at the Swedish Ministry of Foreign Affairs (I no longer recall which). In the course of informal conversation, a Russian mentioned that he had seen the folder-bag with his own eyes and described approximately both its contents and its history.

He had stumbled upon on it by accident, not looking for it at all. Moreover, even had he been looking for Schulz's papers, he certainly never would have found them—the folder did not figure in the archival lists under the author's name, but under that of some Pole whose personal data meant nothing to him. From the enclosures in the folder it was apparent that the person from whom it had been confiscated had been arrested by the Gestapo, and that the folder taken from him had turned up after the war in a former Gestapo archive somewhere in the Soviet zone, later East Germany. In 1947, two years before the formation of the German Democratic Republic, Moscow had taken over the Gestapo archive, transported it to the Soviet Union, and added it to the KGB files.

The depositary doubtless was someone to whom Schulz had entrusted his literary output. The papers were then taken from this person when he perished anonymously at Nazi hands. How then to search for this treasure? In good diplomatic fashion, Jean Christophe Öberg was restrained in his sharing of detailed information. He added, however, that the information he possessed was reliable, that it had been verified through confirmation from other sources, such as, for example, "from Czech Prague," as he enigmatically expressed it. Whether it was from some foreign intelligence service circles, I do not know and will never know now.

Any other knowledge the ambassador had he kept to himself, including such crucially important details as the name of the myste-

Dust jacket from the first edition of **Cinnamon Shops** according to Bruno Schulz's design, Rój Publishers, 1934 (from the collection of Jerzy Ficowski).

A likeness of Bruno's father—Jacob Schulz— illustration for the story "Edzio" ("Eddie") from the volume *Sanatorium Under the Sign of the Hourglass,* about 1934 (from the collections of the Museum of Literature in Warsaw).

"Carried off by the wind," drawing in pencil, a variant of an illustration for the story, "Emeryt" ("The Old Age Pensioner") from the volume *Sanatorium Under the Sign of the Hourglass;* done around 1934. The copy is dedicated to the actress-dramatic interpreter, Kazimerza Rychterówna in 1930 (from the collections of the Museum of Literature in Warsaw).

"*School Boys and the Old Age Pensioner*" (self-portrait of Bruno Schulz), pencil, about 1935, illustration to the story "Emeryt" ("The Old Age Pensioner") (from the collections of the Museum of Literature in Warsaw).

"Bianka with Her Father in a Carriage," drawing in pencil, illustration to the story "Wiosna" ("Spring") from the volume *Sanatorium Under the Sign of the Hourglass;* done around 1935 (from the collections of the Museum of Literature in Warsaw).

"Organ-grinder in the Courtyard," illustration to the story "Księga" ("The Book"), India ink, 1936 (printed in first edition of *Sanatorium Under the Sign of the Hourglass,* 1937).

Bruno Schulz

— 1 —

Druga jesień.

First page of the author's manuscript of "A Second Fall" ("Druga jesień") by Schulz. The complete story comprises six pages in a notebook (from the collection of Jerzy Ficowski).

Julian Tuwim (1895–1953), one of the most outstanding Polish poets of the twentieth century, photograph from around 1930.

Tadeusz Breza (1905–1970), novelist, friend of Bruno Schulz, photograph from around 1934.

Part of one of Schulz's letters to Andrzej Pleśniewicz in 1936 (from the collection of Jerzy Ficowski).

Portrait of Romana Halpern, color pastel by Stanisław Ignacy Witkiewicz, 1938 (from a private collection, United States).

rious Russian who would be in a position to help find *Messiah*. Or the place where the archive in question could be found. He asked me—as Alex Schulz had once before—if I would accompany him as an expert on a voyage of discovery to Ukraine, since it was probably there.

The Soviet Union still existed at the time, although the symptoms of its demise had grown more apparent. The two of us, the ambassador and I, listened closely for promising signs from the east, but we did not believe that the end of the Communist colossus could be so near. At the Soviet diplomatic post, Mr. Öberg put in a request for a diplomatic visa. After a long waiting period and numerous letters, he received a refusal. When he requested an explanation, he was told that Schulz's house in Drohobycz had burned during the war. This was an obvious lie and an absurdity, but the Soviet authorities had the excuse that in his application the ambassador had explained his visa request exclusively by his desire to see the house where Schulz had lived and created his masterpieces, and to visit the town where Schulz had spent all his life. In reply to Moscow's assertion that the goal of his trip no longer existed, Ambassador Öberg submitted to the embassy an illustration from the Polish edition of *Regions of the Great Heresy*, showing Schulz's house in Drohobycz as photographed by me in 1965. Of course, this irrefutable evidence did not resolve the issue satisfactorily, leading only to a face-to-face conversation in which "confidential information" about the dangerous situation of the Soviet Union was now used to discourage the trip. It was a second refusal for Ambassador Öberg. Nevertheless, he continued to plan our trip when he was recalled to Stockholm from his Warsaw post not long after, meeting with me during his short visits in Poland. He was still trying when the Soviet Union ceased to exist and Kiev as the capital of independent Ukraine, rather than Moscow, became the destination for visa requests.

Even more than before, I was constrained from making these revelations known, although I believed without reservation in the truth of the information. Knowledge of the existence of manuscripts, hope for *Messiah*, sealed my lips. Once all-powerful institutions which had existed under different names and in different inhuman forms—Gestapo and NKVD or KGB—destroyed those who preserved documentation. Today from their enormous formerly sealed archives secrets were seeping out a little into the light of day, revealing mysteries incomparably more important than the politically innocent, brilliant prose of Bruno Schulz.

The ill fate which hung over *Messiah* for so long, however, now made itself manifest once again. In May of 1992, not long after a meeting with me, Jean Christophe Öberg died in a Stockholm hospital, of rapidly spreading cancer after a short, terrible illness. True to diplomatic custom, he did not communicate to me data that would permit the continuation of his goals and efforts. The threads were broken, and there is now no clue to where to look, or in what direction to go.

More years have passed, and still nothing has been found. In fact, it may never be discovered. Nevertheless, what remains for me is simply to tell the entire story, believing that people with the power to reach into secret treasures, whether in Ukraine or in Russia, will be able, if such treasures exist, to facilitate their discovery. May they make them available to the world, which will be enriched by the rescue of an unknown masterpiece.

13

⊙━━◆━━⊙

The Last Fairy Tale
of Bruno Schulz

If in addition to the supernatural being known to Christians as the guardian angel one could imagine and believe in a guardian devil—to whom a person in the depths of misfortune would entrust his fate, believing this would save him—this would be the terrifying guardian role of the Drohobycz Gestapo official Hauptscharführer Felix Landau, Bruno Schulz's "protector," as he was known. After all, were it not for Landau, Schulz probably would not have survived until the close of 1942. Emaciated, physically weak, Schulz would not have had long to wait for a bullet. Gestapo murderers did not lack for weapons, and any pretext sufficed (though even that was often unnecessary) to kill someone who had already on principle been denied the right to live, a member of the Jewish nation which the Nazi racial theory had condemned to death.

Neither a desire to break with the principles of Nazism on Landau's part nor a deviation from horrible routine governed his relationship to Schulz. What could have caused Landau to be so apparently kind? Perhaps some feature of his personality or biography restrained him from extreme behavior despite the hideous function he fulfilled in the Gestapo? Perhaps, although he bore one of the most common Jewish surnames in Europe, he was so sure of his unblemished Aryan background, proved by his unswerving faith in the Nazi Party, that the genocidal party had boundless and unreserved confidence in him? Or perhaps the memory of his "father," a Jewish merchant from Vienna, had prevailed? Lest we lose ourselves in suppositions and hypotheses, let us take a look at a brief biography of the Gestapo "protector."

Felix Landau, from what is known, was born in 1910. When he was a year old, his mother married a Jew named Landau, who gave the child his name. Shortly after the death of his stepfather, when the boy was nine years of age, he was placed in a Catholic boarding school run by a religious order. Six years later, in 1925, Felix joined the National Socialist Working Youth. At that time, he was taking craft classes, a course in artistic furniture making. In 1931, at age twenty, he was accepted into the Nazi Party. In the days of Hitler's ascent to the chancellorship of Germany, Landau became a member of the SA,[1] and soon after an SS activist. As a member of the SS he participated in the coup of 1934, during which the Austrian chancellor, Engelbert Dollfuss, was murdered. Landau found himself in prison, where he remained until 1937, after which—fearing arrest again—he fled from Austria to Germany, took Reich citizenship, and in 1938 became an assistant in the criminal police, and subsequently worked in the Vienna central Gestapo. In 1940, a few months after Poland's capitulation to Germany, he became a commandant in the Sichersheitpolizei und Sonderdienst[2] in Radom, Poland. From Radom, Landau went to Lwów, then was transferred in 1941 to Drohobycz, shortly after the takeover of the city by the Germans. In Drohobycz, he was officially responsible for the employment of the local Jews. In reality, he was the co-organizer and the frequent and willing perpetrator of mass killings of the Jewish inhabitants of Drohobycz and its environs.[3] He lived at 12 Jan Street with his new girlfriend and their small son. Witnesses still living after the war recalled how in 1942 he would fire repeatedly from the window of his room on Jews working next door at a *Gärtnerei* (truck garden). He was an excellent shot, and witnesses noted that almost every time his shot was fatal.

Schulz had advantages which made him an ideal protégé for Landau, the master of artistic furniture making: he spoke fluent German, and most important, he was an artist. This impressed the Viennese cabinetmaker, who desired to pass as a chosen of the Muses and a priest of Art. Such aspirations did not seem to conflict with mass murder, something Landau practiced professionally, as an occupation earning him the particular recognition of his superiors.

Periodic meager food rations then began to come Schulz's way, along with the first instructions requiring him to complete various works, not only artistic. For some work, he was paid with bread, jam, or soup. The highest pay was the fact that he could stay alive, that Landau provided Schulz a "guarantee of immunity." Landau burdened Schulz with artistic tasks primarily of the sort which Schulz had never practiced. Schulz was not knowledgeable in all the techniques. To refuse a Gestapo order, however, was unheard of; each one was accepted by Schulz as unavoidable and their completion was an act of struggle for life.

Thus, aside from new portraits of Landau or "presents" of Schulz's previously completed graphics and drawings, Landau was interested in "frescoes," as he imprecisely termed all kinds of drawings and painting on walls that he commanded Schulz to execute. Several such compositions were made on the ceiling and walls of various buildings of German organizations in Drohobycz. In years past, I had made attempts to find this artwork, assuming that it remained beneath layers of paint. Although my information about the existence of the paintings was based on the reliable testimony of witnesses, my search was hampered or blocked, and produced no results.

Long ago in Drohobycz, I had attempted to obtain information about Schulz's paintings in the building which had been the police headquarters before the war and during the German occupation became Landau's residence. The paintings were fairy-tale images meant for Landau's son. The uniqueness of these paintings lay, in my opinion, in the fact that despite Schulz's lack of previous experience of any kind in the execution of wall paintings, in one essential respect the work had a precedent in his many years as a drawing teacher in the Drohobycz gymnasium: the improvisation of fairy tales which he illustrated with drawings on the school blackboard. This was Schulz's way of defending himself against obstreperous boys, and he succeeded because like few others he knew how to reach a child's imagination. By 1942, however, he put his skills to use in the face of a far greater threat. Schulz had a naive faith that through this painting he could buy his life, that he could incline his "protector" to loyalty, to the kindness of a lord toward his slave.

Sometime during spring or early summer in 1942, Schulz began the work, taking one of his former students who had artistic talents as his helper. Between 1978 to 1980, this former student, Emil Górski, wrote out for me the story of his relationship with Schulz, which I then included with various recollections in one of my Polish books about Schulz, *Listy, fragmenty, wspomnienia o pisarzu* (Letters, Fragments, Recollections of the Writer), published in 1984. Górski's recollection includes the story of the wall paintings in the child's room:

> The next order was to paint "frescoes" in the room of Landau's young son, in the living quarters taken over by the Gestapo officer. Schulz took me along to help him at the time, and so in those unusual circumstances—I could get to know directly about his painting in process. . . . We painted scenes from fairy tales— Schulz sketched the composition in its entirety, and I painted certain details. And here Schulz remained somehow faithful to his creative principle: in the paintings on the wall of the child's room, in the fantastic fairy-tale scenery, the characters of kings, knights, squires had the completely "un-Aryan" features of the faces of people among whom Schulz lived at the time. Their similarity to the emaciated and tortured faces that Schulz had captured in memory was extraordinary. Here these tormented people—transported through Schulz's imagination from the world of tragic reality— found for themselves in paintings brilliant richness and pride; as kings on thrones in sable furs, with golden crowns on their heads;

on beautiful white horses as knights in armor, with swords in their hands and surrounded by knights; seated like powerful lords in golden carriages.

Like Górski, I thought that the above description would remain the sole trace of Schulz's fairy-tale paintings forever. Not wanting to part with the last remnants of hope, however, I was still trying find out something in Drohobycz about Schulz's "pictures" as late as the beginning of the 1990s, during the centenary of Bruno Schulz's birth. I queried the current residents of Landau's former quarters; fearful at my inquisitiveness, the occupants replied: "I've lived here for years now, and residents changed three times before me since the war. Each time, the place was done over, the walls painted. By what miracle could something be left on the refurbished walls?"

"But beneath the paint? Beneath three layers of paint?" I asked. Their response was that before each paint job, the previous layer of the wall was scraped away, along with any dirty remnants on the surface of the wall, so any painting must also have been scratched off before the plaster was covered with fresh paint. The explanation seemed reasonable and I did not pursue further efforts to discover the treasures, conceding they must have been obliterated.

Landau disappeared in September 1943, following the complete liquidation of the Jews of Drohobycz. Soon after the German capitulation in 1945, he attempted to hide under a false name, as was the custom with war criminals, but already in 1946, he was recognized in Linz by a Jew from Drohobycz, one of his intended victims. Arrested by the American occupying authorities in Germany, Landau was placed in an internment camp in Glasenbach. In August 1947, Landau escaped, and he remained free for over ten years under the name Rudolf Jaschke, running a firm in the area of Nördlingen for "projects, plans, consultation, interior design, storage." After a second arrest, investigation, and legal process, he was sentenced in Stuttgart in 1963 to life imprisonment. But Landau's varied life does not end with this life sentence, any more than did the history of Schulz's "frescoes" end many years ago with the scraping of walls in Drohobycz.

Life imprisonment was to turn into life freedom for Landau. Just short of ten years after the handing down of the sentence (really sentences, since both had ended in life imprisonment), a Stuttgart court freed him following a review of the charges which had been the basis of the first verdict; on its way to applying an act of leniency, the court then annulled life sentence number two. In this way the murderer from Drohobycz was able to live in freedom for yet another ten years until he died in Vienna in 1983.

At the turn of the 1980s and 1990s, a certain German filmmaker traveled to Drohobycz in order to begin filming a script he had written about Bruno Schulz. At the outset, he conducted a series of conversations and consultations with me to expand his knowledge. I pointed out to him that Schulz had created several polychromes during the time of the German occupation. I mentioned, among other places, the building of the so-called Reitschule (riding school), where wall decorations had once been done under orders; the "Villa Rajmund Jarosz," which had belonged to the Polish mayor of Drohobycz and which later housed a canteen or club for the Gestapo officers, and where one of the walls was covered by a large picture done by Schulz depicting banqueters before a laden table and servants pouring out wine for them; and the ceiling in a building of the prewar Jewish Orphans' Home, later Gestapo and NKVD headquarters. A high-ranking Gestapo officer visiting on inspection from Lwów had remarked somewhat scornfully that the picture in the Gestapo canteen was *typische jüdische Malerei*, a typical Jewish painting. We do not know with certainty whether the picture was painted on the wall or on a canvas suspended from the wall. The film crew found nothing, although it tried; as a result the film was missing a key element.

Years later, a similar path was pursued by a talented documentary filmmaker from Germany, Benjamin Geissler. Arriving in Drohobycz, he went to what had been Jana Street (presently 14 Tarnowski Street), and on February 9, 2001, with information including what I had published, Geissler found a part of Schulz's polychromes—hidden, but slowly beginning to emerge here and there from beneath the whitewash of a painted wall. A one-of-a-kind document, the last trace of the struggle of a defenseless artist and his work against destruction. Film registration and documentation of everything that was peeping, as it were, out from nothingness began. Without art historians, conservators, specialists in polychromes and their restoration from beneath later paint overlays, Geissler himself would not have been able to work on the paintings. The risk of harming the valuable finds would have been too great. The appropriate persons were notified and a group of experts was called together, including representatives from Poland and Ukraine.

From the Polish National Museum in Warsaw came an art conservator, Agnieszka Kijowska, a specialist in polychromes, frescoes, and all works of wall painting threatened with destruction. Wojciech Chmurzyński arrived, an art historian and longtime curator of the Warsaw Museum of Literature, which contains the largest collection in the world of Schulz's artwork. Borys Woźnicki, director of Ukraine's Gallery of Painting, came from nearby Lwów. Other specialists gathered as well. They confirmed the work as authentically that of Schulz. Fragment by fragment, the difficult work of uncovering the paintings began. Material from different samples of paint was prepared and sent to Poland for analysis. Benjamin Geissler took active part in the resurrection processes the entire time.

The participants in the revelatory venture, together with the Polish consul in Lwów, conferred with the minister of culture in Ukraine, at that time a man named Bogdan Stupka. The minister indicated his desire to place Schulz's paintings on the list of protected art and monuments in the territory of Ukraine, thereby assuring the continued cooperation of his office. The Polish minister of culture, Kazimierz Ujazdowski, responded similarly to the situation. By this time, however, the Drohobycz discoveries had given rise to a scandal, one which initially seemed unbelievable. I myself at first denied the reports, which I judged to be slanderous.

And yet the scandal turned out to be true. For many years Yad Vashem has granted the distinction of "Righteous Among the Nations of the World" to those who during the Holocaust risked their own lives to conceal those whom the Nazis denied the right to live—the Jewish citizens of Europe. I myself have a person in my family who was awarded the Yad Vashem medal (and for whom a tree was planted in Jerusalem's Avenue of the Righteous). My wife was saved in 1942 as a child, the sole member of her family to survive. Her rescuer is now long dead, but the Yad Vashem medal is preserved in our house as an inextinguishable memorial to her and out of gratitude for the institution that has honored her sacrifice and heroism with its distinction.

Thus, learning about three mysterious persons presenting themselves to the Drohobycz authorities as employed by Yad Vashem, which had granted "authorization" to seize Schulz's works and transport them to Jerusalem headquarters, I believed that we were dealing with frauds, impostors cloaking themselves in the reputation of a revered institution. Unable to believe in criminal intentions on the part of the patron of the Righteous, I treated the media reports as empty gossip, most likely invented to shake the moral renown of Yad Vashem. I believed too firmly in the unimpeachable integrity and the consistently practiced justice of Yad Vashem to question it. And I was not alone in this.

As it turned out, Stupka, who had promised effective intervention, ceased to be minister of culture in Ukraine, and Ujazdowski ceased to be his counterpart in Poland. Government circles maintained almost total silence, while for a period of time only the newspaper headlines were heard, along with similar reports from experts and responsible figures in cultural life. Only five months after the plunder in Drohobycz did the public prosecutor's office in Ukraine initiate an investigation into alleged corruption in the city government, which had by all accounts aided these three foreigners. Restraining its language with difficulty, the press—and not only the Polish press—wrote that Schulz's frescoes had become the booty of thieves. In an open letter from a Drohobycz resident named Dora Katznelson—philologist and historian, social and cultural activist, and Jewish—we read, "Not only Jews and Poles, but Ukrainians as well, reading daily in the Ukrainian papers about the barbaric theft of Schulz's paintings, cry out in amazement: 'Yad Vashem? It can't be!' And Jews add, 'Israel, our ethical model, our hope? It couldn't do this!'"

Amid this hailstorm of complaints and accusations, Yad Vashem could no longer keep silent, but five days elapsed before it issued its first "clarification." What did we read? "Polish and German media have published reports that paintings by the Jewish artist Bruno

Schulz have been found." Laudatory opinions of the Drohobycz city officials follow, along with information about their active cooperation with the representatives of Yad Vashem. "The best place to preserve them [Schulz's works of art] is Yad Vashem, the Institute of the Memory of Martyrs and Heroes of the Holocaust in Jerusalem."

How could one argue with such an assertion? If we add that when pressing this act of donation upon the residents of the place the uninvited guests sweetened the deal with charity amounting to one hundred dollars, and finally that the entire incident occurred without the use of force, all that is left is to express our amazement and admiration.

From the discovery of the Schulz polychromes in a neglected and decaying building to the moment of their "disappearance"— about which the Ukrainian and Polish authorities learned with some delay on May 25, 2001—nearly four months had passed. Small parts of the paintings, both those discovered and those still hidden under paint, remained in place for the time being. They are, however, rudiments, mutilated remnants of a whole no longer there—like Schulz's literature itself. The early work of the team of three foreigners shows moderate care, indicative of their skill. Later, when the scandal erupted and the affair was publicized, the evidently frightened strangers packed their booty and took off, leaving the rest. Fragments, such as the image of a coachman, considered without evidence to be Schulz's last self-portrait, were pried from the walls hurriedly and crudely, as if the ground had begun to burn beneath the feet of the three gentlemen. Uneven and lacerated traces were left on the wall. A section which portrayed a "queen" (72 by 88 centimeters) was torn from the bricks together with the plaster.

Arguments put forward by the spokesperson for Yad Vashem, Iris Rosenberg, offend logic and common sense and invalidate the work of a generation of Polish intellectuals whose goal it has been to force a nation to come to grips with its past. Rosenberg justified Schulz's belonging to the Jewish nation by recalling that he had been killed in the ghetto by a Gestapo officer—thus the shot of a mass murderer determined the victim's identity. Her second, related argument is simply the obdurate contention that the paintings are better off in Jerusalem because their proper place is there.

In the uproar of the conflict, the goal of creating a Bruno Schulz museum in Drohobycz—for which I have long worked with people of goodwill, proponents of the same idea—was not made easier, nor advanced even a step forward; the city fathers did not even seriously discuss it. Instead, despite local and world protest, a work of art was allowed to disappear, resisted by practically no one, while a blind eye was turned as the intruders—having sized up the friendliness of the Drohobycz authorities—did their work. The office of the public prosecutor of Lwów continues to examine these charges, and there has been no public verdict.

In Drohobycz, in his "one and only town on earth," Schulz had a house in which he spent almost his entire creative life, up until the moment when he was denied a roof over his head, and soon after, life itself. This house stands today, and in it I would see a museum in his name, even though nothing remains of the interior as it was in his lifetime. As late as 1965, I photographed the stairs as they once were, leading from the back to the entrance. I managed to photograph the large, old-fashioned white stove with its decorative metal medallion depicting a mythological scene. Now even this is gone.

At the time of his deportation to the ghetto, Schulz must have bid farewell to his house, just as today he says farewell to his posthumous crypt in Drohobycz where the scenes of his last fairy tale survived in hiding. There exists no other grave which contains his ashes. And now even his last crypt has been violated, while he himself has been deported, banished to other lands, ones foreign to him. Would that I were mistaken, but I fear that the sole, lasting consequence of the discovery of the polychromes is and will long remain reawakened and exacerbated national antagonisms, a xenophobia revived in no small measure by Yad Vashem. A very sad statement, and an unhappy ending to the last fairy tale of Bruno Schulz.

LETTERS

About
Bruno Schulz's
Letters

A s Jerzy Ficowski notes, Schulz was transformed into a published writer through a happy accident of circumstances associated with letters. On the basis of some 150 surviving letters, Schulz is considered—in addition to his place in twentieth-century Polish prose—a major figure in interwar Polish epistolary art. Collected in Jerzy Ficowski's volume *Księga listów* (Book of Letters, 1975), Schulz's letters reveal his creative nature and his personality. Through his letters, we see Schulz as a human being who thrived on creative communication that stimulated his artistic world and provided a pretext to formulate his understanding of it. His letters demonstrate how it was that he made such a strong impression on those whom he encountered. Sometimes importunate or needy himself, he nevertheless was a devoted friend, concerned and sympathetic.

The group of letters here, translated anew (and including one letter never before translated into English), span the period from January 1934, to November 1941—from the publication of *Cinnamon Shops* to just one year before Schulz's death. It was the period of his public life and the prelude to his horrifying murder. While prior to the publication of *Cinnamon Shops* letters had been Schulz's only outlet for literary creation, afterward writing to publish rivaled and even supplanted letter-writing. Yet Schulz's epistolary gift shines through. We see it in his imagery, as in the "Turkish alphabet" of crows in his letter to Zenon Waśniewski. He wrote to women with special sublety. He exposes his vulnerability to Romana Halpern when he describes himself as "an insect pushed out of its chrysalis to face the storm of foreign light and the winds of heaven." His letters to Anna Płockier show his tenderness and his gift for analysis of his own relationship with her, as well as his firm convictions about art.

Any formal traces of epistolary origins are absent from Schulz's fiction; his letters are all the more important as a key to Schulz. In them we find his deep affinity for the short form, for a genre in which he felt at home, a genre in which he could express both his life and his art.

—*Theodosia Robertson*

TO ZENON WAŚNIEWSKI

ZENON WAŚNIEWSKI (1891–1945), *painter and graphic artist, cofounder and publisher of the literary monthly* Kamena *(Camena, Song), published in Chełm Lubelski in the years 1933–39. He studied architecture with Bruno Schulz in Lwów before World War I and, like Schulz, interrupted his studies and became a drawing teacher in Radzyń and Chełm Lubelski. He printed his own graphics and sometimes poetry in* Kamena. *Thanks to renewed contact between the former fellow students after some years, two fragments of Schulz's prose were published in* Kamena, *one of which (a part of "Spring") was later eliminated from the story by the author and has survived solely because of its publication in* Kamena. *Arrested by the Gestapo in 1942, Waśniewski died in Bergen-Belsen on the eve of liberation. Schulz's letters to Waśniewski were preserved by his widow; they are in the collection of Jerzy Ficowski and include twenty-five epistolary texts.*

Dear Classmate!

I deeply apologize for the long silence with which I responded to your beautiful and sad letter shrouded in the atmosphere of All Souls' Day.[1] Where has that funereal tone come from, that coquetry with the terribly seductive and sad Lady of the graves? Could it be perhaps an unconscious recollection of the ancient sacred holy day, the holy day of death and debauchery, of November graveyard baccanalias? Is "taedium vitae" now getting you in its clutches too—the great despondency—passive resistance, urge to sabotage, breaking with the general treadmill? I'm embarrassed in comparison with you, of my teary unmanliness, recividistic doubt—You are so much more active than I and bear your fate in a much more masculine fashion!

For a month now I've written nothing, I haven't painted—and I
sometimes have the feeling that now I will not write anything decent
either. It is a great pity to me to waste the kind of success I had with
Cinnamon Shops, but I waste it if during this year I don't publish something at least at that level. I would write it, if I had obtained leave
time, but not a word is said about it here, the request got buried in
the underground cogs of the Ministry and I am losing hope that it
will ever rise to the surface. For the time being I would like to write
a few articles about books. I'm tempted to analyze Mann's *Joseph and
His Brothers*—an excellent work with which one can demonstrate the
transformation in our understanding of reality and the new view of
the essence of life.[2]

This wonderful autumn (a real "second fall" from the treatise)[3]
ebbs away from me without having been taken advantage of, barely
noticed. Only in the evenings when the air becomes colorful and full
of reflections and all objects, already sinking into dusk, give off colorful emanations, astral bodies, shadow after shadow—I like to look
at the bright verdigris, celadon, topaz skies like a magic book
streaked with black signs, a Turkish alphabet of crows, and watch
those huge crowish assemblies noisy and plaintive, their wide, fantastic flights and circlings, returnings and sudden invasions in the sky
which they fill with a wave of their wings and flickering cawing.
Have you noticed that at moments, having flown off very far, they
become like a barely visible cloud of dust and fall from sight, and
then suddenly on their return, setting the broadness of their wings
toward us, they gather in a black gruel, sprinkle flakes of soot, and
grow ever wider and more violent?

I must let you know that I have falsely or perhaps prematurely
informed you about buying tickets for the class lottery. In the meantime I've received a letter from the lottery office which I am including here, and from which you will see that we didn't play in the first
class at all, since the numbers we bought were already sold. So for
the price of 20 zlotys the lottery office has sent me 1 ticket for the
second-class drawing, because the stakes double in the second drawing. The ticket number is 164 617. Beautiful, that you remembered
to renew the stakes punctually. Should I send it to you, or just keep
it until the December and January drawings? It still seems to me that

as a result of this maneuver we have lost not only the first drawing, but part of the total. Such are the caprices of fate. Does this turn of events discourage you from playing further?

What is new there around you, dear Zenon? Are you painting? Has this autumn inspired you to some new color combinations? Do you have beautiful scenery there? Do you have any news from Leszczyc?[4] Write me at length about yourself!

I embrace you warmly and send good wishes

Bruno Schulz
November 7, 1934

TO TADEUSZ BREZA

TADEUSZ BREZA (1905–1970), *novelist and essayist, debuted with the novel* Adam Grywald *(1936), to which Schulz devoted a review. He was the author of one of the earliest reviews of* Cinnamon Shops, *in which he enthusiastically responded to Schulz's work. A collection of eleven letters, including the two included here, are in the collection of the Ossolineum Library in Wrocław.*

Dear Sir!

I need a companion. I need the closeness of a kindred person. I long for some support of the inner world whose existence I postulate. I persistently cling to it through my own faith alone, heave it despite everything with the strength of its resistance—it is the labor and torment of Atlas. Sometimes it seems to me that despite this strained gesture of lifting I hold nothing on my shoulders. I would like for a moment the power to set down this weight upon someone's arms, straighten up my neck and look at what I have been carrying.

I need a partner for undertakings of discovery. What for one person is a risk, an impossibility, a caprice stood on its head—when reflected in two pairs of eyes becomes a reality. The world waits, as it were, for this partnership—until now closed, confined, without further plans—to begin to mature with the colors of a dahlia, burst and open up inside. Painted panoramas deepen and open into actual perspectives, the wall lets us into a dimension formerly unattainable, frescoes painted on the horizon come to life like a pantomime.

It's good that you are not perfect, that you consume time excessively. You must be full of unofficial events, unregistered activities that eat up time right in front of your eyes, before your official position resolves, after many formalities, to sample it. After all, someone must consume it and it must benefit someone's health.

People's weaknesses betray their souls to us, render them needy. It's that loss of an electron which ionizes them and inclines them to chemical bonding. Without the defect they would be closed in themselves and in need of nothing. Only their failings add flavor and render them attractive.

I'm extremely happy that we will meet. Please come directly to me. I will be here until the first of July. To date I have no specific plans to travel. Maybe together we might come up with something. First I would like to show you Drohobycz and its surroundings, to see anew through your eyes the scenery of my youth. To introduce you into unwritten chapters of *Cinnamon Shops*. Please come.

With warm regards
Bruno Schulz
Drohobycz, June 21, 1934
Address: Floriańska 10

Dear Sir,

I want to thank you sincerely for the letter and let you know that I read your statement in *Rocznik Literatury* which you don't mention in your letter and with which you have thrust me to the forefront of the literary year.[1] I consider it an act of great courage to stand so uncompromisingly and wholeheartedly beside your philosophical kin, to take upon yourself responsibility for their philosophical fancies. I am moved and grateful. This solidarity of people close to me consoles me in my depression. I am very downcast: the leave time upon which I had so counted was not granted to me. I will remain in Drohobycz, in school, where the mob will continue to cut capers on my nerves. You have to know that my nerves are spread like a network throughout the entire handicraft workroom, stretched out across the floor, papered over the walls, and wrapped around the worktable and anvil in a thick braid. It is a phenomenon known in science as *telekinetics*, through which everything that happens on the workbenches takes place to some degree on my skin. Thanks to such a finely developed signal network I am destined to be a teacher of handicrafts.

Since we are sharing with one another the secret failings that plague us, I'll confide to you a particular ailment that persecutes me and which is also connected with time, although it is different from your symptoms of gastric diarrhea that you described. Your alimentary canal lets time through too easily, incapable of holding it in—mine is distinguished by a paradoxical fastidiousness controlled by the *idée fixe* of the *virginity of time*. Just as for some Rajah with a melancholic and unsatisfied spirit each woman who is grazed by the glance of a man is already defiled and worth only a silk noose, so for me, time to which someone else has laid claim, to which someone made the slightest allusion—is already tainted, ruined, inedible. I can't tolerate any rival for time. For me, the scrap that they have touched is made repugnant. I don't know how to share time, I don't know how to live on someone else's leftovers. (Jealous lovers use this same vocabulary.) When I have to prepare a lesson for the next day, buy materials at the lumberyard—the entire afternoon and evening are already ruined for me. I renounce the remaining time with noble pride. All—or nothing—is my motto. And because every school day is profaned this way—I live in proud abstinence and—I do not write. Some feudal mentality resides in such an uncompromising attitude. What do you think, could one breed that mentality out, fatten it up, train this quintessence of chivalry?

In addition, I am letting you know that for the holidays I will probably come to Warsaw, where I plan to spend the midyear break. Will you be at home?[2] I would be delighted to meet you. With respectful regards and warmest sympathy.

Bruno Schulz
Drohobycz, December 2, 1934

PS Could you perhaps suggest some inexpensive lodging in Warsaw?

TO JULIAN TUWIM

JULIAN TUWIM (1894–1953), *poet, cofounder of the poetic group Skamander and one of its most outstanding representatives, sent Schulz a letter expressing his admiration and respect almost immediately after the publication of* Cinnamon Shops. *The letter has not survived. He also showed his high regard for Schulz's writing by putting his name forward as a candidate for the* Wiadomości Literackie (Literary News) *annual award for 1935.*

Dear Sir!

Thank you. I did not expect this, but in the depths of my soul I needed—ardently desired your sympathetic reinforcement. At the root of the passion and pertinacity of this book [*Cinnamon Shops*] was that old longing as well. Today, you have calmed it in me, satisfied and filled me to overflowing. What gratification!

It has come a little late—no fault of yours.

Many years ago when you came to Drohobycz, I was in the hall and looked at you vengefully and rebelliously, full of sullen adoration. Ancient history. At the time, some of your poems brought me to the despair of helpless admiration. It hurt—to read them repeatedly, and each time to push up the hill that heavy lump of admiration which just before the very peak would plunge to the bottom, unable to cling to the steep incline of delight. They annihilated me and at the same time provided me intoxication, a sense of the super-human triumphant powers which a liberated and happy man some-day will be able to control. At the time I carried within myself a kind of legend about "an age of genius" which supposedly once had occurred in my life, not found on any calendar year, rising above chronology and era, in which all things breathed the radiance of divine colors and the entire sky was absorbed in one breath, like a gulp of pure ultramarine. It never happened really. But it was made real and vivid in your poetry, like a peacock eye bleeding azure and thickly lashed—it was like a clamorous nest of hummingbirds. . . .

You taught me that each state of the soul pursued sufficiently far into its depth leads through the straits and canals of the word—into mythology. Not into the congealed mythology of peoples and his-tory—but into the one where beneath an exterior layer our blood throbs, becomes entangled in the depths of philogenesis, and branches out into a metaphysical night.

In this mythological depth you surely have a pact with the devil. Here your poetry becomes transcendent, its craft completely incom-parable, exceeding the measure of man-made things.

Today I have had a great triumphant moment. The spell is bro-ken—what I composed in delight, exalted in attacks of admiration, until now foreign and used against me—confirms and accepts me. Thank you.

Bruno Schulz
Drohobycz, January 26, 1934
Floriańska 10

TO ANDRZEJ PLEŚNIEWICZ

ANDREJ PLEŚNIEWICZ (1909–1945), *literary critic, essayist, author of* Rainer Maria Rilke, Valery Larbaud, Paul Valéry, *and other works, published essays and reviews about Bruno Schulz. He died in the vicinity of Warsaw during the German air bombardment in the last weeks of the war. This letter (today in the collection of Jerzy Ficowski) is one of three to him which have survived.*

Dear and esteemed Andrzej!

Your letter gladdened me, somehow I didn't count on your taking your promise seriously. At one time, I lived through letters; in those days they were my only creative work. It's too bad that we cannot turn our correspondence back to those times. Now I no longer know how to write like that, and that time—not so distant—in perspective seems rich, full, bursting in comparison to the present grayness and distraction. You have a kind of handwriting that I like. I've had good experiences with this kind of handwriting.

You overrate the advantages of my Drohobycz situation. What I miss even here—is quiet, my own musical quiet, a stilled pendulum, subject to its own gravitation, along a clear line of track, undistracted by any foreign influence. This substantial quiet, positive—full—is already itself almost creativity. Those things which I think want to express themselves through me take place above a certain threshold of quiet, they take form in a solution brought into perfect equilibrium. The quiet that I have here, although more perfect than in that happier era—has become insufficient for a more sensitive, more fastidious "vision." It is increasingly difficult for me to believe in it. But precisely these things require blind faith, to be taken on credit. Only united with that faith, do they agree reluctantly to come into being—to exist to some extent.

What you say about our artificially prolonged childhood—about immaturity—bewilders me somewhat. Rather, it seems to me that this kind of art, the kind which is so dear to my heart, is precisely a regression, a return to childhood. Were it possible to turn back development, achieve a second childhood by some circuitous road, once again have its fullness and immensity—that would be the incarnation of an "age of genius," "messianic times" which are promised and pledged to us by all mythologies. My ideal goal is to "mature" into childhood. This would really be a true maturity.

I live entirely alone here. I have taken on the sad obligation of visiting a friend who is dying of cancer.[1] Spring arouses in me the longing for travel with a partner, some high school camping trip. Perhaps one painter-friend may come visit me.

It's better not to write about my work—it's very little and trivial.

If you should see Witold[2] please give him my heartfelt greetings. I don't want him to be angry that I've still not written to him.

I must close now, I thank you sincerely for remembering me, with best regards and a most hearty handshake

Bruno Schulz
Drohobycz, March 4, 1936
Floriańska 10

Please send news soon and continued correspondence

TO ROMANA HALPERN

ROMANA HALPERN (1900–1944), *the recipient of the largest surviving group of Schulz's letters, was a lover of literature and art who moved in Warsaw's journalism and literary-artistic circles. For a period of time she was close to Stanisław Ignacy Witkiewicz, through whom Schulz met her in the winter of 1936 during his half-year leave from teaching. In addition to her enthusiasm for his work, Romana Halpern provided selfless assistance to Schulz on several occasions when he turned to her for help. Their acquaintance and correspondence lasted three years, until the outbreak of the war. During the occupation, she found herself in the Warsaw ghetto with her son. She escaped and, after settling her son in the countryside, moved to Cracow, where she was hired in a commercial firm as an office worker and stenographer under a false name. In September of 1944, shortly before the liberation of Cracow from German occupation, she was arrested by the Gestapo and shot. Her son found Schulz's letters in Warsaw in February 1945. Today they are in the collections of the Museum of Literature in Warsaw.*

[salutation missing]

I have an endlessly guilty conscience in relation to you, although in my own mind I could justify my guilt by the disruption and disorganization of my time in Warsaw. I won't try to exculpate myself; there are motives which the more precisely they desire to convey the real state of affairs, the more they seem artificial and drawn out. It's good that you reminded me about Rilke. When one is desperate about one's defeats in art (about which no one knows)—recalling his name does one good. The existence of his books is a guarantee that the tangled, deaf mass unformulated in us can still rise to the surface wonderfully distilled. The precision and purity of Rilke's distillation is a consolation to us. I am exhausted with my attempts at writing. A writer (at least my kind) is the most impoverished creature on earth.

He must constantly lie, convincingly present as existing and real what inside him is in truly wretched disintegration and chaos. That I might mean to someone what Rilke means to me—seems both moving and humbling to me, as well as unmerited.[1] I don't take it completely seriously either.

Contact with you will be very nice for me. I am curious what the text of this contact will be.

I am sending you a copy of *Cinnamon Shops* by the same mail and add my respects and affection

Bruno Schulz
Drohobycz, August 16, 1936

Dear Madam,

I am letting you know that the misunderstanding between me and Juna[2] was charmed away once more—for how long, I don't know. I sincerely thank you for the information and for the kind warm words. With amazement and joy I ask myself how I gained your friendship, what I did to earn it. Is it not an unmerited and unjustified good fortune that a book brings us—in addition to other benefits—friends as well? But I accept this with gratitude. Today I am having a better day, one of the calming and quieting days. I have a small temperature and am lying in bed, I didn't go to school. Outside it is a cold day, hard and unyielding, full of prose and harshness. But good spirits have gathered around my bed, beside me are two volumes of Rilke that I have borrowed. From time to time I enter his difficult and intense world for a moment, beneath his many-arched skies, and again I come to myself. I don't know if you have read Rilke. I consider *Neue Gedichte* [New Poems] the peak of his creative work. What he wrote afterward: *Duineser Elegien* [Duino Elegies], *Sonette an Orpheus* [Sonnets to Orpheus]—is already too refined and esoteric. I also have my drawings beside me and sometimes it seems to me that they really are good and that I could do still better. My great enemy is lack of faith in myself, an absence of love for myself. Long months pass and nothing that I do earns my approval, no idea that emerges satisfies me, nothing pleases me. This state of discontent with myself condemns me to inactivity. But sometimes I think that this severity is justified and that rightly I condemn to destruction things that are immature and imperfect. This is the weak point about things, that at the beginning one must work with imperfect things in order to get into full swing, to become excited and be transported, and somewhere at the limit of one's powers find things that are perfect. Your fear that life as a couple might wrench me from the climate proper to my creative work—made me think. Perhaps loneliness was the source of my inspirations, but can life as a couple really break through that isolation? Doesn't one remain lonely anyway? And why do all poets in the end trade their loneliness for life with another? I have the human fear of loneliness, of the barren land of an unnecessary and marginal life that I wanted to portray in "Emeryt" ["The Old Age Pensioner"].³ Hence my flight into marriage. Besides, she is the person closest and dearest to me, to whom I mean a great deal—is it not a great thing—to mean everything to someone?

Have you read my "Wiosna" ["Spring"] in the September issue of Skamander?⁴ In October the second part of "Wiosna" will appear, it seems to me, the better part. I would like to know something more about you, about your life and your past. Would you be willing to write me something about yourself? Once again, I thank you sincerely—very devoted and grateful

Bruno Schulz

Drohobycz, September 30, 1936

Floriańska 10

Dear Romana!

Thank you for the news and views which always interest me since they concern my affairs and people are insatiable listeners when others want to speak about them.* Since I wrote you last, things have gotten very bad with me, not externally, but the internal

*This is the source of the success of fortune-tellers, palm readers, etc. [Schulz]

situation has worsened a good deal. My spirits have completely collapsed. I have told myself that I am neither a painter nor a writer, not even a decent teacher. It seems to me that I deceived the world with some sort of brilliance, that there is nothing inside me. I have tried to give up creative work, to live like an ordinary person, and it seems very sad to me. Besides, my daily existence depends on my art, since I support my lame teaching with values borrowed from art. Mentally, I was already without a job and in dire poverty. Looking at the town cranks, at the beggars in rags, I thought: maybe I will look like that soon. You know that I am not cut out for any honest work. I cannot force myself, I cannot find any charm in teaching.† In this I differ notably from my fellow teachers. I would like to waste time, do nothing, wander about—have a little joy in the landscape, in the horizon with its early evening clouds that open into the next world. Then perhaps joy in life would return. Amid this unemployment one hears only imminent danger and dire warnings. Duty grows to some apocalyptic proportions. The threat of layoffs hangs over everyone. A few years ago in our profession one could still feel the confidence of a safe harbor, some mooring in life. There was a little good nature and joy. Now, joy has been banished from our life, and without joy, without a little margin of joy—I don't know how to create. Only please don't say anything to Szturm about my disinclination to work, he doesn't like that in people, although he is so understanding of others.[5]

You are mistaken when you suppose that suffering is necessary for creative work. That's an old cliché—maybe sometimes valid—but not in my case. I need good quiet, a little secret, nourishing joy, a contemplative fondness for quiet, for fine weather. I don't know how to suffer. Suffering doesn't strengthen me. But perhaps I am wrong.

I don't correspond with any woman except Juna. It's too bad that we didn't know one another a few years back. I still knew how to write beautiful letters then. *Cinnamon Shops* emerged gradually from my letters. The greatest number of those letters were to Debora

†But I don't know how to live without some charm, without a little piquancy, without some tasty spice to life. [Schulz]

Vogel, the author of *Akacje kwitną* [The Acacias Are Blooming].⁶
Most of those letters got lost.

Reading current literary journals irritates me. I see how many
people write while I do nothing. Thank you kindly, but don't trouble
yourself to send issues of *Wiadomości*,⁷ I don't know if I will read them.
I don't know what to write to Szturm. I am depressed—without
rational basis, and in this situation I am an egoist, locked in my own
concerns. How could Szturm understand this—he who is totally
devoted to people—without a private life, the antithesis of egoism?

Please don't worry about Stef.⁸ This must last for a while, but it
will pass. You will see.

I send my heartfelt good wishes

Bruno Schulz
November 15, 1936

Do you really still like *Cinnamon Shops*? Do you believe in my creative
ability?

Please convey sincere good wishes to Witkacy.

Could you perhaps do something in the matter of my fictional
registration in Silesia? In the province of Silesia proof of several
weeks registration is enough—as a lawyer from Katowice informed
me. How would one do this? But please don't trouble yourself. You
have enough of your own troubles and Stef is sick besides. I can wait
until he is well.

Dear Romana!

Your letter saddened me. With amazement I recognize feature
after feature of the image of my own depressive states. How essentially similar people are to one another. Just as all have the same
limbs and organs, so too they experience the same [emotional]
states. Were it not for this, would books and works of art, and their
communication, be possible? But your prose sample is a great nov-
elty for me! You write excellently! One question only, do you have
more material, will you have enough breath for a larger work? You
should try! I am struck by the clear narcissism of this short piece. I
would not have attributed it to you. It is a quality which always fas-

cinates me in a woman, as an expression of her fundamental other-
ness, a harmony and self-acceptance that is unattainable for me. This
is what always remains foreign to me, and thus alluring and longed
for. I myself am far from narcissism and it seems to me to be some
metaphysical privilege to give oneself over to it without concern and
without scruples. Please write more! The ending is very good.

What do I advise for your state of mind? Some work! That is the
best narcotic. I speak like a moralist, but I am far from such thread-
bare platitudes. I speak from the point of view of inner health and
techniques for living. This is our sole aid. Ask Witkacy if he could
live for a moment without going crazy or commiting suicide if he
didn't have work.

I am reading Zegadłowicz's *Zmory* [Nightmares] now.[9] It interests and excites me a great deal. Beyond this book I see the outlines
of another book which I would like to write myself. So really I don't
know if I am reading this book, or maybe the potential one not yet
realized. This is the best kind of reading, when between the lines
you read yourself, your own book. This is the way we read in childhood, and why later the same books once so rich and full of pulp—
then in adulthood are like trees shorn of their leaves—shorn of our
additions with which we patched their gaps. The books which we
read in childhood don't exist, they have fluttered away—bare skele-
tons remain. Whoever would still have in himself the memory and
the marrow of childhood—ought to write them anew, as they were
then. A true *Robinson* and a true *Gulliver* would come about.

I'm happy that your son is so well now. You see, it did pass. And
still you are not happy and have other worries. What will happen
with your job? Maybe you can try at Gł[ówny] U[rząd] St[atysty-
czny]?[10] What is Staś doing?[11] Please ask if he can advise me about
registering in the province of Silesia.[12] He has acquaintances there.
Or maybe Szturm might be able to do something? It has to happen
quickly, because around the 20th I want to go to Katowice. Please
remind them. I am now trying for a transfer to Lwów. At the Christ-
mas holidays, I would like to come to Warsaw for a few days. Of
course I will see you. I send very hearty good wishes

                                                          Bruno Schulz

                                        Drohobycz, December 5, 1936

Dear Roma!

Thank you for the prompt reply and for the kind words. When one does not have faith or confidence in oneself—that of others helps a lot, although it can't entirely replace one's own. It's not so much faith in my capability that I lack, but something more general: a trust in life, safely at rest in my destiny, a faith in the ultimate benevolence of existence. I had it long ago, without even realizing it. That faith, that trust, opens reserves of creativity in us, it is the rich, full, and warm climate in which those late and hard-to-reach fruits can grow. Cases in which life's losses, tragic events become creative—are incomprehensible to me. This kind of productivity must be completely different from my own.

If I want to convey my present state, the image of being awakened from a deep sleep comes to mind. Someone awakens to phantoms, still seeing the world of dreams sinking away in forgetfulness, with fading colors still before his eyes and feeling the softness of a dream beneath his eyelids—and now the new, sober, and bracing world of consciousness presses upon him and, still full of inner stupor, he lets himself reluctantly be pulled into its affairs and processes. This is the way my peculiar character, my exceptionality, not unloosened, remains stuck in forgetfulness. The woman who closed me off from the attacks of the world moves away calmly into the distance, while like an insect pushed out of its chrysalis, I am left facing the storm of a foreign light and the winds of heaven, and turn myself over to the elements as if for the first time. Where this will lead me—I don't know. Whether this new sobriety is only an emptiness after the lifting of a creative haze or a new hunger for the world, a new confrontation with the inner element—I don't know. The peculiarity and exceptionality of my inner processes closed me off hermetically, rendered [me] insensitive, averse to the invasion of the world. Now I open myself as if for the second time to the world and all would be well were it not for that fear and inner hesitation, as before a risky venture, leading God knows where.

What is happening with you? What is your inner situation? Whom are you seeing? Has Witkacy written you anything? I don't know now if I will come, I'm expecting news from Rój in this matter. I have a nephew in Warsaw, Wilhelm Schulz,[13] a very capable and

intelligent young man (and very good-looking as well), who would
be wholeheartedly happy to help me with something, should I leave
Drohobycz. Could I send him to you, so that he might seek inspiration and guidance from you regarding work?

I sincerely thank you for so earnestly taking up the problem of
that poor F.[14] He is no relation of mine, just my former student and
an unhappy young man. He has very poor parents who can do nothing for him. I will tell them what they have to do and wait for the
result. Please don't be angry that I have troubled you with this, but
you have not acted in a vain cause.

I send heartfelt good wishes and ask for frequent news

Bruno Schulz

Drohobycz [between August 20 and 26, 1937]

Dear Romana!

Please don't be angry that I repaid your efforts and concern—
with refusal. If you consider my situation more closely, you will agree
that I cannot accept this proposition. I already mentioned once that
I have three persons to support (sister, cousin, nephew), whom I cannot abandon completely to the whims of fate. I am earning about
300 zlotys a month now. If I could obtain work on similar conditions
in Warsaw—I would go, since I could live there for 200 zl., and send
100 to my family. However, at Mr. Ramberg's I would have 2 to 6
hours—I would earn at the most 100 zl. For so few hours I can't leave
a state position (at rank VII) that guarantees me a pension. I don't
have sufficient courage, sufficient stimulus or incentive to take such
a risky step. I delude myself that something still better could be
found were I to attend to this with all my strength. This is not a hint
to encourage you to greater efforts! I know well in what difficult circumstances you work and that you don't have an easy life. I didn't
expect that in addition to everything else you would still find time
and willingness to remember me. In any case, I don't see how you
could do more for me, but even so I don't give up hope. Please excuse
that when referring my nephew to you I allowed myself jokingly to
add for encouragement that he is handsome (which truly is one of

his outstanding qualities). I had no hidden thoughts in this. Anyway, after consideration I gave up the idea of an association with you both, I fear that my nephew is of too independent a nature to work in partnership with someone. Once upon a time, he put forth great effort on my behalf, going with great zeal to Wierzyński,[15] Szturm, Czarski[16] for me. But now he is too absorbed with his own career to occupy himself strenuously with this. As to Gombrowicz, I will try to initiate an acquaintance between the two of you, since it is worthwhile for you to meet him. Can I just write him that you would like to meet him? That would be simplest.

I already don't remember what I wrote about in my last letter. My own diagnosis of my psychic state and my internal situation continually changes and modifies. It seems to me that the world, life, is important for me solely as material for artistic creation. The moment I cannot utilize life creatively—it becomes either terrible and dangerous, or morally vapid for me. To maintain my curiosity, the creative impulse, to resist the process of growing sterile, of boredom—this is my most important and most pressing task. Without that spice of life I lapse into a lethargy of death—while alive. Art has accustomed me to its stimulation and acute sensations. My nervous system has a fastidiousness and delicacy which has not matured to the demands of a life denied the sanction of art. I'm afraid that this year of school work will kill me. As long as I was younger and livelier, I could somehow stand it. Now I am fed up with it. Maybe I should take on a counterweight to this crushing struggle of school—debauchery? This thought has already occurred to me. But it jolts and weakens my nerves too much—(in such difficult and dangerous circumstances as I have here—a small town—a teacher). In order to create, I must have a particularly kindly and encouraging climate around me—good faith in myself, quiet, safety . . . I am more mature and richer now than before when I wrote *Cinnamon Shops*. I no longer have only that naiveté, that carefree quality. I didn't feel any burdens of responsibilities upon me then, no weight, I wrote for myself. That makes it easier. I can well understand how someone like Berent[17] doesn't read any of the criticism about himself, and avoids the press. He produces an artificial solitude for himself, an emptiness in which he creates. It is necessary. True that in Warsaw I wouldn't have that same creative solitude. But then I would not be threatened there by death from monotony, growing boredom, terrible vomitings from the sterility of life. After a certain time I could retreat into quiet in order to write. One can find many contradictions in what I'm saying, but you will understand me if you put yourself in my situation.

Perhaps you might borrow Husserl[18] for me somewhere (a German philosopher). Maybe I will ask Witkiewicz. In general, I would like to subscribe to some large Warsaw lending library that mails books to the provinces. Or maybe it would be better to do this in Lwów?

Are you disillusioned with me? Will you now no longer do anything for me? I feel it, I know and you don't have to convince me, that you would like very much to help me. You are now the only one to whom this is really important. Please remember me and write soon.

I send heartfelt good wishes

Bruno Schulz
August 30, 1937

Dear Roma!

Don't be angry that I did not answer immediately. Physical distance makes the written word seem too weak, ineffective, not reaching its goal. And the goal itself, the person who receives our words at the end of this physical road, seems only half real, as if from a novel, from an uncertain existence. This discourages writing, robs it of reality, makes it seem an activity that's questionable, magic, a gesture of dubious usefulness in relation to the closer reality rubbing closer against us. Maybe such things should not be said, it's better to fight the failure of imagination, which doesn't want to believe in the reality of distant things. It moves me greatly that so weakened and exhausted, you manage to remember me, even for letters, to be interested in my affairs. It is really very lovely that such women exist, that such selflessness exists and such relationships. Can you at least read? Do you have some ailment? I hope that the stones dissolve and disappear from the body. Truskawiec (fifteen minutes from Drohobycz) is very good for that, but you are still too weak for it. I hope that maybe in May you can come to Truskawiec. It's wonderful then. You live amid white cherry blossoms which fill Truskawiec. It is my beloved spot about which sometime I will write a story someday yet. In May it is wonderfully sad and solemn. The nightingales sing and all the trees are white. Korostów[19] is not the place for you. I think that we might get a very good place at Reitman's for 5-6 zlotys a day.

In the meantime such gloomy historical events.[20] Their direction is increasingly worse. It depresses me a great deal. I have been close to despair at some moments, just as before an imminent catastrophe. Spring is so beautiful—one ought to live and gulp down the world. And I spend days and nights without a woman and without a Muse and waste away fruitlessly. I woke up once here from a sudden profound despair and life slips away and I retain nothing from it. Were such despair to last long, one could go mad. But maybe once that despair comes and settles in permanently, then it will be too late for life. Get well quickly and live, because that is the greatest unhappiness—not to live life fully. Are you in Śródborów already?[21] Is it beautiful there? Are you now a little healthier and stronger? I understand that this was an internal operation, without an outside scar? I am now reading a magnificent book by Huxley: *Eyeless in Gaza*.[22] I have read with real admiration for his savage wisdom. Other than that I can't read anything. Nothing interests me. I think that it is because of the lack of a woman.

Write me everything about yourself. Whom have you met in Śródborów? Does anyone visit you? Does Wanda Kragen[23] come by? Do you think that I should thank Wittlin,[24] Kuncewiczowa,[25] and Dąbrowska[26] for supporting me on the jury?

Gombrowicz is not in Warsaw. He doesn't write me at all. I'm not getting any letters now.

I send you the most heartfelt good wishes and I wish you much good health and a good rest

Bruno Schulz
Drohobycz, March 20, 1938

Dear Roma!

I have a bad conscience about you since I haven't written you in so long. I count on your much-tried forbearance and goodness. Several times I have wanted to write, but I didn't know where you were, and I was afraid that a card (I wrote only cards from there [Paris]) wouldn't reach you. I still don't know if you are in Warsaw now, whether Stefanek maybe is there, and who picks up your mail.

I lasted more than 3 weeks in Paris,[27] even though after the first week I had already realized that I would not accomplish the plan I had made here. It was naiveté to set off the way I did to conquer Paris, which is the most exclusive, self-sufficient, closed city in the world. With my language preparation I could not dream of coming into any contact with the French. The embassy didn't take any interest in me at all, and in the future I cannot count on it at all. I did however make contact with one art dealer on rue Faub. St. Honoré, who wanted to do an exhibit, but then I withdrew from the project myself. Despite that I am pleased that I was in Paris, that I saw so many astounding things, and could see the art of great eras up close, instead of through reproductions—and in the end that I have gotten rid of certain illusions about a world career.

I saw beautiful things, disturbing and terrible. The wonderful Parisian women made a great impression on me—both those of proper society and cocottes, their free manner, the tempo of life. I don't want to write more at the moment, while I don't know where you are and how things are going for you. Were you in Krynica? How do you feel? How is Stefan doing? I am waiting for some news from you and for now I send heartfelt good wishes

Bruno

August 29, 1938

Dear Roma!

It really seemed to me that you had forgotten about me. Somehow it's happened that my really numerous and teeming swarm of friends has thinned out considerably, connections have weakened, and once again I am headed as it were toward parts and zones of fate where loneliness reigns. As in the past. Sometimes this fills me with sadness and fear in the face of emptiness, then again it entices me with some confident, long-familiar temptation.

What happened to make you write again? Somehow I'm afraid to travel to Warsaw. I'm afraid of relationships and people. Most willingly I would retreat with some one person into complete quiet and like Proust undertake the final formulation of my world. For some time I was bolstered by the thought that I would take my retirement next year (at 40% salary). Now I have moved away from that idea because I would be unable to support my family.

I am having trouble choosing where I will spend my leave time. I have very limited means—(I still have nothing, I just borrow). I would like quiet and solitude, but not total. One or 2 people comfortable to be with.

What do you plan to do with your vacation?

Gombrowicz asked me to explain to you why he did not greet you. [This] happened because of his fatal visual memory which frequently fails him.

Do you know a good neurologist in Warsaw who might treat me for nothing? I am definitely sick—some breakdown, some beginning of melancholy, despair, sadness, feeling of unavoidable defeat, irretrievable loss . . . I must get advice. But I don't believe in doctors.

I am not writing about my plans and work, I can't write. It makes me too nervous and I cannot talk about it calmly.

Don't neglect me this way anymore. Write something sometime!

I send heartfelt good wishes

Bruno Schulz
[June 1939]

TO ANNA PŁOCKIER

ANNA PŁOCKIER (1915–1941), *graduate of the Academy of Fine Arts in Warsaw, a painter, was the last of Bruno Schulz's erotic fascinations. His letters to her, discovered after her death by the poet Marian Jachimowicz, were bequeathed by him to the collections of the Museum of Literature in Warsaw. She died with her fiancé, Marek Zwillich, a young painter, killed in the second mass pogrom of Borysław Jews carried out by Ukrainian paramilitary formations, under the command of the German occupiers, on November 27, 1941, in the forest outside the health resort Truskawiec near Drohobycz.*

Dear Ania!

I am continually under the spell of your charming metamorphoses. I think that they are so moving because they are so independent of your will, so automatic and unconscious. It is as if someone surreptitiously moved another person forward, replaced you, and you, as it were, accepted this new person and took her for yourself, and played your part further on a new instrument, unaware that someone else is now acting onstage. Of course, I am exaggerating the matter and stretching it to the point of paradox. Please don't take me for someone naive. I know that this is not entirely unwitting, but you don't realize how much of this is the work of more profound powers, how much is some metaphysical puppetry. At the same time, you are unusually reactive, conforming immedi-

ately to a complimentary shape, in wonderful accompaniment. . . .
All this goes on as if beyond intellect, along some shorter and more
direct road than that of thought, simply like a physical reflex. It's
the first time that I have encountered such richness of nature not
confined, you might say, within the range of a single person and
therefore activating auxilliary personalities, improvising pseudopersonalities initiated ad hoc for the duration of the brief role which
you must play. This is how I explain your protean nature to myself.
You may think that I've allowed myself to be taken in, that I am suggesting deep interpretations in the guise of an ordinary flirtation. I
assure you that coquetry is something very profound and mysterious,
and incomprehensible even for you yourself. Of course, you cannot
see this mysteriousness; on your side it must appear unproblematic
and ordinary. But that is a delusion. You do not appreciate your own
powers and ruin the excellent demonism of your nature through a
naive snobbery of saintliness. It's not enough for you to be a demon,
you want to still be additionally a saint on the side, as if this were
possible to reconcile so easily. You who are so sensitive to artistic
kitsch lose your instinct and taste when it concerns the moral sphere
and with a clear conscience you cultivate the serene and unconscious
dilettantism of holiness. No, your holiness is a difficult and bloody
thing, not allowing itself to be attained as a beautiful addition to a
full and rich life. This dilettantism is anyway very charming and
moving in a being who in a step communes with the Precipice. With
the Precipice spelled with a capital "P." I don't know how it happens,
but you are playing with the keys to the Precipice. I don't know if
you know every person's abyss of perdition, or only mine. In any
case, you are moving lightly and madly along that edge which I
avoid in myself with fear and trembling, and where the gravel gives
way beneath one's feet. I have to admit that you yourself are probably safe. Lightly and delicately you are loosening yourself from one
who is receding into the distance and you allow him to slide alone
into the abyss. Even a few steps more you feign that the ground gives
way beneath your feet, certain that at a given moment the parachute
will open and lift you to safety. With all this, you are truly innocent,
somehow without participation in what you do, you are truly the
victim and all the guilt falls upon the one who carries the precipice

within himself, the edge of which you have approached imprudently. I know that all the fault is on my side, for the precipice is mine, and you are only a sylph who has gotten lost in my garden, where my duty is to prevent your foot from slipping. That is why you should have no misgivings. You are always innocent, whatever you do, and here again a new perspective opens on holiness. Your holiness in fact costs you nothing, because you are a sylph and this is not dilettantism, but the unearthly elfic virtuosity of a being who is not subject to moral categories.

Please come, safe and unthreatened as always, and do not spare me anything. I approve you in any case in all metamorphoses. If you are Circe, then I am Ulysses and I know the herb whose charm will render you powerless. But maybe I am only boasting, maybe I am being provocative.

I wait daily until 6 p.m. I have a suggestion for Sunday:[1] let's meet in Truskawiec. I have a morning train there and an evening return, we could spend the whole day at Truskawiec.

Do you agree?

I send you heartfelt good wishes and thank you very much for your coming

Bruno Schulz
[June 19, 1941]

Dear Ania!

I don't know how to justify the delay that I allowed to mount between your letter and my reply. It seems to me that I didn't feel strong enough to unravel the knot of misunderstanding, in which—it seemed to me—you'd gotten tangled, and I wanted to put off the task. It appears to me that realism, as exclusively the inclination to copy reality—is a fiction. It was never that way. Realism became a phantom and a bogy of nonrealists, a veritable devil of the Middle Ages painted on all the walls in glaring colors. For the term "realism," I would propose a purely negative term: it is a method which attempts to fit its devices within the framework of certain conventions; it resolves not to break a convention that we call reality or common sense, or verisimilitude. Within the framework of such limitations a very broad scale of devices remains to it; Mann proves just how broad by exhausting all spheres and hells without violating realistic convention. Mann or Dostoevsky (you should read *The Double* or [*The Brothers*] *Karamazov*) prove how little depends on overstepping or observing the bounds of realism, that it is a matter simply of gesture, pose, style. If by realism we want to understand a certain pedestrian quality, the ordinariness of the reality described, then these authors are a stunning contradiction to this definition. On the other hand, by breaking the realistic convention the battle is still not won. The very fracturing of realism is no service—everything depends on what was accomplished by doing so. Conscious and purposeful violation of realism opened up certain new possibilities, but one shouldn't be deluded that the possession of this trick frees us from the obligation of providing a richness of content, of portraying one's own world. No method, even the most brilliant one, replaces the effort of extracting one's own content. I fear namely that you are headed along the road of opposition, of negation, that instead of doing something yourself, you observe what that enemy-devil did not do, and that tracking the sins and errors of realism doesn't open you up to your own positive production. You know well that I value your work and I believe in your powers and this is precisely why I fear that you substitute a criticism of realism for your own creativity and your own work. Nonrealistic methods have earned their own citizenship rights already, they do not need to struggle for their existence, for their credit. They have only to achieve in their own way what realism has performed in its. This will be their best justification. I liked the attempts which you have read to me very much. I would like you to take courage, the spirit to embrace broader themes, to elaborate the greatest part of your inner world with this method. In the area of creative art, just being in the right is not redemptive. I fear that having achieved a correct and true insight in the matter gives you such a dose of satisfaction that the need to produce evaporates.

About the analysis of Mann, you may be partially right. Perhaps Mann does not portray that condensation of impression, but he redeems it many times over by the breadth and richness of his world.

I wouldn't want to depress you for anything in the world, but I cannot leave you in what I consider to be error. The very fact that I polemicize with you should prove to you how seriously I take you. I have great respect for your painting talent, combined at the same time with a sense of my own incompetence. In literary issues I arrogate to myself a certain competence which you yourself admit—by turning to me with such questions.

I am very curious about what you have written. When will I be able to read it? When will you come? I send hearty good wishes to you and to Marek. Hearty good wishes for Hilda[2] and Marek S.[3]

Bruno Schulz
November 6, 1941

Dear Ania!

Just today I experienced sharp pangs of conscience at the thought of my letter to you in which I felt like indulging mentoring or moralizing tendencies, instead of enjoying the successes and discovery of a person close and dear to me. I also thought that surely you are about to leave for Warsaw and are taking a tarnished and ruined memory of me with you. From your letter I see that I was right, but at the same time I can see that you are not angry, for which I thank you a hundred times over. Your departure[4] is very sad for me. I didn't know how to make the most of your presence, I didn't take full advantage of you, but your presence alone has been a support to some degree, something possible to hold on to. We really never talked about things that matter most. We popularized to ourselves the results of our experiences not like those initiates of the same secret knowledge, but like the profane. Now I see that more confidence in our closeness was needed, that it was necessary to pursue real issues for us and discuss them heatedly, the way we do in monologues to ourselves. Our distance was artificial and conventional, based only upon terminology and the vocabulary of different schools, but essentially identical with regard to spirit and intent.

I would like our close contact not to cease with your departure, that we might communicate with one another, frequently and in a fundamental way. Maybe even such contact at a distance might become productive for us and bear fruit in a kind of marginal creativity. Intuition tells me that we will still meet soon and the history of our friendship is not ended. Objectively, it's only beginning, whereas until now we kept within the confines of privacy.

Would you consider it something hopeless to take me on in your study as a painting student? Take me through, maybe with the help of Marek,[5] a painting course free of academic formalism? In turn, I would share with you my writing experience.

It seems to me now that I would still have much to tell you, unexhausted reserves of things of lively interest to us both. Now, when, in common parlance, I am losing you. Please write again whether you are ready to respond with equal enthusiasm to my proposal that our contact be continued. Would that it be given to us in peace and without surprises to maintain our conversation that is so important and essential. Maybe you will still write something from here. Otherwise, I await news from there[6] soon. I send heartfelt and warm good wishes

Bruno

November19, 1941

How sad to think that at 30 Mazepa where I experienced so much pleasantness, now there will be no one, that all is now only a legend. I don't know why I have a feeling of fault in relation to myself, as if through my own fault I had lost something.[7]

A Chronology of the Life and Works of Bruno Schulz

1892

On July 12, Bruno Schulz is born in Drohobycz, the youngest son of Jacob Schulz, a merchant from Sądowa Wisznia, owner of a textile materials shop in the building at 12 Market Square, and Hendel-Henrietta Kuhmerker, from a Drohobycz family of minor Jewish factory owners and lumber dealers. Bruno's elder siblings are his brother, Izydor (on his birth certificate, Israel), born in 1881, and a sister, Hania. The name Bruno was taken from the calendar, where it appears on the date of his birth. Today in Ukraine, Drohobycz had formerly been in Galicia, territory joined to the Austro-Hungarian monarchy as a result of the partition of Poland by Russia, Prussia, and Austria in 1772.

1902

The beginning of Bruno Schulz's school education at the Drohobycz Franz Josef Imperial-Royal Gymnasium. Throughout his school years, Schulz was a very good student, excelling particularly in the subjects of Polish language and drawing.

1908

Through his father's efforts and with school approval, a postcard is printed in Drohobycz with a photograph of a sculpture, bearing the information "The Work of Bruno Schulz, Student in the Sixth Class of the Gymnasium in Drohobycz."

1910

Final graduation exam with the mark of Very Good. Certificate of graduation carries the notation "with designation for studies at the university."

As a result of family advice and persuasion, particularly that of his brother Izydor, Schulz gives up his desire to study painting and takes the entrance exam at the Polytechnical College in Lwów, where he begins his studies in the department of architecture. In connection with Jacob Schulz's illness, the shop is sold and the family moves to the home of Bruno's sister, Hania, and her husband, Hoffman, on Bednarska (Floriańska) Street.

1911

After getting credit for his first year at the university, Schulz interrupts his studies in Lwów and returns to Drohobycz, where for six months he is confined to bed with a heart and lung illness. His mother cares for her ailing son and for her husband, who suffers from acute arteriosclerosis. Bruno Schulz convalesces in the nearby health resort Truskawiec.

1913

After a two-year interval, Schulz resumes his architecture studies in Lwów.

1 9 1 4

Schulz successfully passes State Examination I at the Lwów Polytechnical College. His studies are interrupted by the outbreak of World War I. He returns home.

1 9 1 5

During the war, several buildings are burned by the Russian army, including the Schulz house on the market square, Bruno's birthplace and the location of the former shop with its sign reading "Henriette Schulz." On June 23, Bruno Schulz's father, Jacob, dies at the age of sixty-nine.

1 9 1 7

Together with a part of his family, Bruno Schulz travels to Vienna, where he makes a short-lived attempt to continue architecture studies and sees the painting collections at museums there. After several months (?) he returns to Drohobycz. Despite mobilization, he is not drafted into the Austrian army; he is considered unfit for army service.

1 9 1 8

Schulz joins the group Kalleia ("Beautiful Things"), made up of young art lovers, representatives of the Jewish intelligentsia of Drohobycz. The cofounders of the group included, among others, Maria Budratzka (Tempele), later an Austrian opera singer; Emanuel Pilpel, a law student, music lover, and connoisseur of literature and art; Michał Chajes, later a lawyer with broad humanistic interests; Stanisław Weingarten, a close friend of Schulz's, and a collector of his artwork; and Otokar Jawrower, a musician and founder of a chamber group he directed, later a translator of Polish literature into Spanish. Bruno Schulz begins a period of intensive and wide-ranging self-education involving many readings in Polish and German, primarily from the large library of Mundek (Emanuel) Pilpel and the bookstore run by his father. This is also a period of concentrated improvement in drawing and painting that Schulz had long desired to accomplish.

Schulz does his first portraits of friends and self-portraits, as well as fantastic compositions.

1920

Schulz begins work on the cycle of graphics (using *cliché verre* technique) entitled *Xięga bałwochwalcza* (*The Booke of Idolatry*), which he worked on for over two years. Twenty or more graphics were finally produced, which Schulz later placed in portfolios bound in linen that he specially prepared himself or ordered at a bookbinder's.

He gave the portfolios title pages decorated with a drawing. Individual portfolios contained some fifteen to twenty graphic works glued onto cardboard, signed by the author, and provided with titles by him. In addition to the portfolios which Schulz gave to friends and acquaintances and those set aside to be sold, graphics from the cycle were displayed individually, but the income from the sale of both the portfolios and single graphics was small and sporadic.

1921

Because of lack of income and the difficult family situation, Schulz decides to seek a permanent position as a drawing teacher in schools. He submits an application to the school from which he had graduated eleven years earlier, now called the King Władysław Jagiełło State Gymnasium. He is hired for a provisional period, but does not begin work because of bad health—and because of his fears of being unable to cope with his new obligations and the vain hope that he might be able to earn a living through art.

1922

In March the group exhibit of Warsaw's Society to Promote Fine Arts includes Schulz's graphic works.

In June, Schulz participates in a group exhibit in Lwów, at the Society of Friends of Fine Arts. In August, Schulz spends a month taking the cure at the then German health resort Kudowa (today in Poland). He meets Arnold Spaet, a Germanist and translator of German poetry into Polish.

1923

Schulz travels to Warsaw. Through the efforts and intervention of an acquaintance made the previous year at Kudowa, a Mrs. Kejlin and her daughter from a family of Warsaw merchants, Schulz does a series of oil portraits: the adolescent Irena Kejlin, her parents, and several of their friends to whom Schulz had been recommended as a portrait painter. This brings him some income, but presumed further requests are not taken on due to Schulz's immediate return to Drohobycz. In Wilno (Vilna) an "Exhibition of Jewish Artists" contains several works by Schulz.

1924

On September 3, Schulz begins work as a contract teacher of drawing at the Władysław Jagiełło State Gymnasium in Drohobycz, teaching drawing for thirty-six hours a week.

1925

Schulz meets Stanisław Ignacy Witkiewicz. While visiting Emanuel Pilpel in Drohobycz, Witkiewicz produced a pastel portrait of Pilpel, a fantastic composition of a head placed on a fish tail.

1926

From March 16 to April 30, Schulz is on leave in order to take an exam allowing him to teach drawing at the gymnasium. On April 27, Schulz takes the exam before a commission at the Academy of Fine Arts in Cracow. He passes with a mark of Very Good. In July, Schulz spends part of the vacation at the pension Piast, in Zakopane, producing oil portraits of unknown guests.

1927

Władysław Riff, a talented beginning writer whose imagination and artistic program seem to have been similar to those of Schulz, dies in Zakopane at the age of twenty-six. Their letters had prompted Schulz's first writing plans and accomplishments. Riff's never-published manuscripts and his substantial correspondence, including numerous letters in which Schulz's kindred creative personality took shape and was expressed, were burned by sanitation workers carrying out disinfection. The death of his friend, his partner in vital, creatively fruitful dialogues, was a great blow to Schulz. Only several years later would Schulz find in the person of Debora Vogel a new creative interlocutor for an epistolary exchange of thoughts

1928

In the summer there is an exhibit of Schulz's drawings, graphics, and oil paintings at the Dom Zdrojowy (Health Resort Club) in Truskawiec. A distinguished senator associated with the Christian Democracy party, Maximilian Thulie, who is vacationing there, proclaims Schulz's work "pornography" and demands immediate closure of the exhibit. The mayor of Drohobycz and owner of Truskawiec, Rajmund Jarosz, responds with a firm and effective refusal.

On August 31, Schulz is released from teaching "because in the course of four years he has not obtained professional qualifications." On October 20, Schulz takes the examination for secondary school teachers at the Commission of the Ministry of Public Education in Warsaw and passes with a mark of Very Good. He is rehired as a contract teacher for the period from November 5 to December 31.

1929

On January 1, Schulz is named a permanent teacher. In addition to teaching drawing, he is now obliged to teach handicrafts.

1930

On January 9, Schulz applies to the Lwów Regional Ministry of Schools for a two-month period of leave "in order to save his threatened health" (according to the doctor's statement, "neurosis of the heart and dyspepsia of the stomach"). The request is denied.

In May, at the Spring Salon in Lwów, one exhibition room presents Schulz's work. In Cracow at the Jewish Society for the Promotion of Fine Arts Schulz takes part in a group exhibit.

During summer vacation in Zakopane, Schulz meets Debora

Vogel, Jewish-Polish poet, writer, and art historian. Their friendship soon becomes a vital exchange of thoughts, and an extensive correspondence begins. Schulz writes Debora letters which contain the first outlines and parts of *Cinnamon Shops*.

1931

A "Showing of Work" by three artists at the Society of the Friends of Fine Arts in Cracow includes Bruno Schulz.

On April 23, Bruno's mother, Hendel-Henrietta, dies. Schulz designs a stone grave marker for both his parents. Years later it is destroyed together with the entire Jewish cemetery in Drohobycz.

1932

On March 8, Schulz receives a " decree of appointment" ensuring him work as a tenured teacher at the gymnasium.

At Stryj, on April 9 and December 3, Schulz takes part in conferences for teachers of handicrafts; he presents a paper there entitled "Artistic Formation in Cardboard and Its Application in School."

In July, Schulz participates in a ministry summer course for teachers in Żywiec. There he meets one of the lecturers, Stefan Szuman, a distinguished psychologist and professor at Jagiellonian University in Cracow. Schulz gives him the manuscript of *Cinnamon Shops*, which Szuman rates very highly, promising to use his influence with a publisher, but nothing comes of his efforts.

1933

In spring, Schulz meets Józefina Szelińska, a teacher of Polish at the local girls' school, and his future fiancée.

On Easter Sunday, Schulz travels to Warsaw with the manuscript of *Cinnamon Shops*. Through the good offices of Magdalena Gross, a sculptor, Schulz is able to persuade writer Zofia Nałkowska to read his manuscript. That evening she telephones with an enthusiastic evaluation that paves the way for its publication.

On April 8, Schulz takes part in a teachers' conference in Stryj.

On June 11, Schulz takes part in the opening of an exhibit of handicrafts and "women's work" in the Center for Methods of the VIII Gymnasium in Lwów.

Schulz's work at the Gymnasium is supplemented by additional employment of ten hours weekly in the Adam Mickiewicz public school in Drohobycz.

In June, Schulz spends several days visiting Zofia Nałkowska in Warsaw. Their correspondence, begun somewhat earlier, becomes extensive.

In August, Schulz spends two days with Zofia Nałkowska in Warsaw and at Na Górkach ("At the Hills"), Nałkowska's family home outside Warsaw, also called Dom nad Łąkami ("House Overlooking the Meadows").

In December, Schulz's literary debut: the story "Birds" appears in no. 52 of the Warsaw journal *Wiadomości Literackie* (Literary News).

Rój publishers in Warsaw prints (with the date of 1934) Schulz's first book, *Cinnamon Shops*.

1934

From January1 to 15, Schulz stays in Zakopane, where he meets Zofia Nałkowska. They begin a romance that lasts about four months.

ABC Literacko Artystyczne (Literary Artistic ABC), no. 1, prints Zofia Nałkowska's response to a questionnaire, *"Jaką najciekawszą książkę przeczytałam w 1933 roku"* ("The most interesting book I read in 1933"). Her response places *Cinnamon Shops* at the top of Polish achievements in prose.

From January to April, Schulz receives letters with the highest and most enthusiastic opinions from outstanding Polish writers and poets—Stanisław Ignacy Witkiewicz, Wacław Berent, Bolesław Leśmian, Zenon Przesmycki, Leopold Staff, Julian Tuwim, Józef Wittlin, and others.

In March, *Wiadomości Literackie* (Literary News), no. 6, publishes Leon Piwiński's review, one of the most perceptive analyses and most accurate evaluations of Schulz's *Cinnamon Shops*.

In March, after reading *Cinnamon Shops*, Zenon Waśniewski, a colleague of twenty years earlier from the Lwów Polytechnical College, writes to Schulz renewing their former acquaintance.

Waśniewski is now a painter and teacher of drawing, as well as coeditor of the literary monthly *Kamena* (Song).

In April, Tadeusz Breza publishes an enthusiastic review of *Cinnamon Shops* entitled "Sobowtór zwykłej rzeczywistości" (The Double of Ordinary Reality), in *Kurier Poranny* (Morning Courier), no. 103.

Schulz spends a week with Zofia Nałkowska in Warsaw. She invites several of Schulz's fans from literary circles to meet him: Błeszyński, Brucz, Wat, Czapski, Rudnicki, Boguszewska, and Kornacki. Schulz also becomes acquainted with Julian Tuwim and meets with Adam Ważyk and Pola Gojawiczyńska.

On May 9, Schulz submits a request to the Ministry of Public Education for a one-year leave of absence to continue his literary work. His request is denied as a result of a recent ruling by the Council of Ministers that discontinues paid leave time.

In response to his request for a month's leave, Schulz obtains a two-week health leave, from August 30 to September 15 (inflammation of the bladder, renal pelvis [pielitis], and prostate).

In December, during the holiday vacation, Schulz spends time with Józefina Szelińska, renews his longtime friendship with Stanisław Ignacy Witkiewicz, and meets several outstanding writers who admire his work, including Witold Gombrowicz and Józef Wittlin.

In the course of 1934, Schulz publishes several stories in journals: "Druga jesień" ("A Second Fall") in *Kamena*, no. 3; "Noc lipcowa" ("A Night in July") in *Signały* (Signals), no. 12; "Genialna epoka" ("Age of Genius") in *Wiadomości Literackie* (Literary News), no. 13.

1935

On January 20 in Lwów, Bruno's older brother, Izydor, dies suddenly of a heart attack. Izydor had been an engineer and codirector of a Polish oil company for many years, and his death leaves Schulz without permanent financial help and necessitates his supporting his sick sister and her son with his own meager income.

Schulz and Józefina Szelińska become engaged.

Schulz helps Józefina Szelińska with her translation of Franz Kafka's *The Trial*.

From March to May, Schulz submits successive requests to the superintendent of the school region in Lwów for a year's paid leave from September 1, 1935, to August 31, 1936.

A group exhibit takes place in the gallery of the Union of Artists in Lwów, in which Schulz's work appears along with that of three other graphic artists and painters.

The literary weekly *Pion* (Probe), no. 34, publishes Stanisław Ignacy Witkiewicz's lengthy essay "Twórczość literacka Brunona Schulza" (The Literary Art of Bruno Schulz). *Tygodnik Illustrowany* (Illustrated Weekly), number 17, publishes his article entitled "Wywiad z Brunonem Schulzem" (An Interview with Bruno Schulz) about Schulz as a graphic artist.

In July and August, Schulz spends vacation with his fiancée in Zakopane. Meetings and conversations with Witkiewicz; Schulz makes the acquaintance of a pianist, Maria Chasin (or Chazen), who visits Schulz several times later in Łódź.

Adolf Nowaczyński, Antoni Słonimski, and Julian Tuwim nominate *Cinnamon Shops* for the annual *Wiadomości Literackie* award; the award goes to another author, however.

In the course of 1935, Schulz publishes the following stories and articles in journals:

"Księga" ("The Book"), *Skamander*, no. 58.

"Dodo," with Schulz's own illustrations, *Tygodnik Illustrowany* (Illustrated Weekly), no. 2.

"Father Joins the Fire Brigade," *Wiadomości Literackie* (Literary News), no. 5.

"Wiosna" ("Spring"), excerpt, *Kamena*, no. 10.

"Sanatorium pod klepsydrą" ("Sanatorium Under the Sign of the Hourglass"), with Schulz's own illustrations, *Wiadomości Literackie*, no. 16.

"Do Stanisława Ignacego Witkiewicza—odpowiedź na zadane pytania—o własnej twórczości" (To Stanisław Ignacy Witkiewicz—a response to a question about my own creative work), *Tygodnik Illustrowany* (Illustrated Weekly), no. 17.

"Powstają legendy" (The Formation of Legends), *Tygodnik Illustrowany* (Illustrated Weekly), no. 22.

"Edzio" ("Eddie"), with Schulz's illustrations, *Tygodnik Illustrowany* (Illustrated Weekly), no. 40.

"Emeryt" ("The Old Age Pensioner"), *Wiadomości Literackie* (Literary News), nos. 51–52.

1936

At the beginning of the year, Schulz writes to the parents of his fiancée, Józefina Szelińska, in Janów (near Lwów) informing them of his intent to marry their daughter; the news is received favorably.

Schulz receives a six-month paid leave from January 1 to June 6. He spends the time primarily in Warsaw, in constant contact with his fiancée and with Polish literary figures, including Zofia Nałkowska and Tadeusz Breza.

In January in Warsaw, Schulz meets Romana Halpern, a journalist, a lover of literature and art with connections to Warsaw literary circles, and a friend of Witkiewicz's. The acquaintance soon becomes a friendship, and they maintain a constant correspondence until the outbreak of war.

On February 8, in order to remove formal obstacles to marriage with a Catholic, Schulz withdraws from the Jewish Religious Community in Drohobycz and receives the status of "without denomination."

Schulz makes plans and efforts to register as a resident in Silesia (never acted upon), where the law allows a civil marriage between a Catholic and a person with no religious affiliation.

On April 4, by a decree of the Ministry of Schools, Schulz receives the title of professor.

Rój publishes Kafka's *The Trial* in book form, translated by Józefina Szelińska with Schulz's help, but under Schulz's name as translator.

During his leave time, Schulz prepares his second book, *Sanatorium Under the Sign of the Hourglass*, for print, and he submits the manuscript and illustrations to the publisher. The book is composed primarily of stories written years earlier.

Schulz writes or completes a lengthy story entitled "Wiosna" ("Spring"), which he adds to *Sanatorium Under the Sign of the Hourglass*, as well as "Jesień" ("Autumn"; published in *Sygnały*, no. 17) and "Republika marzeń" ("Republic of Dreams," published in *Tygodnik Ilustrowany*, no. 29).

On July 2, Schulz submits a request to the Ministry of Public

Education for a transfer to Warsaw. His request is denied because of the lack of open teaching positions in the Warsaw schools.

From August 26 to 29, Schulz goes by ship from Gdynia to Stockholm.

In November, Schulz has contact through letters with the Jewish-German writer Mendel Neugröschl, who is interested in *Cinnamon Shops*. Schulz sends him a copy of the book, suggesting that it be translated into German.

On November 30, Schulz submits an application to the superintendent of the Lwów school region with a request to transfer to a school in Lwów. The transfer never comes about, probably because Schulz's plans for marriage begin to falter and soon are abandoned. His desire to move to another city, to Warsaw or to Lwów, had been connected with them.

For the school year 1936–37, Schulz adds eighteen hours weekly in the Elżbieta Orzeszkowa public school in Drohobycz to his teaching duties.

The *Wiadomości Literackie* (Literary News) editorial board proposes to Schulz permanent cooperation as a regular reviewer of new books translated from foreign languages into Polish.

During this year, *Wiadomości Literackie* publishes two texts by Schulz in this series: in no. 15 "Dzwony w Bazylei" (Cloches de Bâle; Bells of Basel), a discussion of a novel by Louis Aragon, and in no. 50, "Matka i syn" (Mother and Son), on the novel *Genitrix: Mother and Son* by François Mauriac.

In addition to the three new stories ("Spring," "Autumn," and "Republic of Dreams"), Schulz publishes in journals works written earlier which become parts of the volume *Sanatorium Under the Sign of the Hourglass*:

"O sobie" ("About Myself"), entitled "Samotność" ("Loneliness") in the *Sanatorium* volume), in *Studio*, no. 2.

"Ostatnia ucieczka ojca" ("Father's Last Escape"), in *Wiadomości Literackie*, no. 32.

"Martwy sezon" ("Dead Season"), in *Wiadomości Literackie*, nos. 53–54.

In addition, the following literary reviews and essays were published: "Nowa książka Kuncewiczowej" (Kuncewiczowa's New Book), about the novel *Cudzoziemka* (*The Stranger*), *Tygodnik Ilustrowany*, no. 3.

"Wędrowki sceptyka" (Wanderings of a Skeptic), on Aldous Huxley's *Night Music*, *Tygodnik Ilustrowany*, no. 6.

"Aneksja podświadomości—Uwagi o *Cudzoziemce* Marii Kuncewiczowej (An Annex of the Unconscious—Comments on Maria Kuncewiczowa's *Cudzoziemka*), *Pion*, no. 17.

"Mityzacja rzeczwistości" ("The Mythologizing of Reality"), *Studio*, nos. 3–4.

"Nowy poeta," on a collection of poems by Juliusz Wit, entitled *Lampy* (Lamps); *Sygnały*, no. 23.

Wolność tragiczna (Tragic Freedom), a collection of poems by Kazimierz Wierzyński, *Tygodnik Ilustrowany*, no. 27.

"Do Witolda Gombrowicza—odpowiedź na 'List otwarty do Brunona Schulza' W. Gombrowicza" (To Witold Gombrowicz—response to "An Open Letter to Bruno Schulz" by Witold Gombrowicz), *Studio*, no. 7

"Pod Belwederem" (Beneath the Belvedere Palace), on a novel by Juliusz Kaden-Bandrowski, *Tygodnik Ilustrowany*, no. 30.

1937

In January, Schulz's engagement to Józefina Szelińska is broken off.

In July, Schulz spends four weeks in the country, in the village of Boberek, in almost total isolation.

Work on the proofs of *Sanatorium Under the Sign of the Hourglass*, dedicated to Józefina Szelińska.

In August, a visit of several days with Romana Halpern in Warsaw.

As part of an effort to publish *Cinnamon Shops* in Italy, George Pinette, cousin of the pianist Maria Chasin, asks Schulz to write a short text containing information about the book for a foreign publisher. Schulz writes the text in German and sends it to Italy.

School authorities in Drohobycz add five hours weekly (in the Queen Jadwiga and Orzeszkowa public girls' schools) to Schulz's teaching duties for the academic year 1937–38.

In October, George Pinette's efforts to find a foreign publisher for *Cinnamon Shops* end in failure. The Italian publishers which he contacted (Bompiani, Hoepli, and Mondadori) showed no interest in the project.

Schulz finishes writing the novella entitled "Die Heimkehr" (The Return Home), about thirty pages in typescript, thematically similar to the story "Sanatorium Under the Sign of the Hourglass." He writes it in German so that it might have a wider audience. The work was not published and was lost.

In November, Schulz reads Witold Gombrowicz's novel *Ferdydurke*. The Rój publishing house in Warsaw prints the book edition of *Sanatorium Under the Sign of the Hourglass*.

In the course of the year, Schulz's book reviews continue to appear, primarily in *Wiadomości Literackie*:

"Three translated novels: Johan Bojer, *Tułaczka* (The Wanderer), Jo van Ammers-Kuller, *Książe Incognito* (Prince Incognito), Eric Ebermayer, *Sprawa Clasena* (The Clasen Affair), *Wiadomości Literackie*, no. 2.

"A Book About Love," *Adam Grywald* by Tadeusz Breza, *Tygodnik Ilustrowany*, nos. 3–4.

"Otawa Giona," Jean Giono's *Otawa*, *Wiadomości Literackie*, no. 5.

"A novel about a country priest," Georges Bernanos's *Diary of a Country Priest*, *Wiadomości Literackie*, no. 18.

"Czarne anioły Mauriac'a (François Mauriac's *Black Angels*), *Wiadomości Literackie*, no. 19.

Leonard Frank, "Towarzysze snów" (Comrades of Dreams), *Wiadomości Literackie*, no. 22.

"U wspólnej mety" (At a Common Goal), *Cudzoziemka* (The Stranger) by Maria Kuncewiczowa and *Serce mojej matki* (My Mother's Heart) by Karin Michaelis, *Pion*, no. 35.

Irena Niemirowska, *Kariera* (Career), *Wiadomości Literackie*, no. 38.

Ange Seidler, "Paryż. Hotel pod Pięknym Słońcem" (Paris. Hotel Under the Beautiful Sun), *Wiadomości Literackie*, no. 38.

Ivo Andric, "Nowele" (Short Stories), *Wiadomości Literackie*, no. 38.

1 9 3 8

In January, Schulz lectures on Witold Gombrowicz's *Ferdydurke* at the Warsaw Writers' Union.

In February, Artur Sandauer's article "Szkoła mitologów" (School of Mythologizers), on the work of Schulz and Gombrowicz, appears in *Pion*, no. 5.

Natan Spiegel, a Jewish painter and a member of the Łódź artistic group Start, urges Schulz to make a trip to Paris and arrange an exhibit of his drawings there.

In March, Schulz's depression grows over the developing situation in Germany, the Anschluss with Austria, Hitler's takeover of Czechoslovakia, and increasing signs of anti-Semitism.

In April, through an acquaintance traveling to Switzerland, Schulz sends Thomas Mann his German novella, "Die Heimkehr," in a bound typescript with illustrations and encloses a letter to the German writer. (Neither the novel nor the letter was found among Mann's papers and effects after his death.)

Schulz makes a week-long trip to Lwów, meeting with Debora Vogel, the painter Jerzy Janisch, and the writer Marian Promiński.

In May and June, Schulz plans his trip to Paris. Warsaw friends and acquaintances assist Schulz with pre-departure formalities, efforts to obtain foreign currency, and a passport at a reduced price.

On August 2, Schulz leaves for Paris. Maria Chasin has provided him with addresses in Paris and introductions to various persons in France. He takes about one hundred drawings in the hope that he will make artistic contacts in Paris and arrange an exhibit. Schulz chooses the longer and more costly route through Italy in order to avoid traveling through Hitler's Third Reich. Paris turns out to be empty during the summer vacation period; most people with whom Schulz wanted to meet are out of town (for example, Jules Romains). He finds temporary support in Georges Rosenberg, the brother of Maria Chasin, and in Ludwik Lille, a painter he knows. An art dealer, André J. Rotgé, proposes an exhibit from October 1 to 15 in a Paris gallery in the Faubourg St. Honoré, but Schulz withdraws as a result of the cost (sixteen hundred francs), which is beyond his limited budget. Schulz does manage to visit museums and meet with the sculptor Naum Aronson, who admires his drawings. The cultural attaché of the Polish embassy in Paris, the poet Jan Lechoń (a devotee of Schulz's writing), was not in Paris, and Schulz did not receive any help from the embassy.

On August 26, Schulz returns to Drohobycz.

In November, Schulz receives the Golden Laurel of the Polish Academy of Literature.

Schulz's journal publications for the year are:

"Kometa" ("The Comet"), a story, *Wiadomości Literackie* (Literary News), no. 35.

"Egga van Haardt," a column the text of which in an effort at self-promotion E. Haardt half-falsified with clumsy additions and reworkings, *Tygodnik Ilustrowany*, no. 40.

"*Ferdydurke*," an extensive analysis of Witold Gombrowicz's novel, *Skamander*, nos. 96–98.

"Ojczyzna" ("Fatherland") a fragment of literary prose, *Sygnały*, no. 59.

1939

Schulz suffers depressions of varying intensity and frequency because of personal difficulties, failures, disappointments, stultifying work in school, and the mounting threat of the political situation. At the outset of 1939, his depression begins to acquire almost incapacitating dimensions.

In March, in France, A. Grunbaum translates the story "August" from *Cinnamon Shops*. She sends her translation to Schulz, asking for approval and corrections if necessary. Joseph Roth, an émigré Austrian writer living in Paris, ultimately rejects her translation and entrusts a new translation of the entire volume *Cinnamon Shops* to Szaul Fryszman. Having received permission to move to Palestine, however, Fryszman abandons the translation project and emigrates from France. A fragment translated into French, but never published, is found in his papers.

In April, the poet Emil Zegadłowicz visits Schulz in Drohobycz.

Schulz meets with Nałkowska in Truskawiec, where in the park he reads to her from a manuscript of his new essay on literary criticism. According to Nałkowska, it was "full of relevance, and in addition, every intellectual refinement." (The text of the essay was lost.)

Before the outbreak of the Second World War, Schulz managed to place in *Skamander* (nos. 108–10) the last publication of his life:

"Zofia Nałkowska na tle swej nowej powieści" (Zofia Nałkowska in the context of her new novel).

In June, responding to a *Wiadomości Literackie* (Literary News) questionnaire on the topic "W pracowniach pisarzy i uczonych polskich" (In the studios of Polish writers and intellectuals), Schulz writes that he has a book composed of four larger stories nearing completion. (These works are lost.)

On September 1, Germany invades Poland: the outbreak of World War II. In accordance with the Molotov-Ribbentrop pact between the Third Reich and the Soviet Union, the territory of a defeated Poland is to be divided between the two allies.

September 11, German divisions enter Drohobycz and immediately carry out the first killings and atrocities against the local Jewish population.

On September 17, the army of the Soviet Union enters Polish territory.

On September 24, the German army withdraws from Drohobycz and its vicinity, giving way to Red Army units in accordance with the cooperatively devised "demarcation line." Drohobycz, now in the territory occupied by the USSR, is annexed administratively to the Ukrainian Soviet Republic. During this time of Stalinist terror and the mass deportations of hundreds of thousands of people to camps, Schulz has no future as a writer and artist—only a greater chance of surviving than do the inhabitants of the territory occupied by the Germans. He continues to teach in a Soviet school.

1940

At the request of the new authorities, Schulz participates on the local electoral commission during elections for Soviet political authorities.

In July, Schulz begins an acquaintance, friendship, and correspondence with Anna Płockier, a young painter. Anna had fled from Warsaw to Borysław together with her fiancé, Marek Zwillich.

Representatives of the town administration and political authorities engage Schulz off and on to produce painting and drawing work for various occasions, as well as propaganda for the local press and for official Soviet celebrations.

In September, at the order of government authorities, Schulz produces a large oil picture on the subject of "the liberation of the people of Western Ukraine." Schulz is arrested and interrogated by NKVD on the charge of "Ukrainian nationalism," since he used prominently in the painting the national colors of Ukraine, which were absolutely forbidden at the time.

There is an exhibit by the Union of Artists in Lwów which includes several drawings by Schulz, listed in the catalog as "illustrations."

Schulz sends his German novella, "Die Heimkehr," to Inoizdat Foreign Literature Publishers in Moscow. The work was never published and is lost.

Schulz corresponds with an acquaintance, artist and glass painter Tadeusz Wojciechowski, a lecturer in a new school of craft arts in Lwów. Schulz requests help in seeking work teaching drawing and art history in the school, but then drops the idea.

In September and October, Schulz stays in the hospital to have kidney stones removed and then recuperates in Truskawiec.

In November, *Nowe Widnokręgi* (New Horizons), a Polish-language journal published in Lwów, invites Schulz to submit work. Despite reservations that his writing will not meet the demands of "socrealism," he sends one story, a novella having to do with a deformed shoemaker's son, or, according to another report, about a "master of the kaleidoscope." The editorial board returns Schulz's story as not appropriate for print. When queried, a member of the editorial board explains, "We don't need Prousts." Schulz continues to teach drawing and handicrafts in the secondary school ("ten-year" school), located in the building of the former Jagiełło gymnasium.

On June 22, Germany attacks the Soviet Union.

On July 1, the German army takes over Drohobycz. Schools are closed and Schulz is without income. Persecutions, particularly of Jews, begin.

At the end of July, the Nazi occupation sets up the *Arbeitsamt*, which is to apprehend every Jew between the ages of sixteen and sixty-five for forced labor. All Jews aged six years and older must wear an armband on the left arm with the Star of David. Jews are forbidden to use the sidewalk and are obliged to bow before every uniformed German; Jews are not allowed to ride on trains, in automobiles, or in horse-drawn carriages, or to open shops. The first orders are issued forbidding Jews to live on main streets. Jews are paid with a quarter of a loaf of whole-wheat bread for their forced labor (stone breaking, bridge building, working in the forest, street cleaning). The sick are forbidden to use "Aryan" hospitals. There are mass killings of local Jews, executions in groups of one hundred outside Drohobycz, and transports to the death camp at Bełżec. German authorities organize systematic plunder of Jewish possessions.

In the winter, the Germans shoot all the Jewish orphans with their guardians and tutors. The Gestapo officers residing in Drohobycz include a cabinetmaker from Vienna, one Felix Landau, a participant in the assassination of Austrian chancellor Engelbert Dollfuss. An "expert on Jewish affairs," Landau was one of the most zealous murderers of Drohobycz's Jews. He became interested in Schulz's painting talents and demanded various works from him, paying him in bread or soup. Landau styled himself Schulz's "protector" for whom his "charge" performed tasks on demand. At Landau's orders, Schulz decorated the room of Landau's son with wall paintings of fairy-tale scenes. Schulz also painted "frescoes" in the so-called Reitschule and large, multicolored compositions on the walls of the Gestapo casino. Schulz deliberately prolonged this work in order to increase his chances of survival.

On November 27, a great massacre of the Jews of Borysław and surroundings is carried out by Ukrainian fascist paramilitary organizations under Gestapo command. Among the hundreds of those killed are Anna Płockier and her fiancé, Marek Zwillich, who were preparing to flee to Warsaw. At about the same time, together with all the Jews of Drohobycz, Bruno Schulz is forced to leave his home and move to the ghetto, where he and his family occupy a room in a small one-story house at 18 Stolarska Street.

1942

Schulz decides to preserve his manuscripts and art by turning them over to various trusted persons outside the ghetto for safekeeping. He improvises packets out of cardboard and places in them his literary manuscripts, drawings, and graphics and his substantial correspondence saved over many years. The names of the people he entrusted the packets to are unknown.

Schulz becomes sick and gets some treatment as an outpatient at the Jewish hospital. Hungry, emaciated, physically and emotionally debilitated, Schulz is consumed with the worst premonitions about his own fate. He decides to try to save himself by escape and sends out letters begging for help. His Warsaw friends, mainly writers, have false documents prepared for him (so-called "Aryan papers") and send them to him via underground Polish authorities.

Meanwhile, through the help of the Judenrat, Schulz and several acquaintances are given work in the former Jewish Old Age Home, cataloging more than 100,000 books, confiscated first by the Soviets and then later by the Germans. The work protects Schulz from hard physical labor, which he could not manage, and provides him some temporary relative protection.

On November 19, Schulz decides to flee Drohobycz, furnished with false personal identification and money. Around 11 a.m., shooting breaks out in the ghetto and a so-called "wild action" by the local Gestapo begins: random shooting on the streets at anyone passing by. The Gestapo chase after those fleeing into doorways, kill those hiding in stairways and apartments. About 230 persons are killed on the streets of the ghetto that day, called Black Thursday by survivors. Schulz is heading toward the Judenrat for bread when SS-Scharführer Karl Günther shoots him twice in the head, killing him on the spot. According to Drohobycz residents, Günther killed many people that day, and boasted to his friends that he had killed Schulz—whose "protector" was his personal enemy, Felix Landau.

During the night, a friend of Schulz's, Izydor Friedman, buries Schulz's body in the local Jewish cemetery. The location of the grave is unknown. The cemetery survived the war but was later completely destroyed.

—*Jerzy Ficowski*

Notes

TRANSLATOR'S INTRODUCTION: A LIVING BOOK

1. Jerzy Speina's 1974 *Bankructwo realności: Proza Brunona Schulza* (The Bankruptcy of Reality: The Prose of Bruno Schulz) and in 1979 Czesław Karkowski's *Kultura i krytyka inteligencji w twórczości Brunona Schulza* (Culture and Criticism of the Intelligentsia in the Work of Bruno Schulz).
2. Two essays by Władysław Panas in 1974 and Wyskiel's own study of Schulz entitled *Druga twarz Hioba* (The Second Face of Job, 1980) explored Schulz's writing in relation to Hebrew poetic tradition. Władysław Panas also published *Księga blasku: Traktat o kabala w prozie Brunona Schulza* (The Book of Splendor: A Treatise on Kabbalah in the Prose of Bruno Schulz, 1997).
3. The Polish Round Table talks concluded in April 1989, with an agreement leading to the legalization of Solidarity and the first partially free elections in Eastern Europe. In August 1989, Solidarity adviser Tadeusz Mazowiecki became prime minister of Poland with General Wojciech Jaruzelski as president.

4. *A Reading of Ashes*, translated by Keith Bosley and Krystyna Wandycz, introduction by Zbigniew Herbert (London: Menard Press, 1981).

CHAPTER 1: I FOUND THE AUTHENTIC (IN PLACE OF A PROLOGUE)

1. *Cinnamon Shops* is the original Polish title of Bruno Schulz's first collection of stories, and is the title by which it is known in most translations in other languages. This was also the title of the first translation into English done by Celina Wieniewska (published in Great Britain in 1963 by McGibbon & Kee, Ltd.), but it was subsequently retitled *The Street of Crocodiles*.

2. The "Authentic" is the term used in the original Polish text; it is rendered in the Celina Wienewska translation as the "Original." See Bruno Schulz, *Sanatorium Under the Sign of the Hourglass* (Boston and New York: Houghton Mifflin, 1997), p. 25; reprint from *The Complete Fiction of Bruno Schulz* (New York: Walker & Co., 1989).

3. *Cinnamon Shops* comprises fifteen stories, counting the three parts of the "Treatise on Tailors' Dummies" as individual pieces, but excluding the story "The Comet," which was not part of the original Polish collection and was first printed only in 1938. "The Comet" was included as the last story in the Celina Wieniewska translation of *Cinnamon Shops*.

4. The complete text of this letter to Romana Halpern can be found in the Letters section.

5. The reference here is to the Communist era in Poland. Writing was censored, and some types of writing could not be published at all. Official prescriptions for approved socially progressive art called for writing that would deal with the problems of working classes in a realistic manner—that is, according to "socialist realism." Schulz's writing could not be characterized in this way.

6. Stanisław Ignacy Witkiewicz (called Witkacy), 1885–1939; Polish dramatist, novelist, philosopher, and painter; whom Schulz met in the 1920s. Witkacy created the theory of "pure form" in art. His plays have become a permanent part of the theatrical repetoire. Together with Witold Gombrowicz and Bruno Schulz, Witkacy is one of the major writers of the interwar period.

7. Zenon Waśniewski, 1891–1945, an acquaintance of Bruno Schulz's from their student days in Lwów. A painter and graphic artist, Waśniewski was co-founder of *Kamena* (Song), a literary monthly published in Chełm Lubelski.

8. English version *Letters and Drawings of Bruno Schulz with Selected Prose*, ed. Jerzy Ficowski, trans. Walter Arndt with Victoria Nelson, preface by Adam Zagajewski (New York: Harper & Row, 1988).

CHAPTER 2: BRUNO, SON OF JACOB

1. The term "Małopolska" designated southern and southeastern regions of Poland, including at various times in history Cracow, Sandomierz, and Lublin provinces; it was divided between Russia and Austria in the partitions.
2. In 1846 there was a bloody revolt in which Austrian authorities incited peasantry against Polish landowners who themselves were planning an uprising.
3. Sądowa Wisznia lies north of Drohobycz in the vicinity of Lwów, along the route going east from the town of Przemyśl.
4. This was actually an essay composed as a quasi-letter addressed to Stanisław Ignacy Witkiewicz. The complete text can be found in Walter Arndt's translation in *Letters and Drawings*, pp. 110–14.
5. In the German system this would have been equivalent to about the sixth or seventh grade.
6. Truskawiec, a health resort south of Drohobycz, was famous for its mineral waters. Today it is in western Ukraine, whose major city is L'viv (Lwów under Polish rule).

CHAPTER 3: RETURN TO SCHOOL

1. Wojciech Weiss (1875–1950), professor at the Cracow Academy of Fine Arts, was a painter and graphic artist in the styles of Secessionism and later Postimpressionism. Konstanty Laszczka (1865–1956), professor at the Cracow Academy of Fine Arts, was a sculptor. Teodor Axentowicz (1859–1938) was a painter in the style of Young Poland.
2. Julian Tuwim (1894–1953) was one of the most famous prewar Polish poets and a founder in 1920 of the interwar poetic group Skamander. By 1936 he had published four collections of poetry. His 1936 narrative poem *Bal w operze* (Ball at the Opera, published in 1946) was a scathing satire on the ruling elites before the catastrophe of 1939. He survived World War II in France and in the United States and returned to Poland in 1946. Although he had drawn closer to leftist circles, he remained

silent as a poet in the postwar years, devoting his time to translations. The sole surviving letter of Bruno Schulz to Julian Tuwim is included in the Letters section.

3. Stefan Jaracz, 1883–1945; from 1930 to 1939, Jaracz directed and acted with his own troupe at the Atheneum Theater.

4. In 1930 an unmarried secondary school teacher in the provinces would earn a little over 300 zlotys a month after three years. Schulz would have had ten or eleven zlotys to live on per day. In 1934, five zlotys would buy two kilos of sausage or sugar.

5. Drohobycz was in Soviet-occupied territory from September 24, 1939, until the German attack on the Soviet Union, "Barbarossa," began in June 1941, when the area came under German control.

CHAPTER 4: THE PREHISTORY AND ORIGIN OF *CINNAMON SHOPS*

1. The full text of this letter can be found in the Letters section.

2. Adam Ważyk, 1905–1982; poet, essayist, and translator. His poetry was connected with the Polish interwar avant-garde. He coedited *Almanach Nowej Sztuki* (Almanac of the New Art) and contributed to *Zwrotnica* (The Switch). In the 1920s he published two volumes of poetry: *Semafory* (Semaphores) and *Oczy i usta* (Eyes and Lips), and in 1938 a novel, *Mity rodzinne* (Family Myths). A volume of war poetry was published in two editions in Moscow, in 1943 and 1944. He was in Lwów from 1939 to 1941. After being transported to the Soviet Union, he served as a political officer in the Polish army under General Berling. The recollection connected with Schulz and Riff is from Ważyk's *Kwestia gustu* (A Question of Taste, Warsaw, 1966).

3. Stefania Dretler-Flin, b. 1909, was an artist in graphics (in woodcuts) and also in ceramics.

4. Debora Vogel, 1902–1942, was born in Lwów and was a representative of the Galicia's Polish-German-Jewish enclave. She graduated from the Jewish gymnasium in Lwów, traveled in Europe, and studied philosophy and Polish literature in Cracow. She wrote her doctoral dissertation on the influence of Hegel's aesthetics upon Joseph Kremer, a Yiddish poet. She began to write while at the university and gradually became familiar with Yiddish literature. Her father was an officeholder in the Lwów Jewish congregation, director of an orphanage, and a Hebraist. Her uncle, Dr. Mordechai Ehrenpreis, was chief rabbi in Sweden. While Debora visited him, she published an article on Schulz in Stockholm in

1930. She was part of a circle of Yiddish writers and published two volumes of poetry in Yiddish and *Akacje kwitną* (The Acacias Are Blooming) in both Polish and Yiddish in 1935. In August 1942, she was shot together with her mother, husband, and four-year-old son in a street action in the Lwów ghetto.

5. The novel was an important genre in Polish literature during the 1930s, with works written by Maria Dąbrowska, Zofia Nałkowska, Jarosław Iwaszkiewicz, Maria Kuncewiczowa, and others. Writers such as Jerzy Andrzejewski, Tadeusz Breza, and Adolf Rudnicki were beginning their careers. The most famous writers outside Poland from this period, however, are three major figures: Stanisław Ignacy Witkiewicz (his novel *Nienasycenie* [*Insatiability*] was published in 1930), Witold Gombrowicz (his novel *Ferdydurke* was published in 1937), and Bruno Schulz.

6. Zofia Nałkowska (1884–1954), a prolific novelist and playwright, came from an intellectual background. Her father was a well-known scholar of geography. Nałkowska's public career began before World War I and spans the development of the Polish novel up to World War II. Evolving from her first youthful novels and stories about women, she developed into an exponent of the psychological novel and novel of social analysis. Her most famous novel, *Granica* (Boundary Line, 1935), explores the limits of our knowledge about human nature and the world. In the postwar period she became famous for her vignettes about Nazi war crimes entitled *Medaliony* (Medallions, 1946) and her *Diaries*, published in the 1970s and 1980s. Her complete works run to fourteen volumes.

7. The Rój edition bears the following year, 1934, as the date of publication, a standard practice for books published late in the year. The year 1934 is the date customarily given for the appearance of Schulz's first volume of stories, *Cinnamon Shops*.

8. Przedmieście existed as a literary group from 1933 to 1937. Its writers were concerned with social reportage and the documentary novel.

9. A landau is a two-seated open carriage with a top that can be let down on both sides.

CHAPTER 5: THE BOOK, OR CHILDHOOD REGAINED

1. Andrzej Pleśniewicz (1909–1945) was a literary critic and essayist who published essays and reviews about Bruno Schulz.

2. Pan Tadeusz (Master Thaddeus) is the hero of Polish romantic

poet Adam Mickiewicz's 1834 verse epic *Pan Tadeusz.*

3. Goethe's "Erlkönig" is a dramatic ballad (1782) in which a father and son hasten home at night. Held in his father's arms, the boy hears the night sounds—the whisperings of the Erl King, who threatens to take him away by force. When father and son arrive home, the boy is dead.

4. The full text of this letter is in the Letters section of this volume.

5. From "Twórczość literacka Brunona Schulza." (Bruno Schulz's Literary Work), published in *Pion* (Probe) 1935, nos. 34 and 35. Text reprinted in Stanisław Ignacy Witkiewicz, *O znaczeniu filozofii dla krytyki i inne artykuły polemiczne* (On the Significance of Philosophy for Criticism and Other Polemical Articles) (Warsaw: PWN, 1976), p. 195.

CHAPTER 6: SCHULZIAN TIME

1. Tadeusz Breza, 1905–1970, was a novelist and essayist. He had served as press secretary at the Polish embassy in London (1929–32) and after returning to Warsaw directed a theatrical agency. Breza's first successful novel, *Adam Grywałd*, was published in 1936. The complete text of this letter is found in the Letters section.

2. This reminiscence was published in Jerzy Ficowski's *Okolice sklepów cyna-monowych* (Environs of Cinnamon Shops) (Cracow: Wydawnictwo Lit-erackie, 1986).

3. The Polish word *klepsydra* can have either of these two meanings, but this ambiguity does not come through in the English version of the title.

4. Maria Dąbrowska, 1889–1965, was a prolific short story writer, novel-ist, essayist, translator, and dramatist. By the time of this review, she had published her major work, *Nights and Days* (1931–39), a four-volume novel that is a panorama of Polish life from the nineteenth and twenti-eth centuries.

5. Józefina Szelińska's relationship with Bruno Schulz is discussed in Chap-ter 8.

6. Schulz's calendar references have affinities with Jewish timekeeping and have prompted several articles on the Jewish calendar. Articles in Eng-lish include Theodosia Robertson, "Time in Bruno Schulz," *Indiana Slavic Studies* 5 (1990), pp. 181–92, and David A. Goldfarb, "A Living Schulz 'Noc wielkiego sezonu' [Night of the Great Season]," *Prooftexts* 14 (1994), pp. 25–47.

CHAPTER 7: PHANTOMS AND REALITY

1. The complete text of this letter is in the Letters section.
2. "Autumn" is not included in *Cinnamon Shops*; it was first published in *Sygnaty* (Signals) in 1936 (no. 17).

CHAPTER 8: EXCURSIONS ABROAD

1. These lines appear in Mickiewicz's "Epilogue" to his 1834 epic poem *Pan Tadeusz*.
2. This synopsis can be found in *Letters and Drawings*, pp. 153–55.
3. Schulz's July 1938 trip to Paris occurred during a summer of grave diplomatic crisis in Europe. After Hitler's *Anschluss* with Austria in March 1938, he met with Chamberlain and demanded cession of the Sudetenland, a crisis that resulted in the Munich Conference of September 29–30. The Sudetenland was surrendered to the Reich on October 1. It was remarkable that Schulz traveled at all.
4. Józefina Szelińska (1905–1991) probably met Bruno Schulz in spring of 1932 when he asked to do her portrait. She was from Janów near Lwów and earned her doctorate in Polish philology and art history at the university there. She came to Drohobycz in 1930 to teach in a private teachers' seminary for women. In 1935 she moved to Warsaw to work, and Schulz visited her, even planning to move there. This turned out to be impossible for Schulz; he returned to Drohobycz, while Szelińska returned to her parents. At this time their attachment deepened until in 1936 he wrote to her parents about their planned marriage. After the engagement was broken off, SzeliÒska eventually moved to Warsaw, survived the war in hiding, and in 1945 moved to Gdańsk. Her name and the details of her relationship with Bruno Schulz remained secret until after her death.
5. In German folklore a kobold is a mischievous spirit or goblin.
6. The complete text of this letter is in the Letters section.

CHAPTER 9: MAGIC AND DEFINITION

1. The reference is to Adam Mickiewicz's poem "Romantyczność" (Romanticism, 1822), in which an eighteenth-century rationalist doubts the visions of a young girl because such phenomena cannot be appre-

hended by reason.

2. The complete text of this letter is in the Letters section.

3. Stanisław Ignacy Witkiewicz's "narcotic visions" refer to Witkacy's experimentation with various narcotics, especially when he was painting. He "usually marked at the corner of the canvas whether he had taken any drug while working on that particular portrait and if so, its name. Out of those experiments grew his book, *Nicotine, Alcohol, Cocaine, Peyote, Ether + Appendix* (1932)." See Czesław Miłosz, *The History of Polish Literature* (New York: Macmillan, 1969), p. 418.

CHAPTER 10: A SETTLING OF ACCOUNTS

1. Wanda Wasilewska, 1905–1964; writer and journalist, and a political activist; co-organizer of Union of Polish Patriots and the Polish Army in the Soviet Union.

2. *Letters and Drawings*, p. 203.

3. The boundary between the General Government and the region of Eastern Galicia (which included Drohobycz and Lwów) lay just east of Przemyśl. It was under Soviet control from 1939 to 1941—until Operation Barbarossa in June 1941. After July 1941, the region was added to the General Government; the Germans entered Drohobycz on July 3, 1941.

4. More detailed information on Felix Landau appears in Chapter 13.

5. Maecenas was the friend and literary patron of Roman writers in the age of Augustus, most notably Virgil and Horace.

6. Schulz's wall paintings are discussed in Chapter 13.

7. The Home Army (in Polish, Armia krajowa) was the fighting force of the Polish underground state during World War II.

8. Another account of Schulz's death appears in Henyrk Grynberg's story "Drohobycz, Drohobycz" in *Drohobycz, Drohobycz* (Warsaw: Wydawnictwo W.A.B., 1997).

9. On the eve of World War II, the Jewish community in Drohobycz numbered approximately 15,000 to 17,000, or 40 percent of the city population. When the ghetto was established in October 1942, some 9,000 to 10,000 Jews were forced into it. When the Soviet army entered Drohobycz in August 1944, only 400 Jewish survivors emerged. *Encyclopedia Judaica*, vol. 6 (Jerusalem: Keter, 1972); *Encyclopedia of the Holocaust*, vol. 1, Israel Gutman, editor in chief (New York: Macmillan, 1990).

CHAPTER 11: WORKS PRESERVED AND LOST

1. Mór or Maurus Jókai, 1825–1904, was a Hungarian novelist. He was prolific, and was popular in his lifetime and for many years afterward. Several novels were published in English at the turn of the twentieth century.
2. *Letters and Drawings*, pp. 105–6.
3. Ibid., p. 152.
4. The complete text of this letter is in the Letters section.
5. *Letters and Drawings*, p. 243, n. 6.
6. Ibid., p. 73.

CHAPTER 12: AWAITING *MESSIAH*—A POSTSCRIPT

1. Some of this information appears in Jerzy Ficowski's book *Z listów odnalezionych* (From Discovered Letters) (Warsaw: Chimera, 1993) and in English in an interview with Dorota Głowacka in *Bruno Schulz: New Documents and Interpretations*, edited by Czesław Z. Prokopczyk (New York: Peter Lang, 1999).

CHAPTER 13: THE LAST FAIRY TALE OF BRUNO SCHULZ

1. The Sturmabteilung, or storm troopers, founded in 1921 as a paramilitary division of the Nazi Party. Purged in 1934, the SA was succeeded by the SS or Schutzstaffeln ("Defense Echelon"), which had been established in 1925 as a personal guards unit but grew into an enormous state organization under Heinrich Himmler and assumed primary responsibility for the Final Solution.
2. The Security Police (SIPO) and Other Service.
3. Excerpts from Felix Landau's war diary can be found in Ernst Klee, Willi Dressen, and Volker Riess, eds., *The Good Old Days: The Holocaust as Seen by Its Perpetrators and Bystanders* (New York: Konecky & Konecky, 1988). Landau's diary is also cited in Martin Gilbert, *The Holocaust* (New York: Holt, Rinehart & Winston, 1988).

LETTER TO ZENON WAŚNIEWSKI

1. All Souls' Day or Zaduszki in Polish was a traditional feast day combining pagan folk rituals to honor the dead with the Christian holy day celebrated November 2.
2. The reference is to Thomas Mann's use of eternally repeating schemas as in biblical stories.
3. This refers to Schulz's "Treatise on Tailors' Dummies" in *Cinnamon Shops* and his story "A Second Fall" in *Sanatorium Under the Sign of the Hourglass*. "A Second Fall" was first printed in the pages of *Kamena* (1934), and the author's manuscript was preserved in the papers of Zenon Waśniewski. A book edition, *A Second Fall*, based on a facsimile of the manuscript, appeared in 1973, edited by Jerzy Ficowski.
4. Aleksander Leszczyc, an art dealer, owner of a traveling gallery, organizer of exhibits of paintings taken by him on commission at resort areas and seasonal tourist and vacation spots.

LETTER TO TADEUSZ BREZA

1. *Rocznik Literatury*, or properly *Rocznik Literacki* (Literary Annual), began to appear in 1932 and contained discussions of literary works published the previous year. Schulz is not referring to the discussion of *Cinnamon Shops* which Leon Piwiński wrote, but to Breza's column entitled "Na marginesie 'Rocznika Literackiego'—odprawa pesymistom" (On the Margins of Literary Annual—a Retort to Pessimists), which was printed in *Kurier Poranny* (Morning Courier).
2. In December of 1934, Schulz met Breza in person, and their acquaintance, formerly confined to the exchange of letters, developed into a warm friendship.

LETTER TO ANDRZEJ PLEŚNIEWICZ

1. Schulz is referring here to his contemporary and longtime friend Emanuel (Mundek) Pilpel, who died not long after in Drohobycz.
2. The reference is to Witold Gombrowicz (1904–1969), a novelist, playwright, essayist, and diarist. He emigrated from Poland in 1939 after having published some short pieces and a famous novel, *Ferdydurke* (1937). Later novels (especially the parodic *Trans-Atlantyk*, 1953), three

major plays, and his *Diary* (1957–66) have secured his permanent place in twentieth-century Polish writing.

LETTERS TO ROMANA HALPERN

1. Rainer Maria Rilke (1875–1926), Austrian poet, one of the greatest twentieth-century European poets. Schulz considered Rilke to be the patron of his imagination and an incomparable master of poetic expression.
2. Juna was the name Bruno Schulz used for his fiancée, Józefina Szelińska (1905–1991).
3. "Emeryt" ("The Old Age Pensioner") is a story in the volume *Sanatorium Under the Sign of the Hourglass* (first printed in *Wiadomości Literackie* 1935, no. 51/52, z. 6 with illustrations by the author).
4. Printed in two successive issues of the monthly *Skamander* (1936, nos. 74 and 75), the story "Wiosna" ("Spring") was later printed in the volume *Sanatorium Under the Sign of the Hourglass.*
5. Tadeusz Szturm de Sztrem (1892–1968), social activist and member of PPS (Polish Socialist Party), worked for many years in the Main Office of Statistics, where he hired Schulz's fiancée at Schulz's request. A great "social worker," he helped others during his entire life. In the Stalinist period, he spent long years in prison. A friend of Stanisław Ignacy Witkiewicz.
6. Debora Vogel (1902–1942), Jewish poet, theoretician of art, critic, and contributor to *Sygnały* (Signals) and *Wiadomości Literackie* (Literary News), was a friend of Schulz's. The first fragments and beginnings of *Cinnamon Shops* developed in his letters to her. Schulz wrote a review of her prose.
7. *Wiadomości Literackie* (Literary News).
8. Stefan (Stef), Romana Halpern's son, is today a psychiatrist in the United States.
9. *Zmory* (Nightmares) is the best-known novel of Emil Zegadłowicz (1888–1941), poet and prose writer.
10. Główny Urząd Statystyczny (Main Office for Statistics).
11. Stanisław Ignacy Witkiewicz.
12. In connection with efforts to get married, Schulz wanted to register fictionally in Silesia, where it was legal to have a civil marriage without regard to a couple's different religions. (Józefina Szelińska was a Catholic, while Schulz was without religious affiliation.)
13. Wilhelm Schulz (1910–1944) was the son of Bruno Schulz's older

brother, Izydor. In 1938, Wilhelm married Elżbieta Godlewska in the Evangelical Church in Warsaw. He perished with his wife in the gas chambers of Auschwitz.

14. Izaak Feuerberg (1911–1970), a former student of Schulz's, a Communist activist. Schulz turned to friends, including Romana Halpern, requesting advice and help for Feuerberg, who had been arrested in Hungary. After the war, as Ignacy Krzemień, Feuerberg worked in the Polish diplomatic service.

15. Kazimierz Wierzyński (1894–1969), poet from the Skamander group who remained an émigré after the war, living in the United States, Rome, and, finally, London.

16. Wacław Czarski, editor in chief of *Tygodnik Ilustrowany* (Illustrated Weekly), in which Schulz published his stories and essays.

17. Wacław Berent (1873–1940), novelist and translator, author of novels including *Próchno* (Rotten Wood), *Żywe kamienie* (Living Stones), *Diogenes w kontuszu* (Diogenes in a Nobleman's Coat); at that time a member of the Polish Academy of Literature.

18. Edmund Husserl (1859–1938), German philosopher, mathematician, creator of modern phemonenology. Schulz had become interested in him through reading the works of Professor Roman Ingarden, a Polish exemplar of this philosophical school.

19. Korostów was a tourist and vacation spot at that time in eastern Małopolska where Schulz's friend the engineer Jerzy Reitman had established a recreation center described in the poetic-mythicizing vision of Schulz's "Republika marzeń" ("Republic of Dreams").

20. Above all, the so-called Anschluss, the entry of German armies into Austria and incorporation of that state into the Third Reich. The event occurred on March 15, just five days prior to the date of Schulz's letter.

21. Śródborów was a health resort in the vicinity of Otwock, in the Warsaw region.

22. A Polish translation of Aldous Huxley's *Eyeless in Gaza* appeared in 1938. Schulz had become acquainted with Huxley's work earlier, having written a review-essay entitled "Wędrowki sceptyka" (Wanderings of a Skeptic), *Tygodnik Ilustrowany* 1936, no. 6, about Huxley's *Night Music*, published in 1936.

23. Wanda Kragen (1893–1982), translator, primarily of German and Anglo-Saxon literature.

24 Józef Wittlin (1896–1976), poet, novelist, translator. In 1935, he received the PEN Club award for his translation of the *Odyssey* and the *Wiadomości Literacki* (Literary News) award for his novel *Sól ziemi* (Salt of

the Earth). After 1939, he lived abroad, and he died in the United States.

25. Maria Kuncewiczowa (1899–1989), representative of the psychological-moral current in Polish literature. In 1938 she proposed Schulz's candidacy for the *Wiadomości Literackie* award. Schulz published as many as three extensive reviews of her novel *Cudzoziemka* (*The Stranger*).

26. Maria Dąbrowska (1889–1965), novelist, short story writer, essayist, author of *Noce i dni* (Nights and Days), outstanding creator of a great epic novel. Like Kuncewiczowa, she mentioned Schulz as a candidate in the jury discussion for the *Wiadomości Literackie* award.

27. Schulz left for France August 2, 1938, and returned August 26.

LETTERS TO ANNA PŁOCKIER

1. The Sunday that Schulz suggested was the day of the outbreak of German-Soviet war, June 22, 1941.

2. Hilda Berger, some twenty years old at the time, an escapee from Nazi persecution in Germany. Saved by a German, she survived the war and left for the United States. In the 1960s as Hilda Ohlsen she was a witness for the prosecution at the war crimes trial where there also appeared as a witness Berthold Beitz, the person who saved her and many other Jews—for which later he was honored in Israel with the medal "Righteous Among the Nations of the World."

3. Marek Holzman (1919–1982), who then bore the name Singer (his mother's name), director of the library in Borysław, and after the war an outstanding photographer. He died in Warsaw.

4. Anna and her fiancé were preparing to flee from Borysław, intending to get into Warsaw secretly.

5. Marek Zwillich.

6. That is, from Warsaw.

7. Anna received this letter a week before her tragic death.

Index

About Bruno Schulz

BRUNO SCHULZ (1892–1942) belongs to the canon of Polish letters and is an outstanding exponent of interwar avant-garde prose. He was born and died in Drohobycz, a town in the southeastern lands of the Second Polish Republic. His two volumes of stories, *Cinnamon Shops* (1934) and *Sanatorium Under the Sign of the Hourglass* (1937), have established his place in European and world literature. Two stories from the *Sanatorium* collection were part of his projected novel, *Messiah*. Schulz was also a graphic artist and author of several dozen reviews and essays. More than 150 letters survive of his voluminous correspondence. His poetic and fantastic short stories transform the everyday; small details of ordinary reality become powerful and protean forces of beauty living their own life and pursuing their own ends under the somewhat ironic eye of the narrator. He survived the years 1939 to 1942, under Soviet and then Nazi occupation. He was shot by a Gestapo officer on the streets of his beloved town on November 19, 1942.

About the Author

JERZY FICOWSKI (born 1924, Warsaw) is a distinguished poet, prose writer, scholar, and translator. During the German occupation of World War II Jerzy Ficowski served in the Home Army (AK) and took part in the Warsaw Uprising of 1944. He has published some twenty collections of poetry since his debut volume of poetry appeared in 1948. He has written poetry for children and a collection of prose pieces, *Czekanie na sen psa* (Waiting for a Dog's Dream, 1970), as well as essays. During the years which led to Solidarity and martial law, Jerzy Ficowski coedited the literary quarterly *Zapis* (The Record) in the late 1970s and was a member of KOR (Komitet Obronny Robotników; Workers Defense Committee). From 1977 to 1989 his collections appeared either underground or abroad. Jerzy Ficowski's 1979 collection, *Odczytanie popiołów* (A Reading of Ashes, 1981), comprises twenty-five poems devoted entirely to the Holocaust. Jerzy Ficowski is one of the most active translators of Yiddish literature into Polish remaining in Poland. He is a major scholar of

Gypsy history and culture and has published several nonfiction studies, as well as poetry and prose inspired by his knowledge of Gypsy life. He lives in Warsaw, Poland.

Jerzy Ficowski is the major scholar of the life and work of Bruno Schulz. Ficowski began researching Schulz's life and artistic legacy in 1946, and his meticulous and determined efforts recovered and preserved all materials related to Bruno Schulz during the postwar decades. He has documented Schulz's artistic life, all his publications in both books and periodicals, all persons connected with Schulz throughout his life, and the circumstances of his death. Jerzy Ficowski has been instrumental in establishing the substantial collection of Schulziana at the Adam Mickiewicz Museum of Literature in Warsaw, Poland, and in planning for a permanent museum devoted to Schulz in Drohobycz, Ukraine.

About the Translator

THEODOSIA ROBERTSON is Associate Professor in History at the University of Michigan–Flint. She received her doctorate in Slavic Languages and Literatures with a specialization in Polish literature from Indiana University. Her translations include Aleksander Fiut's study of the poetry of Czesław Miłosz, *The Eternal Moment* (University of California Press), and essays in the volume *The Polish Renaissance in Its European Context*, edited by Samuel Fiszman (Indiana University Press). Her articles on Bruno Schulz have been published in both Poland and the United States.